RISK MANAGEMENT IN STUDENT AFFAIRS

RISK MANAGEMENT IN STUDENT AFFAIRS

Foundations for Safety and Success

THOMAS E. MILLER
AND ROGER W. SOROCHTY

JB JOSSEY-BASS™
A Wiley Brand

Cover design by Wiley
Cover image : ©Chad Baker/Jason Reed/Ryan McVay | Getty

Published by Jossey-Bass
A Wiley Brand
One Montgomery Street, Suite 1200, San Francisco, CA 94104-4594
www.josseybass.com/highereducation
Consulting editor: John Schuh

Jossey-Bass books and products are available through most bookstores. To contact Jossey-Bass directly call our Customer Care Department within the U.S. at 800-956-7739, outside the U.S. at 317-572-3986, or fax 317-572-4002.

Wiley publishes in a variety of print and electronic formats and by print-on-demand. Some material included with standard print versions of this book may not be included in e-books or in print-on-demand. If this book refers to media such as a CD or DVD that is not included in the version you purchased, you may download this material at http://booksupport.wiley.com. For more information about Wiley products, visit www.wiley.com.

Library of Congress Cataloging-in-Publication data is on file.

ISBN: 978-1-118-10091-2 (hb)
ISBN: 978-1-118-79151-6 (ebk)
ISBN: 978-1-118-79130-1 (ebk)

Printed in the United States of America
FIRST EDITION

HB Printing   10 9 8 7 6 5 4 3 2 1

CONTENTS

PREFACE

The law as it relates to higher education will continue to develop in its complexity, and student affairs professionals will need to be alert to practices and activities that manage risk. Our society has become increasingly immersed in legal issues, and student affairs staff members at both public and private institutions must be equipped to help manage risk and protect their institutions, the students they serve, and their resources from unintended consequences. There is every reason to believe that the management of those risks will become an increasingly central aspect of the work in student affairs in the future.

This book is intended to present risk management concepts and relevant legal issues in a way that student affairs administrators, who are generally not trained in the law, can readily understand and apply. The need for such a resource is significant, as evidenced by the growth in the number of conferences, programs, and special workshops that are associated with risk management and legal issues in student affairs and higher education. The profession of student affairs does not need another complex, technical book on legal and risk management issues associated with student affairs. The best materials that are already published in these topical areas are serving that purpose. The profession does need, in our view, a resource written by practitioners in the field for practicing professionals, while still addressing the full context of the law and of risk management.

The contribution of this text is less about new information than about organization and tone, which is suited to the audiences for which it is intended. The book is organized around general areas of risk, including issues associated with legal risks, as well as risks associated with resource management. The tone of the book is intended to be more informal than many books related to the subject, with a focus on discussion and views about risk from a general and broad view, rather than pressing into court decisions and the complicated nuances of law. Hence, the reader will find very few footnotes and legal citations, as would be appropriate for other more technical books on the topic. Instead, we provide an annotated reference list of useful general sources for perspective about law, so those interested in more details or context about a matter discussed in the text can conduct further research.

The primary target population for this book is student affairs professionals, principally those who are in the earlier stages of their careers or in middle management in their organizations. A secondary audience is students in graduate programs designed to prepare students to serve as student affairs professionals.

This book is intended to help practitioners understand the sources of risk in their work and the practices and strategies that they can employ to manage risk. The institutions that employ them will derive a secondary benefit, because good practices will help them avoid risk and the associated consequences, which can range from actual losses to increased costs of insurance. In other words, if student affairs professionals can be proactive and help manage risk in what they do, it is more likely than not that the negative consequences of poor risk management will be reduced.

It is clear that student affairs professionals must be aware of how decisions and practices can create risk for themselves and their institutions, and they should be informed about strategies for addressing risk. The work of student affairs has become very complicated, and exposure to risk is much more evident than it was a decade ago. Our intent in producing this book is to provide a framework for understanding and managing risk, and we hope the readers find the text useful as a general guide to decision making as it relates to legal and resource risk management.

Another factor associated with discussing risk management is the variation between states. The culture of a state in New England is rather different from one of a state in the Southwest. The people in those states elect very different sorts of legislators, who write different kinds of laws and select unlike sorts of judges. They also form different juries. Therefore, there is not one uniform approach to managing risk. The context in which a student affairs professional works, including the state and even the local government and norms, can set the tone for the best approach. We wrote this book to help student affairs professional see the basic principles of risk management from high above the clouds, not at street level, because we are all on different streets.

The book is organized into seven parts. Each focuses on an area of law or practice that is a source of risk. The chapters within each part focus on specific ways in which risk presents itself and the strategies student affairs professionals can employ to manage the identified risks.

Part One discusses the framework for the consideration of risk management, detailing the substantial differences between public institutions and private ones and also presenting the factors that may discern between the risk that an individual administrator may face and risk taken by the employing institution.

Part Two covers risk associated with the United States Constitution, specifically principles associated with freedom of expression, weapons policies, search and seizure, and due process. Part Three addresses regulatory challenges that institutions and individuals working in higher education must manage. This part largely covers federal regulatory oversight, but it also addresses private organizations with which institutions may have relationships and obligations.

Part Four covers tort issues, those circumstances under which an individual or a group may feel that a wrongful act has caused them harm and they seek redress. Part Five addresses contract issues, those which institutions have with students, with organizations, and with employees. Part Six covers risk issues associated with resources, from technology and data to physical facilities to finances. Part Seven provides a summary of the material covered.

This book describes risks that student affairs administrators face. Risk comes in many forms. The most obvious of them is risk of litigation in the form of liability for perceived wrongful acts or broken promises. The book explains the sources of liability risk and the management strategies that student affairs administrators can take to reduce risk of this form. Another form of risk is that associated with loss of or damage to property. Part One is dedicated to identifying the nature of risk of this type and the steps that student affairs administrators can take to manage it. A third form of risk is associated with the risk of damaging the reputation of the institution through negative through public relations or damaging publicity. Risk of this form runs throughout this text and can be found in every part. Another form of risk is associated with the health or safety of students and other members of the campus community. Student affairs administrators can also find risk associated with enrollment management. Some activities or events could jeopardize student recruitment or persistence. The alert student affairs staff member will be sensitive to all of these forms of risk and the strategies for managing each.

ACKNOWLEDGMENTS

The authors wish to recognize those in our lives who supported our efforts on this project and also those who gave us insight and perspective to clarify our writing. Anybody who works in higher education and writes for publication finds that the writing complicates the work. This was certainly true for the two of us.

As Roger took on the project, he was in the process of retiring from his senior administrative position at the University of Tulsa. He relocated his home from Tulsa to Indian Rocks Beach in Florida and began a role as an adjunct faculty member at the University of South Florida while continuing to write. Before the project was completed, he began to serve an interim administrative position at California State University, Fullerton, requiring another residential move, completely across the country. His ability to complete the work was only possible because of the incredible support and understanding he received from his wife, Barbara, which is characteristic of the wonderful partner and best friend she's been through forty-four years of marriage.

Tom's work on the project began when he was a tenured, full-time member of the faculty at the University of South Florida, teaching in a master's-level program in college student affairs and a doctoral program in higher education administration. Writing for publication was an appropriate activity for him in that capacity. However, as the project was hitting its stride and the pace of writing was picking up, he was asked to assume a role as interim vice president for student affairs at the university and a few months later was appointed as the permanent vice president.

His work life changed dramatically and became much more demanding and inflexible. Like Roger, he received wonderful support and encouragement from his wife, Carol, as he has in every step of their forty-three years of marriage. Carol also played a significant role in editing the manuscript and used her natural skills to improve the quality of our work.

The graduate students Tom served at the University of South Florida were unflaggingly encouraging and understanding about the book project, as were his faculty colleagues and associates. As he moved into his vice president's role, his administrative colleagues and staff were consistently supportive and encouraging.

We are indebted to Roger's colleagues at the University of Tulsa, Dale Schoenefeld, vice president of information services and chief information officer, and Robert Shipley, associate vice president for operations and physical plant. They provided excellent advice and insight regarding aspects of the project and were very helpful.

Finally, we express our gratitude to the publisher's representatives, who gave us wonderful guidance and support and showed tremendous flexibility and understanding as the project took a series of twists and turns. We thank Alison Knowles, Erin Null, and our good friend, John Schuh.

Thomas E. Miller	**Roger W. Sorochty**
Vice President for Student Affairs	Senior Associate for Higher
University of South Florida	Education, The Center for
	Conflict Dynamics
	Eckerd College

CONTRIBUTORS

The authors wish to recognize two persons who made specific independent contributions to this book. Dionne Ferguson generated a draft of Chapter Fifteen that was very helpful in detailing the principles associated with contract management. Similarly, Joshua Cutchens produced a draft of Chapter Eighteen that helped us see the scope of what might be most useful to address about student conduct systems.

PART ONE

FRAMEWORK

The two chapters in this part present the parameters for the context in which student affairs administrators approach risk. Chapter One describes how private universities and colleges have different conditions associated with risk management than public ones do. Chapter Two explores the ways in which the issues associated with risk and its management are different for the institutions that employ student affairs administrators and the individual administrators themselves.

CHAPTER 1

DIFFERENCES BETWEEN PUBLIC AND PRIVATE INSTITUTIONS

This chapter will detail the essential distinctions in approaches to risk and risk management between public or state universities and colleges and those which are private or independent.

THE CONSTITUTION VERSUS CONTRACTS

A principle difference between public institutions and private ones relates to the areas of law that largely govern their relationships with students (Kaplin & Lee, 2009, pp. 23–49). Public institutions are, effectively, arms of state government. They are established by state authority, funded by state resources, and governed by state authorities. Their employees are employees of the state, and their property is public property. As a result, the principles established by the U.S. Constitution apply to public or state universities and colleges. Since private institutions are not agencies of the state, the U.S. Constitution does not directly establish standards for how they interact with students. The fundamental area of law that governs the relationships between private colleges and universities and students is contract law. The forms of contracts between institutions and students are largely related to published materials and other ways in which services or programs are promised to students. Additionally, contract law greatly applies to state institutions, because a variety of contracts exist between state universities and students. The following section will describe implications of these distinctions.

3

IMPLICATIONS

There are several specific ways in which the contract obligations of private institutions present different risk than is the case at public institutions, given their duties associated with the U.S. Constitution (Kaplin & Lee, 2009, pp. 23–49).

Standard Setting

In Part Two, we discuss specific ways in which the Constitution establishes what government cannot do in its interactions with citizens. Among its provisions is the establishment of rules and procedures associated with student conduct and student freedom of expression. Public institutions are limited, therefore, in the restrictions they can place on students, particularly regarding speech issues and procedural due process.

Sovereign Immunity, Personal Liability

Government may establish limits for its exposure to liability. This is referred to as *sovereign immunity*, and it basically protects government and state entities from unlimited risk. The specific standards for sovereign immunity vary from state to state. Individual states have passed legislation to provide definitions of immunity, and judicial decisions have further defined sovereign immunity in individual states. Many states have passed legislation that establishes specific financial limits of exposure by state institutions to claims of liability. Private institutions are not insulated at all by sovereign immunity, unless, in special circumstances, they are acting as agents of the state, as determined by courts that are reviewing their claim of sovereign immunity.

In addition to the protections associated with sovereign immunity, many states have passed laws insulating government employees, including employees of public universities and colleges, from *personal liability*. This normally applies to employees performing their assigned functions within the scope of their responsibilities as assigned. However, state employees are not protected from intentional wrongful acts. We elaborate on the distinctions between personal liability and institutional liability in the next chapter.

Religious Expression

The First Amendment of the Constitution establishes that government cannot restrict the expression of religion, and neither can it create religion. This applies to public institutions in several ways, some obvious and some not. Chapter Three describes this in some detail, but, fundamentally, public institutions cannot prevent students from expressing religious thought. Neither can public institutions force religion on students. The commonly expressed principle of "separation between church and state" can be confusing and lead administrators to mistakenly violate the former principle associated with preventing student expression.

On the other hand, private institutions have the freedom to require students to participate in religious expression and to limit certain forms of religious expression, but it is safest for them to do so within the context of the institutional mission. Private institutions may require an expression of commitment to faith or student participation in religious ceremonies, for example. In a way, the freedom of expression principle applies to private institutions.

Freedom of Expression

"civility"

There are several ways in which the First Amendment to the U.S. Constitution establishes how public institutions are obligated to permit the free exchange of ideas, even ones that some may find unpleasant or distasteful. Many institutions have attempted to encourage student civility by establishing codes of conduct that regulate speech. There is risk associated with those standards, because the courts would commonly determine them to be content-based restrictions. Student affairs administrators in public institutions should take care to not restrict student speech based on its content. The authors provide a further discussion of this issue in Part Two.

Although the First Amendment establishes a context for the approach regarding free expression at public universities, public statements in codes of conduct and student handbooks provide direct standards regarding the student expression of ideas. Private colleges and universities have more freedom to restrict student expression on their campuses, particularly when the restriction relates to institutional mission or educational purposes.

The freedom-of-expression rights of public institution employees are less restricted when the individuals clearly speak as citizens than when they speak as employees. The rights to free expression by private institution employees can be restricted by contract, loyalty oaths, pledges of religious affiliation, or other conditions associated with the mission or fundamental values of the institution.

Due Process

The Fifth Amendment to the U.S. Constitution (a discussion follows later in this text) obligates state institutions to provide "due process of law" in the student conduct setting, as well as in the review of employee performance. Due process has been defined in case law over the years. Its fundamental requirement is twofold: provide notice of allegations about violations of regulations and provide the accused with a hearing as an opportunity to respond to the allegations (Kaplin & Lee, 2009, pp. 456–474). In some jurisdictions courts have expanded the obligations associated with due process, but notice and hearing apply throughout the United States. However, few public institutions limit their procedures to simply notice and hearing. Many public institutions have several levels of appeal or review regarding student conduct, and many permit students accused of misconduct to be accompanied by attorneys. It is also common for those accused of rule violations to be allowed to hear and respond to those who initiate the charges. Although the Fifth Amendment provides the context for due process in public institutions, the direct definition of due process is located in their published materials. Therefore, contract law, more than constitutional law, guides due process at public institutions.

Private institutions of higher education are generally not bound by the Fifth Amendment to the Constitution. Their definitions of due process are found in their codes of conduct and are the promises of the institutions regarding the rights of students and the procedures that are to be followed in student conduct cases (Lake, 2011, pp. 64–76). It is general practice at such institutions to provide a significant level of procedural rights to students in the conduct setting. Colleges and universities do not generally want to be seen as limiting or restricting the freedoms of, or fairness to, students. Codes of conduct, as a result, are generally written so as to give substantial freedoms to students in the conduct process. Again, as established, those published statements of due process are contractual obligations of institutions to the students they serve. When courts review those procedures, the tests they may apply concern the fundamental fairness of the procedures: whether the institution followed its established process; whether the actions taken were not arbitrary or capricious; or whether the sanction imposed was in proportion to the offense. Private institutions will normally survive legal challenges to their conduct procedures as long as they observe the process and procedures that they have published and their decisions are not made arbitrarily or irrationally.

The same standards apply to the procedures for the review of academic misconduct. As long as the private institution follows its procedures as published and as long as those procedures and the case outcomes are not seen as arbitrary or irrational, little risk would arise as a result.

Search and Seizure

The Fourth Amendment of the U.S. Constitution provides a context for the rights of students attending public universities with regard to freedom from searches (Kaplin & Lee, 2009, pp. 365–371). The Fourth Amendment restricts the rights of government officials to search the property of individuals or to search their person without a properly executed warrant. Government officials, in this case, would include the employees of public colleges and universities. Conducting a search in violation of a student's Fourth Amendment rights could expose employees and public institutions to liability for damages. Any evidence collected during such a search would probably be inadmissible in any subsequent criminal proceeding, but, in some jurisdictions, that may not be a driving factor in a campus judicial proceeding.

Employees of private institutions have more leeway in conducting searches in the absence of law enforcement personnel. However, even in those instances when Fourth Amendment or state law constraints do not apply, a room search that is conducted outside of the parameters of the housing contract between the institution and the student may generate litigation associated with a violation of contract. If a room search is conducted in a fashion that is arbitrary or capricious, a claim of invasion of privacy could result. In theory, private institutions could be more aggressive in searching student rooms, but many of them choose not to be.

Waivers of Fourth Amendment protections offer additional parameters for searches at both public and private institutions. In the case of residence hall contracts, students who executed those contracts are often required to waive their rights to restrict entry into their student rooms for specific purposes of protecting the institutions' interests, including health and safety and protection of property. Likewise, athletes participating in sports sponsored by the National Collegiate Athletics Association may enter into voluntary contracts to waive their Fourth Amendment rights to permit drug testing for illegal substances. Drug testing is, in effect, a search of the body of a person.

Employees of private institutions who conduct searches are generally not considered state actors, and as long as a search is conducted to protect institutional interests, it will normally survive any legal challenge

(Kaplin & Lee, 2009, pp. 365–371). However, at these same institutions, those private security personnel who are licensed or otherwise empowered as agents of the state as peace officers, or special law enforcement personnel, must, as a result, conform to Fourth Amendment restrictions. The purpose for searching a student's room is the test in legal scrutiny. When it is for the purpose of enforcing the law, Fourth Amendment limits apply. When it is for the purpose of protecting institutional interests, constitutional limitations are less applicable.

FEDERAL FUNDING

A number of federal regulations apply equally to public and private institutions, because they are tied to federal aid to higher education. Those regulations include those associated with the Drug-Free Schools and Communities Act of 1989, the Campus Security Act of 1990, and the Campus Sex Crimes Prevention Act of 2000. Those standards apply to all institutions whose students receive federal aid, which has been interpreted as applicable to higher educational institutions. Chapter Six of this text more fully explores the relevant regulatory issues. Every one of these standards applies to both public and private institutions.

PROPERTY OWNERSHIP

There are differences between the rights of those owning private property and rights associated with public property, and these distinctions may come into play for colleges and universities. A private institution may restrict public access to its property. Some private institutions, for example, use guarded entrances to their campuses and regulate visitor traffic. Public institutions are less likely to do so, although access to property can always be regulated, whether it is public or private. For example, public parks and zoos control access by admission only during certain hours, and public college residence halls are typically accessible only to the students who live there and their guests.

A private institution may initiate arrest procedures for any unwelcomed or unauthorized visitor and charge that person with trespass. A public institution—since its property is public—is less able to do so, unless an individual has engaged in unwanted or illegal behavior and has been warned that a subsequent visit to campus may result in a trespass arrest.

TRANSPORTATION

Student affairs staff at public institutions may operate state-owned vehicles to transport students or other persons on or off campus. The institution will have those vehicles insured with liability protection, and there will be procedures governing the use of the vehicles and the procedures to employ in the event of a mishap. Private institutions may be a bit more relaxed about procedures, but will have liability insurance that protects them. Staff members driving vehicles owned by private institutions should be certain that they are informed about their protections in the event of an accident.

At most institutions, both public and private, those using personal vehicles for transporting themselves and others for duties associated with their employment are expected to be self-insured and carry their own vehicle insurance.

CONCLUSION

Student affairs staff members at both public and private institutions have to be aware of how institutional control can affect exposure to liability. In the end, public institutions and private ones are more similar than they are different, largely governed by contract law and the promises they make to students, employees, and other constituents. Risk can be mitigated by those in the public sector of higher education by taking care to not limit religious expression, being conscientious about content-based limits of expression, carefully following established standards for due process, attending to reasonable expectations of privacy, and staying alert to their responsibilities for the property they own. Risk can be mitigated by those working in the private sector by following established procedures and standards in all cases and making no exceptions, unless the process permits it. The authors have described some of the other ways in which public and private institutions differ and how these differences affect the work of student affairs administrators.

REFERENCES

Kaplin, W.A., & Lee, B.A. (2009). *A Legal Guide for Student Affairs Professionals* (4th ed.) (pp. 23–34, 365–371, 456–474). San Francisco, CA: Jossey-Bass.
Lake, P.F. (2011). *Foundations of Higher Education Law & Policy* (pp. 47–89). Washington, DC: NASPA: Student Affairs Administrators in Higher Education.

ADDITIONAL RESOURCE

Pavela, G. (2010, April 23). "Can Students at Private Universities be Dismissed at Will?" In *The Pavela Report*, *15*(13). St John, FL: College Administration Publications.

CHAPTER 2

PERSONAL VERSUS INSTITUTIONAL RISK MANAGEMENT

Many people who bring lawsuits for alleged wrongful acts by college and university officials name only the institutions in their claims. This may have to do with their perceptions of the resources of colleges and universities, compared to those of individual persons. Universities have, in effect, much more capital and financial means than do individual administrators. That perception of "deep pockets" leaves many to bring their claims against only the institutions.

Nonetheless, there are many occasions when individual administrators and staff members are named in lawsuits, either in addition to their employing institutions, or named solely. Many colleges have policies that protect staff members from personal liability for acts performed in the course of their normal duties. Action outside of the normal responsibilities of student affairs administrators, including intentional torts or reckless disregard for the safety and welfare of others, may result in personal liability by those administrators.

PUBLIC VERSUS PRIVATE DISTINCTIONS

Many states have laws that shield them and their employees from litigation under the doctrine of state immunity. Governmental, or sovereign, immunity shields public institutions from many forms of liability claims. Under some circumstances, that immunity may be extended to employees at public institutions. Typically, official immunity protects senior-level administrators at public institutions. In some circumstances it may be possible that, when governmental immunity is successfully claimed by the institution, individual administrators may be more exposed to liability risk. The alert student affairs administrator will be familiar with state law regarding governmental immunity and the protection of government employees.

Officials at private colleges and universities are generally not protected by sovereign immunity or by official immunity. The principle of charitable immunity, protecting charitable organizations from legal liability, might be used to insulate private institutions and their employees, but it is not a typical defense strategy, and it is not often successful.

TORT LIABILITY

Torts are wrongful acts that result in harm or loss (Kaplin & Lee, 2009, pp. 109–127). They can be acts of omission or failure and they can be acts of commission. We discuss tort issues in more detail in Part Four. Tort liability arises for a student affairs administrator when a person believes that a wrongful act or failure to act by the administrator has caused the person injury or harm. When the act in question is within the scope of responsibility of the administrator, action may be initiated against both the institution and the individual. If the act in question is outside the normal duties of the administrator, the individual is more seriously exposed to the claim. The typical tort claims come from students (or from employees or former employees). Examples of tort claims by students are injuries they experience while participating in organized activities or while using campus facilities. Claims of violations of their civil rights or failure to warn them of hazardous conditions are other examples. In some circumstances, students who believe that their First Amendment rights have been violated may bring suit against individual administrators.

Some high-ranking student affairs administrators, particularly at public institutions, may be able to claim official immunity from liability when acting within the scope of their responsibilities and making a judgment relative to policy. Middle managers and junior-level staff members are less likely to successfully claim immunity in this respect.

Claims against student affairs administrators for negligence will usually be principally brought against their employing institutions, but individuals may be found liable if their acts contributed to the claimant's injury. An example of such circumstances is the death of a student, the most horrific experience a student affairs staff member can have. When surviving family members come to believe that the faulty judgment of an administrator is to blame, an action against the individual can be pursued. A serious and permanent injury is a similar example with the same possibilities. Administrators are not insulated from liability for intentional torts, so a purposeful act that causes harm or injury can certainly result in personal risk. It is always possible that alleged criminal acts by administrators can expose them to civil liability, too. The development of social media brings the possibility of communication producing exposure to risk, and student affairs administrators should be sensitive to claims of threats, disturbances, or unwelcome activity of any sort through the use of social media.

An additional area of possible individual risk is associated with writing reference letters. A former employee or a student may find that a reference letter creates a barrier to employment, and the letter's author may be exposed to a tort liability risk. Similarly, a reference letter that fails to disclose a significant limitation of a candidate or a danger posed to those whom the candidate might serve may also expose the author to risk. In any event, writing reference letters is a normal activity for student affairs staff, and supporting those whom we serve in their career exploration is natural. Balancing the effort to assist in advancing an individual's career with any associated risk should also be natural and normal.

A claim of a tort may arise when an employee feels wronged by the institution or the supervisor. Those who supervise others, either staff or students, need to recognize the risk associated with taking advantage of them or asking them to do things outside of their position responsibilities. We discuss this in more detail in Part Five.

Those who counsel or advise students must be sensitive to the risks associated with providing direction and steering students toward specific actions. Students often confide in student affairs administrators, and, as a result, student affairs personnel have to be alert to information that might suggest a health or safety risk for an individual student or others. An individual administrator may acquire some duty to warn or protect others based on a student confiding in him or her. On the whole, however, confidential information that presents no risk of harm to any person should generally be protected (Kaplin & Lee, 2009, pp. 454–456).

Some student affairs administrators assume roles as classroom instructors. As such, they must be sensitive to copyright infringement when they use printed or online materials that are copyrighted. Being sensitive to intellectual property issues may not be natural for student affairs professionals, but when they enter the classroom, they must be alert to those issues.

CONTRACT LIABILITY

Contract liability arises when institutions are unable to satisfy their contractual obligations when their employees have committed them to those obligations (Kaplin & Lee, 2009, pp. 244–252). Contracts with students in the form of published materials, residence hall assignments, and promises of services become relevant for student affairs staff. One of the key issues in determining institutional versus individual liability is the question of authority: whether the individual making a commitment on behalf of the institution has the authority to do so. The informed student affairs administrator will take care to know with certainty where the burden for making promises lies.

In institutional residence halls, residential administrators typically require students to sign physical contracts that make their duties and obligations clear and specific. Student affairs staff members who work in residence halls have to be alert to potential violations of local housing code, fire code, and federal housing laws through the Fair Housing Act. Individual exposure to risk may accompany institutional exposure. The same may be true for violations of health codes through dining services, particularly if the dining service is a self-operated one or if insufficient oversight is given.

PROFESSIONAL LIABILITY INSURANCE

Some administrators transfer their liability risk by purchasing professional liability insurance. Some student affairs professional associations offer liability insurance to their members. The coverage afforded by liability insurance can be more complex than it seems. The law associated with the duty to defend an insured person varies from state to state, and case law often defines that duty. Some insurers may wish to make a business decision to settle a case rather than defend it. In many instances, it can be much less expensive to resolve a dispute by offering a cash settlement than by proceeding to a trial. However, it may be possible that the insured would prefer to be defended and exonerated from the wrongful behavior claim. The informed student affairs administrator must be aware of state law associated with the duty of the insurer to defend the insured against liability claims. It is also prudent to be familiar with the terms of the policy in order to know the rights of the individual associated with responding to liability claims.

The principle of *respondeat superior* establishes that those who supervise can be held responsible for the actions of those who report to them.

This gives the supervisor the duty to train, monitor, and give oversight so as to manage the risks associated with how staff behave and perform their responsibilities. For reasons established in the previous chapter, those employed in private higher education may be less insulated by their institutions and should become informed about their personal risk of liability.

Student affairs administrators who serve on boards of directors or other organizations may find themselves exposed to risk. If a disgruntled employee brings an action against the organization through the board, members may find themselves individually exposed. Those serving in such capacities should know whether they are insured by the organization or by their employing institution and, if neither is the case, then they should consider purchasing insurance.

LIABILITY INSURANCE AND INSTITUTIONS

Although some states require insurers to defend cases against the insured, the obligations on institutions are less restrictive. Some institutions, both public and private, purchase insurance that covers the institution as well as employees acting in good faith and in accordance with their assigned duties. The purchase of insurance is, in effect, risk transfer. Many institutions do not use insurance in the face of smaller claims but, rather, self-insure. An institution that is self-insured will often favor a settlement with a payment of damages, rather than proceeding to trial, even if officials are confident regarding the case. These are financial decisions, because defending a charge in civil court can be very expensive. Settling cases, therefore, is a reality; but it may cause frustration on the part of an involved administrator.

CONCLUSION

Student affairs staff should be familiar with institutional policies and procedures, as well as the limits of their own duties and responsibilities. Being ill-informed or unaware of institutional policies is not a strong defense in litigation. Good record-keeping and documentation inform best intelligent practice. Individual staff members should consult with their supervisors to determine institutional policies and protections associated with personal liability of employees. Student affairs administrators at public institutions should know about the extent to which their exposure to liability is limited by sovereign immunity or statutory limitations of exposure. Those who work at private institutions should learn about the existence of liability insurance held by the institution, as well as policies for the protection of employees from exposure. Of course, being in contact with legal counsel when questions about personal and institutional liability arise is a good practice.

REFERENCE

Kaplin, W.A., & Lee, B.A. (2009). *A Legal Guide for Student Affairs Professionals* (4th ed.) (pp. 109–127, 244–252, 454–456). San Francisco, CA: Jossey-Bass.

ADDITIONAL RESOURCES

Kaplin, W.A., & Lee, B.A. (2009). *A Legal Guide for Student Affairs Professionals* (4th ed.) (pp. 149–158). San Francisco, CA: Jossey-Bass.
Lake, P.F. (2011). *Foundations of Higher Education Law & Policy* (pp. 1–46). Washington, DC: NASPA: Student Affairs Administrators in Higher Education.

PART TWO

THE U.S. CONSTITUTION

The U.S. Constitution has a substantial impact on student affairs practice, particularly in public institutions. In this part, we discuss the particular ways in which the Constitution affects student affairs practice. Specifically, in Chapter Three we address First Amendment issues: freedom of speech, freedom of religion, limits on restricting religious expression, and freedom of the press. In Chapter Four we address both Second Amendment and Fourth Amendment issues relative to, respectively, the right to bear arms and search and seizure. Chapter Five details Fifth Amendment issues, particularly as related to employment review matters and other procedural issues.

CHAPTER 3

THE FIRST AMENDMENT

Congress shall make no law respecting an establishment of religion, or prohibiting the free exercise thereof; or abridging the freedom of speech, or of the press; or the right of the people peaceably to assemble, and to petition the government for a redress of grievances.

INTRODUCTION

The First Amendment of the U.S. Constitution serves a number of essential purposes in a free and democratic society. Principally, it allows for the expression of minority viewpoints or unpopular opinions (Kaplin & Lee, 2009, pp. 478–480). The open discourse that follows helps ideas to form and permits the clarification of individual thinking. The First Amendment also has the effect of limiting the authority of government and opens the door to protests against government action. In the institutional setting, the public university is, for all practical purposes, government. Therefore, First Amendment rights of citizens, particularly students, faculty members, and members of the university community, fully apply at public institutions. The employees of public institutions are employees of the state, and campus property is public property. These conditions have been further defined and refined by the courts over the years, and we discuss them in this chapter.

RELIGIOUS EXPRESSION

The first clause of the First Amendment, related to the expression of religion, is important to student affairs professionals from two different perspectives (Kaplin & Lee, 2009, pp. 35–49). First, what is commonly referred to as the "establishment clause" prohibits government from creating religion or forcing religion on citizens. Case law has established that public institutions cannot force persons to pray, partake in religious services, or be subjected to religious readings. A number of decisions by the U.S. Supreme Court have provided useful context for this aspect of the Constitution, including findings of clarity regarding school prayer.

The second part of that clause prohibits government from preventing the expression of religion, and this is where student affairs professionals at public universities might become confused. The casual understanding of this aspect of the Constitution has commonly been characterized as the "separation of church and state." Some student affairs administrators might believe that the Constitution does not allow religious expression on public university campuses. To the contrary, case law rather firmly establishes that a public institution that prohibits students from gathering to express religion or religious beliefs is acting in a way that is contrary to the First Amendment. Such restrictions are, in effect, restrictions of speech based on content. Not only should public institutions avoid prohibiting students from expressing religion, but they also should not fail to fund activities associated with the practice of religion. Some public institutions have misinterpreted this issue in fear of violating the establishment clause of the First Amendment, but failing to permit or fund religious expression is a violation of the free exercise clause.

Since a public university that prohibits religious publications on campus is also "prohibiting the free exercise" of religion, student affairs professionals should give careful consideration regarding the rights of students who wish to express religious views or engage in religious ceremonies. At the same time that students should be permitted to engage in religious expression, university officials cannot force that on them at public institutions. For example, if a group of students at a public institution wants to use a residence hall lounge for a Bible study, it should be permitted. However, if the Bible study is organized by a resident director, a professional employee of the institution, it may be subject to challenge. Similarly, if a student is assigned Bible readings as part of a disciplinary sanction at a public institution, it probably entangles the institution with forced religious practice.

FREE SPEECH

The second clause of the First Amendment prohibits government from unreasonable restrictions of freedom of speech. This aspect of the First Amendment has received much attention from the courts over the years, and case law has helped to form standards and clarify rights that are associated with free expression (Kaplin & Lee, 2009, pp. 478–508). An important aspect for student affairs professionals to understand is the principle of a "public forum." A public forum is a place in which government does not regulate speech, and a key condition of speech regulation is that it cannot be content-based. In other words, a student affairs administrator cannot permit one form of speech outside of the student union building, such as student election campaigning, and regulate against another form of speech, like a pro-life protest, without risk. By permitting the student election campaigning, the administrator has created a "public forum" at that location and would be wise to not prohibit at that same place other forms of speech based on content.

Some challenges have arisen where students have acted as though their First Amendment rights were restricted by their institutions because they were forced to express things they did not wish to say (Kaplin & Lee, 2009, pp. 306–310). A student in the theater department, for example, may be required to speak words in a performance that she finds offensive. Courts have indicated that, in this particular instance, acting necessarily involves saying or doing things that one might not naturally say or do, although the student's right to freely express religion may prevail over the argument about acting. Likewise, a student in a counselor education program might be dismissed from the program if he refuses to work with gay students.

Although this clause of the First Amendment permits citizens to protest in public places, the right of expression does not extend to the right to disrupt the fundamental purposes of universities. The courts have determined that reasonable restrictions on free expression can be made in the form of *time* limitations, *place* designations, and *manner* of speech. For example, institutions may govern when and where amplified speech may be allowed. Institutions may also restrict speech that is inside of or near classroom buildings and any other speech that interferes with the purpose of the university. A regulation that requires speech or printed work to be "wholesome" risks a constitutional challenge, as might one that prohibits "offensive speech." Further, restrictions of time, place, and manner must be reasonable. An administrator who directs a group of protesters to a remote part of campus so they do not disturb or disrupt the normal traffic in a busy part of campus may be imposing an unreasonable restriction which, in effect, is based on content.

Although this practice has recently become less common, a number of institutions have created what are referred to as "free speech zones." The notion of such a designation is that there are no content restrictions in those spaces. A complication is that any other space that becomes by designation or default a public forum would also have no content restrictions. Some have argued that free speech zones have the effect of regulating the content of speech, and, of course, one might wonder about the openness of speech at all places that are not free speech zones.

Many student affairs professionals have faced requests from students to organize around a cause or belief. Colleges and universities usually encourage social activism and student expression of opinion or values (Pavela, 2014). Free expression has been so highly valued on college campuses that they have been referred to as the "marketplaces of ideas." Some university leaders have attempted to restrict students from organizing around subjects or in affiliation with groups that are believed to be supportive of violence or at least disruptive behavior. Courts have determined that the suspicion or fear associated with some risk of future disruption is not sufficient reason to not allow students to organize. The standard that courts have imposed is greater than "suspicion." Instead, courts have said that institutions must reasonably forecast that a disruption or illegal behavior is imminent (Pavela, 2014).

Some universities have policies that require student organizations to open their memberships to all students in order to be eligible for funding. Such a requirement may restrict some types of organizations from accessing funds and may result in complicated tests of free association and free expression. It is not clear at this time whether such a restriction is a failsafe approach to guide the funding of student organizations. However, a decision by the U.S. Supreme Court allowed a restriction of the funding for a student organization that was open only to students who subscribed to the group's beliefs.

Some court decisions have indicated that the rights of visitors on college campuses may be different from those of members of the university community, such as faculty members and students. Some institutions have set limits on time and place restrictions for visitors that are different from those restrictions on student or faculty speech. Those limitations are most likely seen by courts as permissible, as long as they are not based on content. Some institutions have required persons to receive prior approval before an event or public expression is allowed. The challenge to prior-approval restrictions would probably be based on prior restraint on free expression, motivated by a content restriction, so that, in some jurisdictions, prior approval may be impermissible.

Among the foundational principles of student affairs work are those that emphasize civility and respect for others (Young, 1997, pp. 71–85). Possibly as a result of this sort of thinking, and in an effort to protect students and others from harm, some institutions have attempted to regulate speech with rules that limit the kinds of expression that are allowed. These speech codes can be risky because they can be seen as an unreasonable restriction of speech based on content. A code that regulates against speech that is harmful or hurtful obligates the speaker to know when harm or hurt might take place. A code that regulates against speech that is "offensive" or speech that is "upsetting" may be overly broad and not supported in a court test. A code that regulates against speech that is "disruptive" might seem on its face to be contradictory with the fundamental principles of the First Amendment, which, at its core, protects unpopular speech and minority viewpoints.

For similar reasons, to promote civility, student affairs administrators may be inclined to restrict actions by students or others that disrupt programs or speeches. Heckling or interrupting speakers may be seen as uncivil or discourteous, but courts may determine that the behavior advances the purposes of the First Amendment. It can be difficult to know where the line is between the right to express disagreement with the speaker's position and the rights of audience members to hear the expressed views. At public institutions, in particular, student affairs staff members must be sensitive to the rights of those who wish to express opposition to a viewpoint.

Hate speech is difficult to regulate because it is defined as speech that has the purpose of humiliating or causing hurt more than communicating ideas. Establishing a motive or purpose for such speech may be a very challenging enterprise. Hate speech that is not directly threatening nor falling under the doctrine of "fighting words" (addressed later in this chapter) is probably best left unregulated. An additional context is that courts have determined that emotional content is as much protected by the First Amendment as is cognitive content, and the offensiveness of speech is no reason to restrict it.

An institution of higher education may be challenged if it regulates against obscenity or cursing. The challenge associated with obscenity is that it is hard to define and regulate, and cursing is a form of speech that exists in the public forum, in media, and in many aspects of communication between adults. There may be some sites on college campuses where obscenity can be regulated, such as a chapel or an elementary school located on campus property.

Universities can reasonably limit expression in a variety of conditions (Pavela, 2014). Commercial speech, for example, does not enjoy the same level of protection as does the communication of ideas or opinions about issues. Universities are not obligated to permit commercial speech at the same level and under the same conditions as other speech. As described previously, institutions are also not obligated to allow speech that disrupts the academic environment or the fundamental purposes of the university. Commercial speech is limited, for example, in the classroom, as this is the fundamental teaching and learning environment.

Further, universities are not required to permit speech that encourages or has the direct result of unlawful behavior (Pavela, 2014). The test for limiting this type of speech, however, is rigorous. Lawlessness must be immediately imminent before the provoking speech can be prohibited. A form of expression that falls in this category is that of "fighting words," expression that has a tendency to provoke an immediate violent reaction. Courts rarely apply this doctrine. Another form of speech that can be limited is a true threat of violence. The threat must be genuine and an expression of a serious tenant to commit harm.

In addition, several forms of speech can be regulated that might affect a student's ability to learn or an employee's ability to work productively, including sexual or racial harassment. Regulations against harassment must be clear, and violating speech must be severe enough to limit an individual's ability to participate in a program or work setting. Institutions may also regulate against defamatory expression that is communicated to someone other than the subject and would harm the subject's reputation.

Courts have also recognized the principle of "individual privacy," and institutions may regulate against invasions of privacy whereby individuals may be subjected to unwelcome speech in their homes or, perhaps, in residence hall rooms. A principle associated with individual privacy is the notion of a "captive audience." This has been broadly applied. Places in which individuals may be "captive" include private residences and their work environments, but generally not other places that are more public. Further, even in captive-audience environments, courts have permitted limits on expression in the form of oral speech, but they have been less inclined to prohibit expression that is written. That may be because oral expression with a captive audience is expression the audience cannot escape, but written expression can be avoided. An additional point that the courts have made clear is that expression may be in the form of the spoken word or the written word, but it may also be symbolic in nature. A black armband, a Confederate flag, and a Nazi swastika are all symbolic forms of expression. Those examples of symbolic expression are as closely protected by the First Amendment as are spoken and written words.

Besides having the capacity to regulate forms of speech as described previously, institutions may also establish regulatory conditions that limit expression in other ways. For example, although such regulations cannot be based on content, institutions can clearly regulate against graffiti or the defacing of buildings and interior walls. Again, these regulations must be viewpoint neutral, so it might be risky for an institution to permit sidewalk chalking for some purposes and not for others. Of course, institutions can regulate against expression that causes harm to people or property, so the reader can see that institutions are not required to permit every form of expression in every setting. Viewpoint neutrality is essential, and speech cannot be regulated based on content, except as detailed above.

The First Amendment applies to public institutions as it protects speech rights of employees. Generally, those employed by public higher educational institutions are free to criticize governmental entities, including their employing institutions, as long as they speak as private citizens (Pavela, 2013). However, they may be subject to consequences, including dismissal, if their speech is as employees or associated with their official duties.

FREEDOM OF THE PRESS

The freedom of the student press has been tested over time in the courts. Prior approval of student publications may be a form of a prior restraint based on content, so a public university is best served to not engage in prior approval. Some university leaders have suspended the publication of student newspapers because of the expression of controversial views. Again, the expression of controversy is the fundamental purpose of the First Amendment. Some university leaders have taken disciplinary action when publications or student organizations have engaged in expression that is tasteless and sophomoric. There is risk in such practice, largely because tastelessness exists in many forms in the media and in entertainment and, of course, it is always subjective and in the eye of the beholder. Some student government organizations have attempted to withhold funding from student publications because the views expressed were unpopular. Such efforts to restrict funds have typically failed in tests in courts, because they are content restrictions.

OTHER ISSUES

Almost everything that has been addressed in this chapter applies fully at public institutions, but less so at private colleges and universities. The relationships between students and private institutions are largely governed by published materials that describe student rights, regulations, and associated procedures (Pavela, 2014). Many private institutions have standards and procedures that appear similar to those at public institutions. That may be because private colleges have the same viewpoints about open expression and free thought that is required of public colleges and universities. The principles of the First Amendment are grounded in the rights of citizens, and they are honored and treasured in our society. For private colleges to respect them and afford to students the same rights that students at public institutions enjoy seems to some to be natural. In any event, the published standards and procedures at private institutions are part of the contractual relationship with students.

Private institutions have often made the mistake of not following their own established rules and procedures and, effectively, violating their contractual obligations to students (Pavela, 2014). The standards that are written are, in effect, promises made by institutions to students. A simple rule of integrity should guide institutional actions that are consistent with published rules, regulations, and procedures.

Some private institutions have acted in ways that might fall under the doctrine of "state action." This condition applies when private organizations act on behalf of government or when they perform functions normally considered associated with the role of government. Although state action can legitimately be applied to private organizations, it is not commonly associated with court decisions with respect to private colleges and universities.

A number of organizations have become involved in disputes associated with the freedom of expression. One such group, the Foundation for Individual Rights in Education (FIRE), has as its purpose defending individual rights in higher educational settings that deal with freedom of expression and other constitutional rights. FIRE has effectively challenged institutional practices or regulations that have the effect of limiting First Amendment rights. Another group, the Student Press Law Center, advocates for the rights of student publications and provides information and advice at no charge. The informed student affairs administrator should recognize that students and those who represent them have access to expert advice and opinion regarding their First Amendment rights from these and a number of other sources.

CONCLUSION

College students are a very diverse collection of people, and they often gravitate to argument and dispute. Some have deeply held religious beliefs, and some have none at all. Almost every campus has some students who might be considered activists or dissenters who impose their views on others in ways that some might consider annoying. The views and expressions of extremists are afforded as much protection as the positive, agreeable messages some might prefer. The values of those in the student affairs field often revolve around harmony, civility, and agreement; but we must value more highly the freedom for the expression of unpopular ideas that fuel debate and discussion and help students refine their own beliefs. What better place than a college or university campus for such activities to occur! Student affairs staff members should recognize that dispute and disagreement, even when it is disturbing and upsetting, is usually protected by the U.S. Constitution, particularly at public institutions. Religious expression is similarly protected, as is the freedom of the student press. Those at private institutions, as established in this chapter and in Chapter One, operate under slightly different conditions and must be aware of how their published policies inform practice and decision making.

REFERENCES

Kaplin, W.A., & Lee, B.A. (2009). *The Law of Higher Education* (4th ed.) (pp. 306–310). San Francisco, CA: Jossey-Bass.

Pavela, G. (2013). *The Pavela Report, 18*(29). St. Johns, FL: College Administration Publications.

Pavela, G. (2014). *The Pavela Report, 19*(4). St. Johns, FL: College Administration Publications.

Young, R.B. (1997). *No Neutral Ground* (pp. 71–85). San Francisco, CA: Jossey-Bass.

ADDITIONAL RESOURCES

Bird, L.E., Mackin, M.B., & Schuster, S.K. (2006). *The First Amendment on Campus: A Handbook for College and University Administrators*. Washington, DC: NASPA: Student Affairs Administrators in Higher Education.

Foundation for Individual Rights in Education (FIRE). Available at http://thefire.org/

Hutchens, N. (2012). "You Can't Post That . . . Or Can You? Legal Issues Related to College and University Students' Online Speech." *Journal of Student Affairs Research and Practice, 49*(1), 1–15. Available at http://journals.naspa.org/jsarp/vol49/iss1/art1/.

Kaplin, W.A., & Lee, B.A. (2009). "Students' Freedom of Expression." In W.A. Kaplin & B.A. Lee, *A Legal Guide for Student Affairs Professionals* (4th ed.) (pp. 478–510). San Francisco, CA: Jossey-Bass.

Pavela, G. (2010, July 9). "'All Comers' Equal Access Policies and the First Amendment." *The Pavela Report, 15*(22). St. Johns, FL: College Administration Publications.

Pavela, G. (2012, November 2). "Campus Newspaper Regulation: A Case Study in Too Much Law." *The Pavela Report, 17*(32). St. Johns, FL: College Administration Publications.

Pavela, G. (2010, December 17). "Funding Religious Programs at Public Colleges." *The Pavela Report, 15*(39). St. Johns, FL: College Administration Publications.

Pavela, G. (2011, February 18). "Itinerant Preachers and the First Amendment." *The Pavela Report, 16*(5). St Johns, FL: College Administration Publications.

Pavela, G. (2010, October 15). "When Can Student E-mail Messages Be Punishable 'Fighting Words'?" *The Pavela Report, 15*(31). St. Johns, FL: College Administration Publications.

Wolf-Wendel, L.E., Twombly, S.B., Tuttle, K.N., Ward, K., & Gaston-Gayles, J.L. (2004). *Reflecting Back, Looking Forward: Civil Rights and Student Affairs*. Washington, DC: Student Affairs Administrators in Higher Education (NASPA).

CHAPTER 4

THE SECOND AMENDMENT AND THE FOURTH AMENDMENT

THE SECOND AMENDMENT

A well-regulated militia, being necessary to the security of a free state, the right of the people to keep and bear arms, shall not be infringed.

The Second Amendment of the U.S. Constitution relates to the right to bear arms. Although the amendment is in the federal Constitution, interpretation of it has been in the hands of the states, and there is great variation in how the states have responded, particularly in the past several years. The states have varying cultures, and state lawmakers hold varying ideological beliefs in regard to protecting the welfare of their citizens. Many states have laws that ban guns from college campuses, and quite a few states permit colleges to develop their own policies regarding firearms on campus. Some states have passed or are considering legislation that ensures that citizens can possess guns on public property. States have passed or will consider legislation that allows guns on public property in locked trunks of cars or that permits guns in the hands of employees, but not students. As legislation and litigation associated with these matters will surely unfold over the coming years, the alert student affairs professional is encouraged to stay informed about associated state law that can affect the rights of students and employees regarding the possession of firearms.

Safety on campus is a major issue for student affairs administrators (Kaplin & Lee, 2009, pp. 383–390). There have been horrific incidents of campus shootings and grave concern about weapons on college property. Gun control has not been a prominent issue historically in American higher education; however, legislative concern about campus safety in today's climate has led to several states exploring the possibility of laws that at least partially open the door to gun possession on college campuses. A heightened sensitivity derived from recent college shootings may change legislative interest in allowing guns on campus, as well as affect future judicial decisions. Courts have recognized that Second Amendment freedoms can be reasonably restricted, and banning firearms from places like schools has been allowed through court decisions. Courts have understood that college campuses may have a significant number of persons in their communities who are minors, that is, persons under eighteen years of age. At the beginning of an academic year, many incoming students have not yet reached the age of majority and are considered minors, members of a protected class. Additionally, universities commonly host groups of younger persons as part of summer camps and programs and prospective student tours and visits. The vulnerability of minors on campus may affect legislative initiatives associated with Second Amendment rights, as well as court decisions. There are strong emotions associated with this issue. Advocates for permitting guns on college campuses argue that it would allow potential victims to fight back against an active shooter. Those who take this position often present the matter as a Second Amendment issue and suggest that students are being stripped of their constitutional rights when they arrive on campus (http://concealedcampus.org). Those who argue against guns on campus suggest that allowing guns would make the risk of violence even higher (http://keepgunsoffcampus.org).

The well-informed student affairs administrator is aware of state law that governs the possession of weapons on campus, as well as any local or municipal law. Any proposed or actual change in these laws should be carefully monitored for their possible impact on campus life. It is probable that the debate about Second Amendment rights on college campuses will continue. Courts will make rulings, and laws will be passed and challenged, and the issues will be explored and discussed for some time before there is clarity on this matter. The varying cultures and norms of the fifty states may be the most significant factor in this issue, and the states will have some measure of independence as legislation unfolds and is debated. Few would argue that guns on college campuses present no liability and safety risks, but student affairs administrators and their colleagues on campus will have to manage whatever risk is presented. Court decisions and legislative proposals may be monitored by student affairs professional associations and other interested groups, and the informed professional should use those connections to stay as current as possible and respond intelligently and thoughtfully to what could be a changing landscape.

The issues that enter the debate on campus guns control from the student affairs perspective center on student alcohol use, student mental health, residence hall arrangements, and safe storage of guns and the typically free, open climate of college campuses. The presence of alcohol on college campuses and its prominence in the student culture and social experience may give student affairs staff pause when considering weapons on campus. The combination of risks associated with student alcohol use and the presence of guns presents serious consideration. Colleges are enrolling greater numbers of students with mental health issues. For the same reasons associated with student alcohol use, the combination of a portion of the student community struggling with challenges of mental health and the presence of weapons on campus should create some concern for any student affairs professional. In college residence halls, there is usually a significant amount of shared space. The resulting limits of privacy and control of space make the safe storage of weapons problematical. Finally, universities are places where the free and open discussion of ideas is encouraged and highly valued. Sometimes, the resulting debates and discussions can become heated, because of the wide-ranging ideologies of students and others. Bringing weapons into a heated disagreement can lead to unwanted consequences. The student affairs administrator must struggle with these matters and, in the context of state law, help produce and promulgate policies that keep campuses and their communities safe.

It is essential to ensure that the campus public, employees, students and families be well-informed about the campus policies associated with guns. Making sure that the campus community understands the expectations associated with firearms is an essential first step toward compliance. The use of various communication processes may make sense. Of course, the policies have to be in codes of conduct, but encouraging conversation about the policies in residence hall meetings or other student and staff gatherings may be wise. The use of social media is an additional way to communicate with campus community members about guns and institutional policies relevant to gun control. Additionally, campus policies must be enforced (and, of course, able to be enforced). Policies should be evaluated for these criteria. Having a policy, but failing to (or being unable to) enforce it, is not good practice and exposes the responsible party to risk.

THE FOURTH AMENDMENT

> The right of the people to be secure in their persons, houses, papers, and effects, against unreasonable searches and seizures, shall not be violated, and no warrants shall issue, but upon probable cause, supported by oath or affirmation, and particularly describing the place to be searched, and the persons or things to be seized.

The Fourth Amendment of the U.S. Constitution protects citizens from government intrusion when individuals have an expectation of privacy. That expectation clearly extends to residence halls on college campuses and also to other places where privacy is assumed. Where the expectation might exist, "persons, houses, papers, and effects . . ." can be clarified. "Persons" has been interpreted by the courts to include an individual's clothing, materials and pockets, and bodily fluids. "Houses" includes rental property, such as an apartment, a porch, and a mobile home or camper in which one lives. "Papers" includes a diary, a journal, a book, and letters. "Effects" would typically include a backpack, a purse, a personal computer, and mobile communication devices such as cell phones and tablets.

The key legal test for Fourth Amendment challenges is the matter of what is reasonable as opposed to unreasonable. One of the primary tests of reasonableness relates to the expectation of privacy. If an individual is in an environment in which privacy might reasonably be expected, an intrusion into that environment may be seen as a violation of her rights. However, an expectation of privacy isn't necessarily a binding aspect of this matter. For example, an individual may have an expectation of privacy, but an objective assessment of that may find the expectation to not be reasonable.

Under typical circumstances, government officials need to secure a warrant, based on probable cause, from a court before executing a search. Courts have issued rulings that clarify this standard and establish exceptions. For example, if a police officer is in a place where the officer has a right to be, incriminating evidence or contraband that is in plain view may be seized. This "plain view" exception extends not only to police officers but to persons who represent government. Resident hall searches at public institutions are obligated by these legal principles.

In conducting residence hall searches, a residence hall administrator or other official of an institution (or a landlord) may not waive the Fourth Amendment rights of another person and grant permission for a warrantless search. Furthermore, other persons, including one's roommate, cannot waive a person's Fourth Amendment rights. In such circumstances the "plain view" doctrine still applies, but not beyond these limitations.

Most institutions have a residence hall contract that students sign as a condition of moving into the residence halls. That contract can allow for students to waive their Fourth Amendment rights in limited circumstances. For example, a contract may state that institutional officials reserve the right to enter rooms for educational purposes, such as the protection of the university property, but not for the enforcement of criminal law. Residence hall contracts may also create an exception for room entry for health and safety reasons. These exceptions, however, would extend under typical circumstances only to campus officials, not police officers.

Most residence hall administrators employ courteous, ethical practice and inform students when room entries might take place for health and safety reasons. They also describe in residence hall contracts or published materials the procedures that will be used when student residence hall rooms will be entered. Those contracts and published handbooks present the fundamental guidelines for administrators at private institutions, but they are just as relevant at public institutions, supplementing and defining processes that conform to the Fourth Amendment.

At private institutions, administrators are not subject to Fourth Amendment restrictions, unless police or other government officials are active participants in room entry or search. The Fourth Amendment restricts search and seizure by government or government officials. It does not address the actions of private individuals or organizations. Police, as observers, may be allowable participants, but the Fourth Amendment applies if they become party to a search. The role of campus security is an important variable in this matter. If campus security personnel are licensed police officers or licensed "special" police officers, they are bound by all of the restrictions of police and government officials. However, if campus security personnel do not act with police powers, but solely with the rights of normal citizens, which is often the case at smaller, private institutions, they may act in the same way as student affairs staff when it comes to residence hall room entry and search and seizure. Any involvement by licensed police or government officials, even after the fact, may expose those involved and the private institution to risk of liability.

The expectation of privacy has been determined to extend to hallways in residence halls, where students might share common bathrooms and walk to them without being fully clothed. The privacy expectation of hallways would seem to be particularly well grounded if exterior entrances of buildings are locked or if visitors are monitored or regulated by staff. The informed student affairs professional should be alert to this condition and realize that students may enjoy privacy rights, not just in residence hall bedrooms.

Sound student affairs practice should include a general sensitivity to the issues associated with student expectations of privacy. Students probably have a reasonable belief that their purses or their backpacks are free from institutional intrusion. They may also expect that their lockers in recreational facilities and their personal computers and other electronic devices are free from search and seizure.

A practice that may receive attention is the increased use of video surveillance for security purposes. Technology in this area has made significant improvements, and the capacity for undetected video surveillance has grown significantly. This may bode well for improving security and solving crime, but if the practice continues to grow and become more widespread, it may well bring with it some Fourth Amendment and privacy legal challenges. Warnings that an area is subject to video surveillance may be a way around this concern, but police personnel may not favor that approach.

An additional area that may provoke Fourth Amendment controversy is the growing use of social networking sites. Actions taken by college officials for things that appear on social network sites may provoke freedom of expression challenges or invasion of privacy claims. It may be difficult to predict the actual effects of this growing trend, but student affairs staff members should stay alert to the issue and to best practices associated with it.

In late 2001, the U.S. Congress passed the Patriot Act in response to the national security risks evidenced by the September 11 tragedies. The Patriot Act broadened the federal government's surveillance powers and modified Fourth Amendment rights in several areas. It allowed for the expansion of the federal government's ability to examine records of an individual's activity that are held by a third party. In other words, a federal agent may ask to review students' records held by a university without a subpoena or other judicial review, if the request is related to national security. It also allowed for searches of a person's effects without notice to the owner. Additionally, the Patriot Act expanded the federal government's rights regarding the interception and collection of communication, from phone records to computer communication. The Patriot Act has been in effect for more than a decade, but heightened attention to national security may easily produce growing application of federal powers, to which all student affairs administrators should be sensitive.

The Fourth Amendment also covers another form of search, drug testing. Courts have determined that the collection of urine or blood for the purpose of testing for drugs is a search, as defined by the Fourth Amendment. Student athletes in colleges and universities may be asked to waive their Fourth Amendment rights for the purpose of drug testing. Policies that guide drug testing for athletes may be based on the reasonable suspicion of the use of a non-allowed drug by an individual student athlete. Policies may also be based on no suspicion at all, but a random practice. Waivers signed by students for such purposes should be clearly voluntary and, in the best practice, with some advance notice.

Students may encounter other forms of drug testing during their educational experiences. For example, a student may be engaged in an off-campus internship for which the employer requires drug tests. Students may also be given the opportunity to waive their Fourth Amendment rights and submit to voluntary drug tests as a result of conduct proceedings to monitor continued avoidance of illegal substances. This practice, as a matter of fact, is often part of a drug testing policy in intercollegiate athletics.

CONCLUSION

Student affairs administrators should stay alert to the dynamic nature of legislative initiatives and court decisions that are related to the Second Amendment and guns on college campuses. The pace at which the law is changing, either by new legislation or through court decisions and case law, is challenging. This is one of those issues for which there is great variation between states, driven entirely by the distinctions in culture in different parts of the country. Courts and legislatures in, for example, the Rocky Mountain states differ greatly from those in New England states. Student affairs professional associations may be good resources for up-to-date information on these issues.

Issues and concerns associated with the Fourth Amendment are more stable, and case law has been more consistent in recent years, but good student affairs work includes being alert to the privacy rights of students and managing the risks associated with those rights. The key test may be the expectation of privacy of the student, and thinking in that context will help student affairs staff manage the risks associated with practice related to search and seizure.

REFERENCES

Kaplin, W.A., & Lee, B.A. (2009). *A Legal Guide for Student Affairs Professionals* (4th ed.) (pp. 383–390). San Francisco, CA: Jossey-Bass.
Keep Guns Off Campus. Available at http://keepgunsoffcampus.org/
Students for Concealed Carry. Available at http://concealedcampus.org/

ADDITIONAL RESOURCES

Kaplin, W.A., & Lee, B.A. (2007). *A Legal Guide for Student Affairs Professionals* (2nd ed.) (pp. 365–371). San Francisco, CA: Jossey-Bass.
Pavela, G. (2013). *The Pavela Report, 18*(1). St. Johns, FL: College Administration Publications.
Pavela, G. (2013). *The Pavela Report, 18*(35). St. Johns, FL: College Administration Publications.

CHAPTER 5

THE FIFTH AMENDMENT

No person shall be held to answer for a capital, or otherwise infamous crime, unless on a presentment or indictment of a grand jury, except in cases arising in the land or naval forces, or in the militia, when in actual service in time of war or public danger; nor shall any person be subject for the same offense to be twice put in jeopardy of life or limb; nor shall be compelled in any criminal case to be a witness against himself, nor be deprived of life, liberty, or property, without due process of law; nor shall private property be taken for public use, without just compensation.

The Fifth Amendment of the U.S. Constitution has a substantial bearing on the work of student affairs. The application of the Fifth Amendment to student affairs work is fundamentally associated with the principle of due process. It relates to employment matters, student social conduct, and other student rights matters. We treat the due process issues associated with student social conduct in Chapter Twelve; this chapter will focus on due process associated with various other student rights issues and with matters of employment.

DUE PROCESS IN EMPLOYMENT

The key issue associated with due process in higher education is the presence of a property interest, as universities pose no threat to an individual's life or liberty. In employment matters, due process issues apply whenever the property of an employee is affected. Wages, benefits, leave time, and other compensation are all forms of employee property.

Employee property interests first surface in the candidacy phase. Student affairs professionals who are hiring persons to fill vacant positions need to be sensitive to the hiring process and the rights of candidates. The initial step is determining qualifications for the position. When specifying qualifications, the hiring authority must take care to discern between *required* qualifications and ones that are *preferred*. The associated risk is having identified a requisite qualification and the successful candidate falling short of it. This puts the hiring authority in a compromised position, because all other candidates who fall short of the requirement, as well as those who meet the requirement and were not selected, have a cause of action.

Some institutions require their employees to sign "loyalty contracts," promises to not publically criticize the institution or to adhere to certain beliefs or practices (Roth, McEllistrem, Brown, & Weinman, 2004, pp. 162–166). The institutions most commonly employing these practices are private institutions, but, no matter the type of institution, responsible student affairs administrators must be alert to the risks associated with expecting a prospective employee to waive his or her First Amendment rights. Loyalty contracts that have no conditions of exceptions for certain circumstances may expose the supervising, or requiring, authority to some risk.

New law regarding health care reform affords some part-time employees full health benefits (www.healthcare.gov/). Any decision to restrict an employee from health insurance may be subject to a complaint, and due procedural processes must be established to ensure objective review of such decisions. Supervisors also must be alert to hours and wages issues, when employees are asked to work for extended periods without appropriate adjustments in compensation. Again, a procedure to permit employees to make an official complaint about this matter must have due process embedded within it.

Another form of property interest is tuition benefits afforded to employees or their families. Any change in tuition benefits or uneven administration of such programs can result in some risk of liability. Health and safety hazards may expose employees to personal danger, and supervising authorities who are responsible for protecting against hazards, or at least for not modifying them, could be at personal or professional risk. Any grievance regarding either of these matters must receive a response that has due process embedded in it.

The property rights of graduate students serving as graduate assistants, research assistants, or teaching assistants can be complex in nature, because determining the status of graduate students can be complicated. Under some circumstances, they are principally employees; in others, they are principally students; and in still others, they may be a combination of the two. The establishment of their due procedural rights in property claims may vary, or at some institutions may be established by a collective bargaining agreement. The alert student affairs administrator should be aware of the circumstances surrounding such individuals and should know what due procedural elements determine the approach to disputes. The same is true for off-campus interns. A general rule of thumb is that, if the individual intern is the primary beneficiary (from an educational perspective) of the internship, the relationship to the overseeing organization is educational in nature, not employing. If, however, the principle beneficiary of the relationship is the sponsoring organization, the relationship is more of an employment one (www.dol.gov/whd/regs/statutes/FairLaborStandAct.pdf).

When an employer wants to bring change to provisions of property because of some act or alleged misconduct by the employee, there must be due process afforded the employee. Particular job duties or scope of responsibility would not generally be considered property and can usually be changed without applying due process. Due process rights of employees are usually defined by contract in employee handbooks or manuals, but minimal rights in employee discipline, in the form of notice of allegations and an objective opportunity to be heard in response, must be afforded.

The circumstances described above certainly apply to all full-time regular employees, both hourly and salaried. They also apply to student employees, for whom standards of performance may be less likely to be written. If the termination or penalizing of a student employee is affecting the property rights of that student, then some aspect of due process should be afforded the student.

Some institutions make decisions about employees based on financial exigency, a fiscal crisis that makes retaining all employees on the same terms impossible. When those circumstances occur, a fair and reasonable process for decision making should be articulated, and those affected by it should understand it. Alternatives to termination can be explored, and institutions can consider negotiating early retirements, furloughs, job sharing, and so forth in order to manage the risks associated with an acrimonious collection of terminations (www.aaup.org/report/financial-exigency-academic-governance-and-related-matters).

Sexual harassment charges must be carefully investigated and explored with a close eye to due process. Usually, entirely different procedures are employed for sexual harassment claims than for other employment environment complaints. That is the case, in part, because there are usually two employees (or more) involved, and they would commonly have conflicting interests. Property rights of both parties must be protected, so the process employed in the investigation and resolution of the claim must be carefully described, clearly understood, and address the due process rights of all subjects. The failure to respond effectively to a claim of sexual harassment can be very consequential to a supervisor and the employing institution, so a carefully considered process is essential to attaining a fair and effective resolution.

DUE PROCESS RIGHTS OF STUDENTS

The Fifth Amendment rights of students come into play whenever their property interests are at stake. Property can come in the form of financial aid, tuition charges or extended time to degrees, enrollment, and access to programs and services. This section will describe several ways in which challenges to the property of students relate to their Fifth Amendment due process rights.

The financial aid that institutions provide to students is most certainly property. If an institution intends to reduce the aid provided to a student, it would seem that some process is due, some fair review of the decision. That would be the case less if the decision to reduce or eliminate financial aid is due to a contractual agreement, such as state aid tied to academic performance. A specific example of a reduction in aid which merits due process is the case of a student athlete whose financial aid is linked to athletic performance. If the athlete's performance were deemed less than satisfactory and his financial aid were subsequently reduced, it would be good practice to permit the student to grieve that decision and request review by an objective party.

It is possible for a mistake in academic advising to cause a student to lose property in the form of required additional coursework. For example, if an academic advisor suggests that a student should enroll in a course that turns out to not be necessary, and the student did not instead enroll in a course that is essential for graduation, the student may be burdened with a tuition payment for an extra semester of enrollment. Some process for the review of such circumstances should be afforded, so students can be treated fairly and objectively. Institutions should have some process in place in the event that an error by an employee, or a flaw in procedures or published materials, leads to a consequence for a student in the form of additional cost or time to degree completion.

Allegations of academic misconduct can present significant challenges to institutions and students. At some institutions, student affairs administrators are responsible for the process for responding to charges of academic misconduct. Procedures for managing such allegations should be readily understood and widely promulgated. They should include clear notice of the allegation and an opportunity for the student to respond to it. Because fairness and objectivity are essential components of due process, a faculty member who is bringing a charge of cheating should probably not be the final authority on the matter, and some review of the proposed determination is advisable. The stakes for students charged with academic misconduct can be very high, because their access to academic programs or graduate and professional schools may be affected. It is essential that procedures for responding to academic misconduct charges have due process afforded to students (Kaplin & Lee, 2009, pp. 466–474).

The Fifth Amendment rights of students impact requests for accommodations for disabilities. The law requires institutions to make reasonable accommodations, and there may be a dispute between the authority representing the institution and the student who is affected. That dispute will usually revolve around what is reasonable. Due process is employed in securing accommodations for students (and employees) with disabilities. An individual who requests an accommodation of a disability and is denied has a right to due process and an objective review of the decision, particularly if the denial has an effect on a student's access to education or results in a loss of money for either a student or an employee.

MEDIATION OPTIONS

Many institutions employ a person who serves in a role as ombudsman to give students and employees an opportunity to grieve an adversarial circumstance when there is no institutional review process offered. An ombudsman has to be able to function independently without interference and must be neutral and impartial (www.ombudsassociation.org/). Sometimes, an ombudsman can negotiate a dispute to resolution in a way that is not adversarial. This sort of dispute resolution is not necessarily tied to due process, and is not an alternative to providing process that is due. However, it can be an informal avenue for managing a dispute without going through a process that can become adversarial. The presence of a mediation alternative can be an effective way to manage risk associated with student grievances.

CONCLUSION

Sound student affairs work involves knowing when students and employees have property rights at risk due to institutional policies or practices and being able to apply procedures that protect their due process rights. It may not be necessary to have written policies for grievances or the review of property risks; however, it is essential to know when it is correct to allow persons with property claims to grieve the outcome of lost property and be afforded appropriate due process rights. An important tactic in dealing with such matters is keeping good, thorough, accurate records. Much of the risk mitigation in this area is institution-specific, so knowing and adhering to the rules and standards of the employing institution is fundamental to good practice.

REFERENCES

American Association of University Professors. (n.d.). "Financial Exigency, Academic Governance, and Related Matters." Retrieved from www.aaup .org/report/financial-exigency-academic-governance-and-related-matters

Affordable Care Act. (n.d.). Retrieved from https://www.healthcare.gov/

Fair Labor Standards Act. (n.d.) Retrieved from www.dol.gov/whd/regs/statutes/ FairLaborStandAct.pdf.

International Ombudsman Association. (n.d.). Retrieved from www .ombudsassociation.org/

Kaplin, W.A., & Lee, B.A. (2009). *A Legal Guide for Student Affairs Professionals* (4th ed.) (pp. 466–474). San Francisco, CA: Jossey-Bass.

Roth, J.A., McEllistrem, S., Brown, C.J., & Weinman, C.S. (2004). *Higher Education Law in America* (pp. 162–166). Malvern, PA: Center for Education and Employment Law.

PART THREE

REGULATORY CHALLENGES

The three chapters in this part present the exposure to risk faced by student affairs administrators in the context of regulations of government associated with protecting student interests or the rights of employees, as well as the regulatory relationships with private organizations. Chapter Six provides a review of federal regulations that relate to student affairs practice, as well as the regulatory matters left in the hands of the states. Chapter Seven details the government standards associated with discrimination and the risk management issues that are related. Chapter Eight examines the risk management issues regarding the private agencies and organizations that regulate institutional practices.

CHAPTER 6

FEDERAL AND STATE REGULATIONS

INTRODUCTION

There are many ways in which government regulations affect or impact the work of student affairs administrators. Some such regulations affect society at large, including higher education, and other regulations are specifically designed for application in colleges and universities. This chapter will describe a variety of regulatory and legislative initiatives with which student affairs administrators should be familiar.

IMMIGRATION LAW—SEVIS

The most significant federal regulation associated with immigration law that impacts student affairs is the Student and Exchange Visitor Information System (SEVIS). SEVIS is a web-based utility designed to track and monitor students and exchange visitors and their dependents who have been approved to participate in the U.S. education system. More detailed information can be found at www.ice.gov/sevis.

SEVIS provides information to the Department of State, U.S. Customs and Border Protection (CBP), U.S. Citizenship and Immigration Services (USCIS) and U.S. Immigration and Customs Enforcement (ICE). The information that institutions are required by law to keep updated in SEVIS for any international student entering the United States on a student visa is name, address, major field of study, education degree level, and sources of funding. This means that those responsible for reporting that collection of information must be current about the status of all such students. The law and associated enforcement of it are under the umbrella of the Department of Homeland Security.

COPYRIGHT LAWS

Copyright laws exist to protect the rights of authors and inventors regarding their writings and inventions. For almost 200 years, copyright law was relatively stable. During that period, the exclusive rights to a creator of a unique work lasted for fourteen years and were renewable for a second fourteen years. In 1976, duration of copyright rights was extended to the creator's lifetime, plus fifty years. In the past thirty years there has been a substantial amount of legislative activity and private litigation. Much of that activity can be attributed to the increased access to information, largely attributed to the Internet, as well as to the dramatically growing use and application of technology. Court decisions have been governed by what is called a "fair use" doctrine, but more recently, courts have become quite rigorous in protecting the rights of copyright holders.

Student affairs administrators should be careful about photocopying copyrighted material for distribution to others, such as for a staff training exercise. The variables that might put such behavior at risk include the relative portion of material that was copied and whether the copying reduced the market for the published material. Copying computer software or music can present similar problems. The copying of music on the Internet is a common practice by students, and student conduct officers are familiar with their obligations associated with informing violators of the law and the rights of copyright holders.

In the past decade, the Recording Industry Association of America (RIAA) has been employing various strategies to protect the rights of copyright holders (www.riaa.com/physicalpiracy.php?content_selector=piracy_online_the_law). The motion picture industry has been less aggressive, but that may change. The informed student affairs administrator should take necessary steps to educate students about the law in this area and consequences for violations. Within this area of the law, universities are also exposed to risk as Internet service providers (ISPs) and, as such, can be given particular duties associated with warning violators, taking corrective action, or being held accountable for copyright infringement by student users of the Internet.

LAWS LINKED TO FEDERAL AID

A number of federal laws are enforced for institutions of higher education through a connection to federal aid. Federal aid to an institution includes all forms of funding, including financial aid to students. This has the effect of making this class of federal legislation applicable to virtually every college and university in the United States.

Drug-Free Workplace Act

The Drug-Free Workplace Act of 1988 applies to all universities and colleges that are federal grant recipients. The law requires that institutions publish statements about illegal drugs and the risks associated with their use, and it obligates institutions to establish educational programs and support systems for those seeking help associated with drug use or abuse.

Drug-Free Schools and Communities Act

The Drug-Free Schools and Communities Act of 1989 is more aggressive and comprehensive than the Drug-Free Workplace Act. It requires institutions to have written policies that include conduct standards, legal sanctions, health risks, helping programs, and disciplinary sanctions associated with the use of illegal drugs. It also requires the annual distribution of those policies to all students and employees. Schools are obligated to enforce those standards and to conduct a biennial review of their policy statements.

Student Right-to-Know Act

The student right-to-know law requires institutions to report graduation rates for their student bodies. By accessing this federal data set, individuals can compare graduation rates among colleges and universities.

Equity in Athletics Disclosure Act

Institutions that offer student aid to athletes are required to submit a comprehensive collection of information about expenditures, staffing, and student participation in sports and to make a distinction between men's sports and women's sports on all items. The report produced by the institution must be submitted to the Secretary of Education, but must also be available to prospective student athletes, their parents, and high school officials.

Campus Security (Clery) Act

The Campus Security Act of 1990 requires colleges and universities to annually report statistics regarding crimes that took place on campus and on property adjacent to or accessible from campus (Kaplin & Lee, 2009, pp. 387–390). The categories of crime are drawn from the FBI list of crimes. The annual security report must indicate the policies associated with campus security that are in place for the campus and must include crimes that took place in the three most recent years. The report must be submitted to the U.S. Secretary of Education, and it must also be provided to all students and employees. Prospective students and parents must be informed about the existence of the report. Further, it must be made available to applicants for admission to the institution.

Additionally, campus officials must provide timely warnings about crimes that have taken place and that pose a threat to the safety of individuals on campus. They must maintain a public log of all reported crimes. Crimes must be reported by all campus officials except counselors and clergy.

Campus Sex Crimes Prevention Act

This law requires campus officials to notify the community when a registered sex offender is in the vicinity and where sex offender information is available. One of the challenges with this law is that laws associated with sex offenders vary from state to state. What is a sex crime in one state might not be in a state where the sex offender is residing. Chapter Thirteen has a thorough review of this legislation and the associated requirements.

Title IX

Title IX of the educational amendments of 1972 is enforced by the Office of Civil Rights and obligates institutions to provide opportunity to either gender that is underrepresented in a particular activity. Much of Title IX legal activity has hovered around intercollegiate athletics, but it applies to co-curricular programs, academic programs, and so forth.

Originally, institutions measured their compliance with Title IX based on a three-part test. The elements of the test were: having the percentage of male and female participants substantially proportionate to the percentage of male and female students enrolled at the institution; having a history in continuing practice of expanding participation opportunities for the underrepresented gender; and demonstrating the accommodation of interests and abilities of the underrepresented gender (Kaplin & Lee, 2009, pp. 735–738).

Title IX liability has recently been extended to colleges when they have shown "deliberate indifference" to a student's grievance associated with sexual assault or harassment. In order for an institution to be held liable, the following conditions must apply: the harassment is so significant that it can prevent the victim from accessing educational opportunity; the college has control over the circumstances where the harassment took place; the college has control over the perpetrator of harassment; and the college was notified of the harassment and did not respond in an appropriate fashion.

The application of Title IX to sexual assault changes the landscape for such matters for colleges and universities (Pavela, 2011). It brings the federal government and its attorneys into the dispute and makes for a much more challenging circumstance than a simple, private lawsuit might. In recent years the federal government has been much more aggressive in the application of Title IX to sexual assault matters. High-profile cases have raised awareness of the usefulness of Title IX in the pursuit of resolution of sexual assault charges; it is predictable that more cases of this nature will occur. The responsible student affairs administrator must carefully evaluate assault cases that have a Title IX element and take great care to pursue facts diligently and thoroughly. Initiating a Title IX investigation is a serious matter, and the institution is best advised to proceed quickly and not wait for resolution of any associated criminal investigation or proceeding. Those involved in the investigation should have training and experience in responding to complaints of sexual violence, and they should understand the grievance procedure and requirements associated with confidentiality. Additional information on Title IX is found in Chapter Seven.

VIOLENCE AGAINST WOMEN REAUTHORIZATION ACT

The Violence Against Women Reauthorization Act (VAWA) was signed into law by President Obama in 2013, and it gives institutions of higher education substantial responsibility (www.whitehouse.gov/sites/default/files/docs/vawa_factsheet.pdf). One of them is the obligation to report incidents of domestic violence, dating violence, and stalking. This duty to report these classifications of crime goes beyond those required by the Clery Act.

Another set of responsibilities associated with VAWA pertains to the student conduct process. Institutional policy must include information on the rights of victims to seek assistance from law enforcement and campus authorities. Policy must also make clear the rights of victims regarding judicial no-contact, restraining, and protective orders, which serve to isolate victims from the accused. VAWA also prescribes standards for student conduct proceedings in domestic violence, dating violence, sexual assault, and stalking cases.

Under VAWA, institutions are obligated to offer prevention and awareness programs that promote awareness of rape, domestic violence, and associated behaviors. Such training programs are expected to include definitions of the offenses and of consent regarding sexual offenses and a statement that the institution prohibits the offenses. Programs must also include information on bystander intervention in the recognition of signs of abusive behavior. Institutions are expected to provide prevention and awareness campaigns on an ongoing basis; these programs must be made available to new students and new employees. Much of the responsibility for compliance with VAWA will fall on student affairs professionals, and they must be alert to the law and its requirements.

RIGHTS OF HUMAN SUBJECTS

Laws associated with the protection of human subjects may impact those student affairs professionals who conduct human subject research. Surveys of students or focus group research initiatives, particularly when the researcher intends to publish results, may be subject to human subject research rules. Student affairs practitioners should communicate with officials serving on institutional review boards responsible for reviewing proposals for human subject research.

ENVIRONMENTAL LAW

Environmental law can affect student affairs practice associated with managing waste in student health centers and the disposal of computers and printer cartridges—the fastest growing form of trash. Older buildings may have asbestos around pipes or in ceilings, and student affairs practitioners who are responsible for property should be alert to removal standards. Detection and removal of mold in buildings has become a growing part of the enforcement of the Environmental Protection Agency, and student affairs personnel responsible for buildings should be alert to the possible presence of mold.

MISSING STUDENT NOTIFICATION

An amendment to the Higher Education Opportunity Act of 2008, the Missing Student Notification Policy and Procedures, requires the notification of a parent or guardian, or other emergency contact person, when a resident student who is under twenty-one years of age is missing for twenty-four hours (http://counsel.cua.edu/missing.cfm). When campus police report a resident is missing, they must conduct a preliminary investigation. If they cannot verify that the student is safe within twenty-four hours of making the report, they must notify the student's parents or any other individual listed as an emergency contact person for the student. They must also notify local police agencies and give full cooperation to local police officials in their investigation.

LAWS ASSOCIATED WITH THE RIGHTS OF PERSONS WITH DISABILITIES

The rights of persons with disabilities have largely been shaped in the last forty years by two separate laws: The Rehabilitation Act of 1973 and The Americans with Disabilities Act (ADA) of 1990.

The Rehabilitation Act of 1973

Section 504 of The Rehabilitation Act is one of the first civil rights laws protecting the rights of persons with disabilities, and it established that any organization that receives federal aid must use affirmative action in employment when any person who is "handicapped" is a candidate. The law paved the way for the more comprehensive and far-reaching Americans with Disabilities Act.

The Americans with Disabilities Act

The ADA was intended to assure equal opportunity, full participation, independent living, and economic self-sufficiency for any person with a disability (www.ada.gov/). Key terms in the ADA include the judgment that persons with disabilities are "otherwise qualified" for participation in an activity or service and that institutions must make "reasonable accommodations" for persons with disabilities. Institutions are required to have a person designated to coordinate compliance with the law, and they must have a grievance procedure for persons who believe they have been denied accommodation. This law is enforced by the Office of Civil Rights, and compliance with it is arranged by litigation and penalties up to $100,000. In addition, forced compliance conditions are allowed.

The ADA Amendments Act of 2008 provided additional interpretation. In that legislation, the definition of disability was adjusted. Previously, disability was defined as "a physical or mental impairment that substantially limits one or more major life activities of such individual." This more recent legislation changes "substantially limits" to "materially restricts." It also expands "major life activities" to not just "learning," but to "thinking" and "concentrating." The bill also excludes impairments that are both transitory and minor, while the original legislation excluded impairments that were either transitory or minor. As a result, more conditions are defined as disabilities and covered by the ADA. Chapter Thirteen provides additional coverage of this subject.

Persons with any one of a variety of learning disabilities are protected by the ADA, as are persons with mobility disabilities or hearing and vision limitations. In providing accommodations, institutions must make adjustments to their requirements, such as providing course substitutions, permitting tape-recorded lectures, and allowing extended time on examinations, and they cannot charge fees for said accommodations. The student is obligated to provide medical documentation of the disabling condition, including a diagnosis and a description of the accommodation addressing the condition. At many institutions, the departments that provide support to students with disabilities are part of the student affairs division. Student affairs staff may be part of a grievance procedure or dispute resolution regarding accommodations or the quality of documentation that students provide.

One of the challenges facing departments that provide support to college students with disabilities is helping those students make the difficult transition from adhering to the law that governs the secondary and primary educational systems to the ADA that binds schools of higher learning. The Individuals with Disabilities Education Act (IDEA) encourages K–12 schools to keep students with disabilities in regular classrooms. It also mandates parental inclusion in educational planning for students. K–12 schools have the burden of assessing students with disabilities and making appropriate accommodations if eligibility for services has been determined. At the college level, those obligations to the educational institution do not exist. The college student has the responsibility of demonstrating the existence of a disability and the appropriate accommodation, and the parents are not directly involved, at least not at the same level they might have been in the K–12 schools. This transition can be difficult for students with disabilities if they have not been prepared and oriented to how disability support functions in higher education.

Another phenomenon facing student affairs professionals, specifically those who work in student residence halls, is associated with "service" and "assistance" animals. Most college campuses restrict students from having pets on campus, particularly in residence halls. However, the ADA does define "service" animals as allowable accommodations for persons with certain types of disabilities. Under that definition, service animals are animals trained to do work or perform tasks for the benefit of a person with a disability. Under the ADA, service animals must be permitted to accompany the persons whom they service in residence halls or anywhere else on campus. Furthermore, the ADA is clear in that it does not consider companion animals to be service animals. In a broader application, the U.S. Department of Housing and Urban Development (HUD), which enforces the Fair Housing Act, considers "assistance" animals to be a form of reasonable accommodation for a person with a disability. As defined, an assistance animal may provide emotional support that alleviates symptoms or the effects of a person's disability. Although HUD's definition technically falls outside of the strict requirements of the ADA, it may affect how college housing authorities respond to requests for companion animals. The alert student affairs professional must consult with counsel when faced with such a question; a follow-up with HUD may be appropriate.

FAMILY EDUCATIONAL RIGHTS AND PRIVACY ACT OF 1974 (FERPA)

FERPA gives college students the right to control the disclosure of their education records, to inspect their education records, and to seek amendment to their records if they wish (Ramirez, 2009, pp. 27–62). Students, not parents, hold these rights, irrespective of their age. The law has the effect of protecting the privacy of college students. There are several exceptions to FERPA that permit disclosure to parents, including a health or safety emergency, a violation of alcohol or controlled substance laws, and financial reporting for income tax purposes in the case of dependency. The enforcement of FERPA is the responsibility of the Family Policy Compliance Office of the Department of Education. Although the consequences for FERPA violations are potentially grave, that is, the loss of all federal aid, the compliance office seeks to help institutions adjust policies and practices and fix problems associated with violations, rather than punish institutions.

FERPA is frequently misunderstood and may sometimes be misrepresented. For example, when student affairs staff tell parents that federal law prevents them from answering the parents' questions about the student, it is often not true. For example, students who are under twenty-one years of age and dependents of their parents for tax purposes may find that educational information may be shared with their parents in no violation of FERPA. The truth is that many student affairs staff members do not want to share information with parents, seeing the student as the principle constituent. In emergencies or when a student is in some risk of harm or injury, parents can certainly be informed. In any event, falsely hiding behind FERPA is not the best practice.

The responsible administrator knows the purpose of FERPA and what its limitations are and treats student educational records, as defined by the law, appropriately.

THE PATRIOT ACT

The United States Patriot Act is a significant piece of legislation that passed shortly after the attacks of September 11, 2001. There is a FERPA waiver for the disclosure of records and permitting of wiretaps, electronic surveillance, and review of telephone records and stored voicemails. It does not require judicial review, and a subpoena is sufficient, as long as it is relevant to an investigation associated with national security.

OCCUPATIONAL SAFETY AND HEALTH ACT (OSHA) OF 1970

OSHA protects workers from safety and health hazards. As applied to higher educational institutions, it requires them to train employees on workplace health and safety risks, to keep employees informed about workplace hazards, to report injuries in the workplace to the federal government, and to maintain records of injuries and illnesses. Student affairs staff members who supervise employees must be aware of workplace risks and hazards and ensure they are in compliance with OSHA standards.

AFFORDABLE CARE ACT

The Affordable Care Act, signed into law by President Obama in 2010, requires employers to pay for health insurance for a group of part-time employees who were not previously eligible for those benefits. Student affairs staff members supervising departments employing persons made eligible for health care under this law must ensure that they are complying with the law. Most human resource department heads are informed about the law and can help student affairs professionals reach compliance.

STATE REGULATIONS

The states have the principal regulatory responsibility for education, and the ways in which they use that authority vary substantially. How, and whether, states regulate matters associated with higher education is at great variance. For example, some states have laws associated with hazing, immunizations, or insurance, and some do not. Informed student affairs professionals must be familiar with the state laws that apply to their work and employ reasonable risk management strategies so as to conform to those standards.

CONCLUSION

Federal and state laws that affect the practice of student affairs are abundant. Governmental regulation of higher education will continue as long as it is perceived as being in the public interest and as long as public money is invested in it. The informed student affairs practitioner has to be alert to changes in public law and to new developments that alter the practice of student affairs. Acquiring familiarity with government regulations is a key first step, but the responsible student affairs administrator must also be aware of and responsive to reporting requirements and deadlines, the duty to objectively investigate and respond to claims, the obligation to educate and inform students and the broader institutional community, and the need to protect the interests or students and, in some situations, their families. Knowing the regulations is a first step, but making the correct response to them is crucial.

REFERENCES

Fact Sheet: The Violence Against Women Act. Retrieved from www.whitehouse. gov/sites/default/files/docs/vawa_factsheet.pdf

Information and Technical Assistance on the Americans with Disabilities Act. Retrieved fromwww.ada.gov/

Kaplin, W.A., & Lee, B.A. (2009). *A Legal Guide for Student Affairs Professionals* (4th ed.) (pp. 387–390; 735–738). San Francisco, CA: Jossey-Bass.

Missing Student Notification Policy and Procedures 20 USC 1092. Retrieved from http://counsel.cua.edu/missing.cfm.

Pavela, G. (2010, July 9). "The April 4, 2011 OCR 'Dear Colleague' Letter." *The Pavela Report, 16*(12). St. Johns, FL: College Administration Publications.

Ramirez, C.A. (2009). *FERPA, Clear and Simple* (pp. 27–62). San Francisco, CA: Jossey-Bass.

Recording Industry Association of America. Retrieved from www.riaa.com/
physicalpiracy.php?content_selector=piracy_online_the_law

ADDITIONAL RESOURCES

Family Educational Rights and Privacy Act (FERPA). Available at www.ed.gov/
policy/gen/guid/fpco/ferpa/index.html.

Kaplin, W.A., & Lee, B.A. (2009). "Affirmative Action." In W.A. Kaplin &
B.A. Lee, *A Legal Guide for Student Affairs Professionals* (4th ed.)
(pp. 182–189). San Francisco, CA: Jossey-Bass.

Kaplin, W.A., & Lee, B.A. (2009). "The Federal Government." In W.A. Kaplin &
B.A. Lee (Eds.),*A Legal Guide for Student Affairs Professionals* (4th ed.)
(pp. 672–757). San Francisco, CA: Jossey-Bass.

Ramirez, C.A. (2009). *FERPA, Clear and Simple: The College Professional's
Guide to Compliance.* San Francisco, CA: Jossey-Bass.

The Catholic University of America, Office of General Counsel. FERPA.
Available at http://counsel.cua.edu/ferpa/questions.

Pavela, G. (2010, July 9). "Questioning Accepted Beliefs on School and College
Violence, the Bullying 'Epidemic,' and the 'Tide of Societal Violence.'" *The
Pavela Report, 15*(22). St. Johns, FL: College Administration Publications.

Smith, G.M., & Gomez, L. (2012, Fall). "The Labyrinth of Title IX: Clarifying
the Dear Colleague Letter." *Leadership Exchange.* Washington. DC:
NASPA: Student Affairs Administrators in Higher Education.

Student and Exchange Visitor Information System (SEVIS). Available at www
.ice.gov/sevis/.

The Catholic University of America, Office of General Counsel. Available at
http://counsel.cua.edu.

CHAPTER 7

DISCRIMINATORY PRACTICES

S tudent affairs administrators, given the norms and values of the work, may be very unlikely to act in ways that discriminate against persons from a protected class. However, well-intentioned acts may appear discriminatory, even though they are unintentionally so. This chapter reviews the laws and regulations associated with discrimination and presents practices that can manage the risk that could result.

PROGRAMS AND SERVICES FOR STUDENTS

Certainly, no effective student affairs professional wishes to be accused of discriminating against students; however, many practitioners are not fully informed about the law and may rely too heavily on their own good faith and fair-mindedness. Good judgment is a useful tool in student affairs work, but, where discrimination is concerned, it might be wise for it to be enhanced by an understanding of how laws regulate against it. In addition to being familiar with the laws regulating discrimination, student affairs administrators must be familiar with institutional policies and promises relative to discrimination. Many institutions publish statements of non-discrimination that establish the conditions and human characteristics around which the institution will not discriminate. It is quite possible that these statements would include characteristics that are in addition to what is prohibited by law.

Title VI of the Civil Rights Act of 1964

Title VI prohibits discrimination on the basis of race, color, and national origin in programs and activities that receive federal financial assistance

(Kaplin & Lee, 2009, pp. 726–735). Violations of Title VI can result in the loss of federal funding or legal action initiated by the U.S. Department of Justice. Of course, racial discrimination is antithetical to student affairs, but the alert administrator will guard against unintended discrimination in every aspect of student life. Issues of discrimination may arise in many student affairs functions, from roommate assignments in residence halls, to student conduct administration, to student organization memberships, to campus entertainment.

Title IX of the Educational Amendments of 1972

Title IX protects the rights of persons on the basis of gender, and it holds institutions accountable rather than individuals (Kaplin & Lee, 2009, pp. 735–738). It permits the recovery of monetary damages and allows for individuals to bring private causes of action. The principle areas of litigation regarding Title IX have been associated with women's opportunities in college sports; employment conditions for women faculty members, administrators, or sport coaches; and sexual harassment of students by faculty members or other students. Title IX has also been applied to sexual assault cases when institutional officials have been given actual notice of a claim of a sexual assault and have responded with "deliberate indifference." It is also possible for a pregnant student who alleges gender discrimination because of her pregnancy to use Title IX as an avenue for redress. Title IX protects the rights of students to return to academic programs and positions they held in student organizations before they took leave for childbirth. The power of Title IX in protecting the rights of pregnant students may not be widely known. Furthermore, some institutions do not employ persons as Title IX coordinators, so information about Title IX protections may be scarce or unavailable.

Another issue covered by Title IX is associated with gender identity. Title IX covers gender identity discrimination and access, so student affairs administrators must be sensitive to this form of discrimination. Additional information on Title IX is covered in Chapter Six.

Section 504 of the Rehabilitation Act of 1973

Section 504 prohibits discrimination against persons with disabilities. Discrimination may come in the form of limiting access to programs by persons with disabilities, failing to communicate effectively with persons with vision or hearing disabilities, and failing to make new construction or remodeled construction accessible.

The Age Discrimination Act of 1975

The Age Discrimination Act prohibits discrimination against older Americans, persons over forty and, in some instances, younger persons (Kaplin & Lee, 2009, pp. 174–176). Students who are denied college admission or the opportunity to participate in certain activities simply because they are too young or too old may be able to make a good discrimination claim. If there is some other factor, irrespective of age, such as a younger or older person having limited physical capacity to be part of a particular activity, then the denial may be allowed. For example, an older student in poor physical condition may be excluded from a fundraising distance run, not due to age, but to physical condition.

EMPLOYMENT

Student affairs leaders are often responsible for a significant number of employees, so it is wise for them to understand the laws that govern discrimination in employment.

Title VII of the Civil Rights Act of 1964

Title VII prohibits discrimination in employment on the basis of race, color, religion, sex, or national origin. Differential treatment is allowed for religion, sex, or national origin if it is a genuine occupational qualification. Title VII was amended in 1978 to also prohibit discrimination on the basis of pregnancy, childbirth, or related illness employment. Title VII also prohibits retaliation against employees for making claims of discrimination. If an employer initiates an adverse employment action against an employee who has claimed discrimination, Title VII makes it clearly unlawful. The informed student affairs administrator will be careful to avoid decisions in employment that appear to be discriminatory, even if unintentional.

The Family and Medical Leave Act of 1993

The Family and Medical Leave Act provides qualified employees with up to twelve weeks of unpaid leave in any twelve-month period for the birth and care of a child during the first year of life, the adoption of a child, or the serious health condition of the employee or a family member of the employee.

Other Considerations

Chapter Six described several regulatory principles that apply to employment, including the Drug Free Workplace Act, Title IX, Environmental Law, the ADA, and OSHA. Chapter Five addressed due process in employment regarding grievances and employment conditions. The Equal Employment Opportunity Commission is the enforcement agency for most grievances associated with employment, when the Office of Civil Rights is not involved.

The student affairs administrator should be sensitive to other practices associated with hiring employees. In conducting searches to fill vacant positions, it is important to be consistent in specifying minimum qualifications. If minimum qualifications are published, the employer may be exposed to liability upon hiring a person who does not meet the minimum qualifications. It is important that the selection process be fair and unbiased: each candidate should be treated equally and have the same opportunities as all others to compete for the position.

In the search process to fill positions in student affairs, it is likely that students are involved in the interviewing process. It is important that students who engage with candidates be trained and educated about the law associated with searches. Many topics cannot be addressed in employment interviews because they have a discriminatory effect. Questions that can lead to charges of discrimination include those related to age, religion, plans to start a family, or native language. It is essential to train those who are interacting with candidates.

SEXUAL HARASSMENT

Two forms of sexual harassment are "hostile workplace harassment" and "*quid pro quo* harassment" (Kaplin & Lee, 2009, pp. 410–426). Hostile workplace harassment is a pattern of unwelcome verbal or physical conduct of a sexual nature that has the effect of substantially interfering with an individual's work performance or creates an intimidating or hostile working environment. *Quid pro quo* harassment can be unwelcome sexual advances or a request for sexual favors that is a term or condition of an individual's employment or used as a basis for employment decisions.

Institutions become liable for sexual harassment of either form when they are notified of a complaint, either in person or in writing. Institutions are not liable for sexual harassment if the harassed individual has not given them the opportunity to respond and take corrective action. Institutions are most liable when they have taken action, but the action has been ineffective in stopping the offending behavior. As discussed further in Chapter Seventeen, responsible student affairs administrators must take the proactive step of ensuring that all employees are trained on sexual harassment. Training employees effectively can reduce the incidence of sexual harassment and also serve as a defense against the claim of indifference.

A challenging issue related to sexual harassment that student affairs professionals may face is associated with consensual relationships. When employees engage in intimate relationships with other employees or with students, there is substantial exposure to claims of harassment. Consensual relationships can be viewed fundamentally as conflicts of interest. Establishing and promulgating policies that address consensual relationships are intelligent practices and can reduce exposure to liability. Student affairs staff members are particularly vulnerable to consensual relationship issues; because they often work to establish trusting, helping relationships with students, their intentions can be misunderstood or misconstrued.

AFFIRMATIVE ACTION

Legal challenges and judicial interpretations of affirmative action have largely been associated with college admissions practices and policies. A number of states have passed or introduced legislation associated with affirmative action. The law in this regard is still taking shape. Although the future of affirmative action is unclear, most courts have been unequivocal in their recognition of the value of diversity in higher education.

However, affirmative action in employment has been less frequently challenged. The original intent of affirmative action was to provide a way to remedy past discrimination against minorities, women, and others protected by law against discrimination. Many institutions have established affirmative action plans, providing specific action steps to diversify the workplace.

Many colleges and universities can easily identify groups that are underrepresented in their employment. Student affairs administrators can readily establish characteristics of students whom they serve that are in different proportion to the staff providing service. Several strategies can be employed for affirmative action or enhancing diversity in the workplace in student affairs. A review of recruitment, promotion, and compensation practices may uncover biases, such as unnecessary job requirements. Mentoring programs and training programs can be instituted to stimulate advancement by persons from underrepresented groups. Race or gender can be among the factors considered in evaluating candidates for employment. Conducting outreach programs to underrepresented groups can establish networks that can be employed to increase diversity.

CONCLUSION

Student affairs administrators are usually characterized as having sound judgment and fair-minded instincts. They are sensitive to differences and accustomed to supporting persons from underrepresented groups. However, making judgments and choices associated with diversity and inclusion is soundest when informed by the standards and regulations associated with discrimination. The administrator wishing to comply with existing laws is most effective when she is familiar with the laws and current on court decisions that relate to discrimination. Sound risk management practices can be employed in that context. Accurate record-keeping in this arena is essential.

REFERENCE

Kaplin, W.A., & Lee, B.A. (2009). *A Legal Guide for Student Affairs Professionals* (4th ed.) (pp. 174–176, 410–426, 726–735, 735–738). San Francisco, CA: Jossey-Bass.

ADDITIONAL RESOURCE

Kaplin, W.A., & Lee, B.A. (2007). *A Legal Guide for Student Affairs Professionals* (2nd ed.) (pp. 159–181). San Francisco, CA: Jossey-Bass.

CHAPTER 8

PRIVATE AND VOLUNTARY ORGANIZATIONAL REGULATIONS

Institutions of higher education have relationships with external organizations, some of which are of a voluntary nature. Most of them offer peer review of services, programs, activities, and outcomes. Student affairs administrators are usually engaged in aspects of that peer review. This chapter will describe institutional connections to accrediting associations, athletic associations, and educational and professional associations, and how they affect the work of student affairs administrators.

ACCREDITING ASSOCIATIONS

There are two basic forms of accreditation: the institutional accreditation that is managed by the regional accrediting associations and the program or discipline accreditation that is managed by licensed agencies associated with the institution's programs and disciplines.

Regional Accrediting Agencies

The accreditation process verifies that the institution meets established standards and also has the effect of protecting the institution against harmful internal and external pressure (Kaplin & Lee, 2009, pp. 760–762). The process creates goals for self-improvement and often results in the raising of standards among educational institutions. It involves faculty and staff in institutional evaluation and planning.

The regional accrediting associations assume the responsibility for institutional accreditation. Standard setting for regional accreditation is conducted by the accrediting agency and its institutional members. All regional accrediting agencies have standards associated with student life, persistence, and services that directly bear on the work of student affairs administrators.

The accreditation process typically begins with an institutional self-study in which the institution candidly and honestly measures itself against standards for accreditation. Typically, student affairs administrators bear responsibility for the part of the self-study that details student life. The self-study is reviewed by an accrediting agency evaluation team that includes faculty members and professional staff from comparable institutions. Following review of the self-study, a team visits the campus for an in-person review of the institution to draw comparisons with the self-study.

Institutional accreditation is used as a basis for determining eligibility for federal assistance, and it determines the acceptability of transfer of credit between institutions. More importantly, it is tied to the authority provided by states to grant degrees. Clearly, institutional accreditation is of the utmost importance to colleges and universities, and student affairs administrators have a significant role. A critical institutional review and an adversarial outcome are made public. The risk of such an outcome is substantial for its impact on the recruitment of students and the faculty. A negative finding by a regional accrediting association can have a lasting effect on the institution's ability to attract students and the willingness of prospective faculty and staff candidates to accept offers of employment. Few informed professionals want to work at an institution for which the accreditation is seen to be at risk, so the student affairs staff members who are responding to the accrediting association's teams must be honest and candid and quick to address concerns that are uncovered.

Student affairs administrators who participate in the self-study process and the accreditation review must be honest and forthright and unafraid of objective, constructive criticism. The accreditation process can produce high levels of institutional understanding and appreciation for student affairs work. Suggestions for improvement can help the student affairs operation grow and develop.

Program or Discipline Accreditation or Certification

Another form of accreditation is specialized for programmatic accreditation, normally associated with specific academic disciplines, such as nursing and psychology, or collections of disciplines, such as business or teacher education. Student affairs staff members are not typically involved in the accreditation of academic disciplines and programs.

However, there are several functional areas within student affairs that may experience a peer review that is similar to the accreditation process. Such peer reviews are typically sponsored by professional associations associated with the respective functional areas. Student affairs departments that may experience such reviews from the appropriate associations include counseling centers, health centers, campus law enforcement, and campus recreation. Again, student affairs administrators may find themselves benefiting from an objective review by a group of peers. Being measured against reasonable, objective standards would seem to be a wise process. The risk associated with criticism would seem to be worth the benefit of potential improvement.

ATHLETIC ASSOCIATIONS AND CONFERENCES

Most colleges and universities that sponsor intercollegiate athletics affiliate with an umbrella organization; the largest proportion of them are members of the National Collegiate Athletic Association (NCAA), which administers standards and regulations that members must adhere to or face sanctions. Additionally, institutions often join smaller groups, athletic conferences, which also have rules and enforcement procedures to which their members are bound.

National Collegiate Athletic Association (NCAA)

The NCAA provides oversight to intercollegiate athletics (Kaplin & Lee, 2009, pp. 762–780). It sponsors championship events in each of the sports and disburses revenue to its member institutions. It publishes a manual of rules to which institutions must adhere in order to remain eligible for championship play. The NCAA employs a number of professional staff members who investigate allegations of NCAA rules violations, and the Association has a process to penalize institutions for rules infractions.

The NCAA requires its member institutions to adhere to the following: conduct regular audits of their practices and programs to ensure they are in compliance with NCAA rules, apply appropriate approaches to governance of athletics, attend to student athlete welfare, and abide by the principles of gender equity and diversity in their sport offerings. This athletics certification process is, in some ways, similar to the institutional accreditation process. It involves a self-study, external review of the self-study, and a campus review by a team of peers.

Student affairs administrators may inadvertently violate NCAA rules in their interactions with athletes, sports boosters, or even faculty members. Alleged NCAA rule violations are vigorously investigated, and penalties to institutions can be significant, including the loss of funding or ineligibility for post-season play. It is unlikely that a student affairs staff member will attempt to become familiar with the complex and extensive rules of NCAA. However, those who work with students, including student athletes, can be briefed by athletic administrators about risks associated with NCAA rule violations and groups of rules and standards that might inform the relationships between student affairs staff and student athletes.

Other Athletics Organizations

The National Association of Intercollegiate Athletics (NAIA) is composed of almost three hundred institutions of higher education. Most of its members are smaller schools with athletics programs of more limited scope than those of the typical NCAA member institution. Like the NCAA, the NAIA has regulations that hold the institution accountable for compliance, and student affairs administrators at NAIA institutions should be familiar with those regulations and work to ensure adherence to them. At many NAIA schools, the athletics department might report to student affairs, so compliance becomes doubly important in those circumstances.

Another national athletics association is the National Junior College Athletic Association, which serves community colleges. It has similar regulatory authority, compared to the NCAA; and it also sponsors post-season tournaments and championships.

Athletic Conferences

Institutions may belong to athletic conferences, often organized around geographic areas; athletic conferences also have standards and rules associated with athletic competition. They do not generally exert the same amount of power as the NCAA, and, typically, their pursuit of an alleged rule violation would not be adversarial. When athletic conference personnel conduct an investigation of an alleged institutional rule violation, it may result in a modified approach from the NCAA. For example, if a conference conducts a thorough review of an allegation and proposes a sanction, the NCAA may adopt a less confrontational or adversarial position. Student affairs staff members should be sensitive to the existence of athletic conference rules and seek perspective and insight from campus athletic administrators.

OTHER ASSOCIATIONS, EDUCATIONAL AND PROFESSIONAL

A number of other associations contribute to the establishment of best practice in student affairs and establish norms for performance and outcomes of the work. The National Association of Student Personnel Administrators (NASPA) and the American College Personnel Association (ACPA) are general student affairs associations that provide professional development opportunities for their members and represent the profession to the general higher education community (Kaplin & Lee, 2009, pp. 758–759). They have developed statements of policy on sound professional practice, and the prudent student affairs administrator must be aware of those standards and make efforts to conform to them. The associations have developed statements of key competencies for student affairs work, framing a set of guidelines for hiring and professional development in the field. An aspect of intelligent risk management in student affairs work would be membership in one of these associations and participation in its activities. Staying abreast of the changing nature of student affairs work and the latest issues in serving students is sound behavior.

Several of the associations to which student affairs professional staff members may belong have published standards of ethical practice. It is good practice for those working in student affairs to stay well informed of ethics in the field and in specific functional areas. Although those standards are not binding, the embarrassment of violating the ethical expectations associated with student affairs work invites unwelcome risk associated with image and public relations.

The Council for the Advancement of Standards (CAS), an organization composed of representatives from various student affairs associations, publishes a handbook of standards for professional practice in various functional areas within student affairs. Using those standards as measures for accountability by student affairs programs and services is an appropriate risk-management activity. The CAS Standards do not obligate institutions to perform at a certain level, but they present an opportunity to conform to best practice in student affairs.

CONCLUSION

The practice of student affairs does not exist without context. The context includes the associations and organizations that are external to institutions of higher education, but that have an impact on the work of campus-based student affairs professionals. Understanding that impact and its scope is key to the management of risk. Common risks associated with the accreditation process include damage to one's reputation. Risks associated with athletic rules violations are also in the form of reputation, but violations may also bring serious financial consequences, such as fines or loss of championship eligibility or athletic scholarships.

REFERENCE

Kaplin, W.A., & Lee, B.A. (2009). *A Legal Guide for Student Affairs Professionals* (4th ed.) (pp. 758–759, 760–762, 762–780). San Francisco, CA: Jossey-Bass.

PART FOUR

TORT ISSUES

The five chapters in this part present the exposure to risk faced by student affairs administrators in the context of torts, or civil wrongs for which a remedy may be obtained. Chapter Nine explores the management of risk associated with student activities and events. Chapter Ten examines student organizations and how their behaviors can expose the responsible student affairs administrators to risk. Chapter Eleven reviews risk and its management as associated with alcohol and other drugs. Chapter Twelve details the risks surrounding the functions of counseling, advising, and helping students. Chapter Thirteen addresses safety and security, injuries to students and others, and assaults.

CHAPTER 9

STUDENT ACTIVITIES AND EVENTS, RISK LEVELS, SUPERVISION

INTRODUCTION

The scope and variety of student programs, events, and activities on any given campus is virtually limitless. Such programs contribute to the quality of campus life and engage students in the collegiate experience that research has shown contributes to their commitment to their institutions (Kuh, Schuh & Whitt, 1991). This results in not only student satisfaction, but also, and more importantly, a broader, more comprehensive educational experience that ultimately contributes to student retention and completion (Tinto, 2012).

While many programs, events, and activities are developed and offered by various departments within the institution, including, of course, those within the student affairs division, this chapter focuses on those that are developed and offered by student organizations. Naturally, the same issues related to managing risk associated with those programs, events, and activities apply to those developed and offered by any entity within the institution.

The first section that follows addresses the various relationships that can exist between an institution and its student organizations. The second section examines the various considerations that enter into granting institutional sponsorship, recognition, and/or approval for a program, event, or activity. It is through this process that those involved have the opportunity to attempt to reduce the risks involved. The third section of this chapter offers suggestions for what should be done following any approved program, event, or activity in order to make any necessary improvements for the future, particularly if problems arose during the approved activity.

UNDERSTANDING THE RELATIONSHIP BETWEEN THE INSTITUTION AND ITS STUDENT ORGANIZATIONS

The term "student organization" can mean many different things. Being clear about its meaning is critical to understanding not only the organization's relationship to its institution, but also the parameters within which it functions within its institution. Those parameters also have a bearing on the risk-management measures the institution should consider in connection with the organization's activities.

Most would immediately recognize an institution's student government as a student organization. A student government generally receives funding from a variety of possible sources, and its elected members usually engage in passing legislation and/or resolutions aimed at improving the quality of student life, in addition to often developing and conducting a range of programs for the benefit of the student body. There is a certain level of risk involved in any program or activity provided by a student government.

While sometimes not characterized in the same way, an institution's intercollegiate athletic teams are also student organizations. Naturally, the type and degree of risk associated with such teams' activities are much different from those associated with, for example, a program involving a speaker brought to campus by the student government.

However, there are other types of student organizations for which the distinctions described above are not as apparent. For example, most residential colleges and universities, and even some that are not, have intramural teams that may or may not receive funding from the institution and/or from student activities fees. While those teams generally compete on campus with the inherent risks associated with the various sports, some campuses also have club sports teams that compete with club teams from other campuses with similar inherent risks, combined with the added factor of traveling.

Campuses, of course, have numerous other types of clubs and organizations that are not involved in sports but which, depending on the organizations' purposes, can also be involved in activities that have a range of risk levels associated with them. Consider the following student clubs and organizations and think about the different levels of risk that could be involved in their activities: the chess club; the Spanish club; Habitat for Humanity; class-level honor societies such as Scroll and Mortar Board; national honor societies such as Phi Beta Kappa or discipline-specific honor societies such as Beta Gamma Sigma (business); student ambassadors who host visiting prospective students and provide campus tours; a paintball club; the student newspaper; et cetera.

For those institutions that have fraternities and sororities on their campuses, the fraternities and sororities are also considered student organizations unless an institution has specifically defined the relationship as one that is not recognized in any way by the institution. In other words, a fraternity might exist on a college campus without being officially recognized by officials of the institution. However, that tends to be the rare exception, rather than the rule.

More examples could be offered; however, the reader would be well served to have a thorough understanding of the different types of clubs and organizations on his or her campus.

In virtually every instance, for a student club or organization to use an institution's name, reserve space for activities on campus, and certainly to receive funding from the institution, the club or organization must be officially recognized by the institution (Kaplin & Lee, 2009). Each institution has its own process for granting official recognition. However, some typical steps for becoming an officially recognized student organization are the following: submission of a charter or constitution; submission of a request for, and receipt of, institutional funds; and selection of an advisor, usually a full-time employee (either faculty or staff member).

It is important to address one other type of student organization. These "organizations" are those whose members are students enrolled at the student affairs administrator's institution. These "organizations" can be engaged in a number of types of programs and activities. However, these "organizations"—which may be more aptly referred to as student groups—have not received official recognition from their institutions.

In some instances, such groups form as a result of a specific issue or concern that has arisen. Social media make it very easy to identify an issue and ask people to come together around it. In other cases, such groups may have a longer-term agenda, but for a variety of reasons may opt not to seek formal recognition from their institutions. Whatever the groups' agendas, there are a variety of potential risks of which the student affairs administrator must be aware and attempt to address proactively. Consequently, the student affairs administrator should be fully aware of her institution's policies about reserving space, as well as legal precedents for doing so. Many of those precedents are related to time, place, and manner considerations, which are more thoroughly addressed in Chapter Three.

Even though those issues were discussed there, they warrant some attention in this chapter. Among the most important things to keep in mind in order to avoid the potential liability of a legal challenge is the following. At the vast majority of institutions both public and private, but especially at public institutions, students have the right of freedom of association and freedom of expression guaranteed by the U.S. Constitution (Kaplin & Lee, 2009). Thus, only when certain criteria are met can student groups on those campuses be denied the right to schedule an event. As identified in Kaplin and Lee (2009, pp. 514–515), these include:

o Requiring all recognized groups to comply with reasonable campus regulations concerning conduct;

o Denying recognition to a group that would create substantial disruption on campus; and

o Preventing organizational activity that is itself illegal under local, state, or federal laws, as well as activity that is directed to inciting or producing imminent lawless action and is likely to incite or produce such action.

Another issue to consider is whether any student can reserve space for an event, or can that only be done by representatives of officially recognized student organizations? Especially at public institutions, virtually any enrolled student should be able to schedule an event and/or reserve space if the student does so in compliance with the institution's procedures for doing so, unless the event can be found to meet the criteria mentioned above for not granting approval (Kaplin & Lee, 2009).

Another factor to consider is whether or not the group can use the institution's name in relation to its activities. An example of such an issue is the creation of an alternative "student" newspaper.

Some campuses have such a publication, and under the name of the paper on the front page, or in the masthead, there likely is a phrase along the lines of "a [or the] student newspaper of" followed by the name of the college or university. The word "of" conveys an official connection to the institution that an alternative publication probably should not use.

ACHIEVING INSTITUTIONAL SPONSORSHIP/ RECOGNITION AND APPROVAL FOR A PROGRAM, EVENT, OR ACTIVITY

This section will examine the processes that are generally followed when a recognized student organization plans and delivers programs, events, or activities for its members or the campus in general. It is during these processes that student affairs professionals have an opportunity to take appropriate steps to minimize risk.

As mentioned earlier, knowing, paying attention to, and following the institution's policies and procedures for granting institutional sponsorship or recognition and approval for a program, event, or activity will help minimize the risks associated with them. The following are among the various questions that should be asked once a student organization desires to offer a program, event, or activity.

Who Is Authorized to Grant Approval?

The nature and type of event usually determine who and what office(s) is (are) involved in granting approval. For example, if the Spanish Club wants to reserve space in the student union for its regularly scheduled meetings, it is likely that a staff member in the facility can arrange for that to occur without the involvement of anyone else. However, often different buildings on a campus have different reservation procedures, so if the Spanish Club wanted to meet in an academic building, the process and those involved could be different.

There are a number of scenarios, of course, in which the approval process is necessarily more complex in order to minimize risk and protect one's institution. An example of such an event would be that of the student government entering into a contract with a band to perform a concert during homecoming. Such an event would involve such things as: a contract with the band and/or perhaps an agent representing the band; arranging for space in a facility on campus that could accommodate such events; working with a ticket seller if the event was also open to the public; arranging for security during the event; and so forth.

More information about the nature of such contracts is included in Chapter Fifteen on contract management. Suffice it to say here that the overall goal is to protect the interests of the student organization and the institution. Because of this, institutions often have their office of general counsel or another attorney (if such an office does not exist) review the contract.

Is the Activity on or off Campus?

Most institutions make it clear to their student organizations that the process for approving an event is the same, whether the event is on or off campus. One important difference when an event is off campus is that there are usually additional steps involved, including, perhaps, a separate contract for use of the off-campus venue. Such a contract spells out the relationship between the venue and the student group whose event will be held there. Here, too, it is important for such a contract to be carefully reviewed in order to protect the interests of the student organization and the institution.

Is an Off-Campus Group or Organization Also Involved in the Activity?

A wide variety of events and activities could involve a recognized student organization and an off-campus group. For example, a student organization could partner with the American Cancer Society's Relay for Life program. In the same way, the student chapter of Habitat for Humanity could partner with the local Habitat for Humanity chapter to build a house in the community. While there may be more risks involved in the latter activity than the former, there are certain elements of risk involved in a Relay for Life event, too.

Another such example would be the various philanthropy events that fraternities and sororities often sponsor to raise funds for local or national charitable organizations. These events could range from something as "simple" as a dinner to something as complex as an athletic competition. Each, however, has certain elements of risk associated with it. Therefore, in activities that involve off-campus groups or organizations, it is especially important to have a contract or agreement that spells out the responsibilities of the off-campus group compared to those of the student organization and its institution.

Some student organizations contract with vendors to provide such activities as carnival-type rides or fireworks displays in connection with major campus events. Usually, in addition to the contract between the vendor and the student organization and institution, various permits and/ or licenses are required, including those that demonstrate that the vendor is licensed to provide the particular service. Not only do those add another layer of risk that needs to be addressed, but also securing some permits involves working through local town or city governmental departments, which can take time.

Will Alcohol Be Available at the Event?

Laws at the local and federal level are in place that address providing, serving, and consuming alcoholic beverages generally, and specifically at college and university activities. This is true because such events arguably present a high degree of risk should alcohol be consumed illegally or in excess, including by those who are at least twenty-one years of age. As a result, colleges and universities have devoted significant resources to developing policies and procedures that address such events. These policies and procedures invariably are in place, whether the event is on or off campus.

Student affairs professionals should be very familiar with their institutions' policies and procedures regarding events at which alcohol is present. Among the considerations are whether the alcohol is sold by the institution under its license or if those of legal age bring their own. If the latter is the case, is the amount allowed limited? Are there limits on the amount that can be consumed in any given time period? If so, how is that managed?

Also, what, if any, requirements are in place for nonalcoholic beverages to be available, along with appropriate types of food? What understandings are in place to refuse service to someone who appears to have had too much to drink, especially if such a person becomes belligerent because of being refused service?

Many campuses have taken advantage of a variety of programs offered by third parties designed to help address the issue of alcohol consumption among college students. Among those are the TIPS program (www.gettips .com/), which is designed to prevent intoxication, underage drinking, and drunk driving. Another is the Red Watchband program (www.stonybrook .edu/sb/redwatchband/), which trains students to recognize when someone is approaching drinking at a "toxic" level and how to intervene. Also available is AlcoholEDU from Everfi (formerly Outside the Classroom) (www .outsidetheclassroom.com/solutions/higher-education/alcoholedu-for-college.aspx) and eCHECKUP TO GO (www.echeckuptogo.com/usa/) These are online alcohol misuse/prevention programs that can be used in a variety of ways, from being included in an orientation program to being an educational component of an institution's conduct process associated with violations of an institution's alcohol policy.

Paying attention to the alcohol policies and procedures of one's institution, with the help of resources from others, is also essential to minimize the risk associated with not being in compliance with the Department of Education's Drug Free Schools and Communities Act of 1986 and as amended in 1989 ("The Drug Free Schools. . ."). This law requires colleges and universities that receive federal financial assistance (student aid and research grants) to establish alcohol and drug abuse prevention programs for students and employees.

The law also requires that institutions conduct a biennial review of their programs to include: the number of drug- and alcohol-related violations and fatalities in connection with the institution's activities; the sanctions imposed; a determination of the effectiveness of its polices; and the fact that the institution has made revisions to the policies if such revisions are determined to be needed. Failure to comply could result in the loss of all federal financial assistance to the institution. It should be noted that the Department of Education has become more active recently in monitoring institutions' compliance with this law.

When Can Institutional Oversight Become Censorship?

As discussed elsewhere in this book, the courts have addressed (and will continue to do so) the issue of students' rights of freedom of assembly and expression. As a result, it is recommended that student affairs professionals remain current on this aspect of the law.

As an example, a student organization may want to bring a speaker to campus whom some at the institution consider to be "controversial." Also, the student newspaper may decide to publish a story on a topic that is also seen as "controversial" by some or not in keeping with the values of the institution. Student affairs administrators should be very cautious about intervening in such situations, especially if the student organizations involved have followed the appropriate procedures in such situations.

On the other hand, if the student affairs administrator has the responsibility to approve (or not) a contract with a vendor supplying carnival-type rides to be used during homecoming week activities, she most certainly has a duty to not approve it if she believes that approving it presents the likelihood of risk to those who would use the rides based on the terms of the contract. While one certainly wants to provide appropriate oversight where such oversight is reasonable and expected, one probably does not want to create a duty to care when one is not necessary. Therefore, these situations must be reviewed carefully, case by case.

Can the Method and Time of Payment for an Activity Help to Minimize Risk?

When payment for an event occurs, the method and time of payment can be factors in reducing associated risk. Following are several scenarios to illustrate how these factors enter into play.

A vendor requires a deposit (in some cases a substantial amount) toward the total cost of the service provided. If the deposit is paid and the service is not performed, obtaining a refund of the deposit could be a long, drawn out, and costly process, depending on the terms of the contract. And if the vendor were to go out of business before completion of the service, recovering the deposit could be impossible. To avoid this, student affairs administrators should not agree to pay a deposit toward any service. Given the institution's standing in the community, reputable vendors should know that they will be paid once the service is provided.

Another scenario involves a musician, band, speaker, or other individual who agrees to provide a service but whose contract calls for prepayment at the beginning of the engagement rather than at the conclusion. If payment is made at the beginning and the individual does not fulfill the obligations of the contract (such as a musical performer not performing the full length of time given in the contract), recovering a portion of the prepaid fees could be very challenging.

Payment for services under the terms of a contract should always be made by a check drawn on an account in the name of the institution. Cash payments and payments from an individual's bank account always should be avoided. The use of an institutional check affords the institution the recourse of stopping payment on a check, even when payment has been made at the end of an event, if the institution has reason to believe that some aspect(s) of the contract was not delivered.

THE PROCESS TO BE FOLLOWED AFTER AN EVENT HAS OCCURRED

A prudent risk management strategy or framework certainly involves considering where vulnerabilities (or the possibilities for risks to occur) exist. One might refer to that as the risk assessment step in a risk management strategy. After the event, it is good practice to take steps to try to reduce the likelihood that something undesirable will occur. That would likely be referred to as the risk management step. A key next step in the risk management process is conducting a post-event review. This provides an opportunity to consider whether anything might be done differently the next time the event, or one like it, is proposed.

Generally, such a review would be conducted by student affairs administrators and others who were involved in approving the event. The review should address all stages of the process and identify those changes that might improve the process for the future. Naturally, the review could be quite perfunctory or rather complex, depending on the nature of the event or activity.

The post-event review would reasonably become more complex and could require the involvement of others at the institution in the event that problems occurred as a result of the event or activity. The problems could be relatively minor, such as finding a larger venue for the next similar event, or be rather serious, such as injuries and/or arrests of students on alcohol violations. Based on the severity of the problem, the post-event review could lead to recommendations for changes to the institution's policies.

CONCLUSION

Student activities and events require various degrees of supervision by student affairs professionals, because they present varying levels of risk. Factors involved in determining where an activity falls on a continuum of risk include: whether the student group is officially recognized by the institution; whether the event is on or off campus; whether third-party vendors or suppliers are involved; the terms and conditions if contracts are associated with the event; and whether alcohol is present. Having sound, tested institutional policies and procedures in place regarding the approval of and execution of events, together with an appropriate risk management process, will help mitigate the possibility that problems will occur in connection with such activities in the future.

REFERENCES

Kaplin, W.A., & Lee, B.A. (2009). *A Legal Guide for Student Affairs Professionals* (4th ed.). San Francisco, CA: Jossey-Bass.

Kuh, G., Schuh, J., & Whitt, E. (1991). *Involving Colleges: Successful Approaches to Fostering Student Learning and Development Outside the Classroom*. San Francisco, CA: Jossey-Bass.

The Drug Free Schools and Communities Act Amendments of 1989. (n.d.). Retrieved from http://counsel.cua.edu/fedlaw/dfsca.cfm

Tinto, V. (2012). *Completing College: Rethinking Institutional Action*. Chicago, IL: The University of Chicago Press.

ADDITIONAL RESOURCES

Kaplin, W.A., & Lee, B.A. (2009). "Institutional Tort Liability." In W.A. Kaplin & B.A. Lee, *A Legal Guide for Student Affairs Professionals* (4th ed.) (pp. 109–127). San Francisco: Jossey-Bass.

Kaplin, W.A., & Lee, B.A. (2009). "The College and Student Organizations." In W.A. Kaplin & B.A. Lee, *A Legal Guide for Student Affairs Professionals* (4th ed.) (pp. 511–604). San Francisco, CA: Jossey-Bass.

Sandeen, A., & Barr, M.J. (2006). "Who has responsibility for the lives of students?" In A. Sandeen & M.J. Barr, *Critical Issues for Student Affairs*. San Francisco, CA: Jossey-Bass.

CHAPTER 10

HAZING AND STUDENT ORGANIZATIONS

INTRODUCTION

This chapter continues the discussion in the previous chapter that addressed supervision and risks associated with student activities and events. While that discussion covered a broad range of such activities and risks that apply to virtually every type of student organization, this chapter addresses the risks to students, student affairs administrators, and their institutions when student organizations' behaviors involve hazing. This issue has been prevalent on college and university campuses for a very long time, and it can create such serious risks to students, student affairs administrators, and others—and even to the institution itself—that this chapter is devoted to it.

The first section offers a number of definitions of hazing in an effort to show that such behavior is not narrowly defined. The second section describes the ways in which varying types of student organizations might engage in hazing behavior. The third section of the chapter describes the serious risks to students, student affairs administrators, others, and the institution itself, associated with exposure to a hazing incident.

HAZING DEFINED

Unfortunately, hazing has long been associated with membership in Greek organizations on college campuses (Nuwer, 2002). As a result, every national Greek fraternity and sorority and its coordinating body, as well as many local fraternities and sororities, have taken strong, clear positions that denounce hazing in any form as counter to the founding mission and values of those organizations. Additionally, at the current time, forty-four states have anti-hazing laws that make hazing a crime in addition to being a violation of fraternity, sorority, and institutional policies ("State anti-hazing laws," n.d.). Therefore, student affairs administrators would be well advised to be informed not only of their institutions' policies regarding hazing, but also of their states' anti-hazing laws.

Most national fraternities and sororities are also members of national organizations that take similar positions against hazing. Many fraternities are members of the North-American Interfraternity Conference (NIC) (www.nicindy.org). The following description of the NIC was found on its website: "Founded in 1909, the North-American Interfraternity Conference is the trade association representing 75 International and National Men's Fraternities" ("North-American Interfraternity Conference," n.d.).

Many sororities are members of a similar organization, the National Panhellenic Conference (NPC) (www.npcwomen.org). The following description of the NPC was found on its website: "The National Panhellenic Conference provides support and guidance for its 26 member inter/national sororities/women's fraternities and serves as the national voice on contemporary issues of sorority life" ("National Panhellenic Conference," n.d.).

A third organization, the National Pan-Hellenic Council, Incorporated (NPHC) represents historically African American fraternities and sororities. It was formed in 1930 and represents a total of nine fraternities and sororities. According to its website: "The stated purpose and mission of the organization in 1930 was 'Unanimity of thought and action as far as possible in the conduct of Greek letter collegiate fraternities and sororities, and to consider problems of mutual interest to its member organizations'" ("National Pan-Hellenic Council," n.d.).

Another national organization that focuses much of its efforts on reducing risk within the Greek community on college and university campuses is the Fraternal Information and Programming Group (FIPG) (www.fipg.org). The following description of the FIPG was found on its website: "Our mission is to promote sound risk management policies and practices, to be the leading resource of risk management education, programming, and information to the broad-based constituency involved in all aspects of Greek Life" ("Fraternal information and," n.d.). Like the previous organizations mentioned, FIPG seeks to work not only with fraternities and sororities but also with the student affairs administrators and others at the campuses on which their member organizations exist.

As a result of FIPG's focus on risk management and sound management policies, FIPG has created a fifty-page *Risk Management Manual* ("FIPG Risk Management," n.d.) which was updated in January of 2013. The introduction to the manual provides some interesting information on the origins of the organization. According to the manual, nearly 70 percent of all undergraduate fraternities and sororities have adopted FIPG's risk management guidelines, which impact all aspects of their functioning. The policies included in the manual include those that address alcohol and drugs, sexual abuse and harassment, fire, health, and safety, education, and of course, hazing.

On page thirty-three of FIPG's *Risk Management Manual*, hazing activities are defined as:

> ... any action taken or situation created, intentionally, whether on or off fraternity premises, to produce or that causes mental or physical discomfort, embarrassment, harassment, or ridicule. Such activities may include but are not limited to the following: use of alcohol; paddling in any form; creation of excessive fatigue; physical and psychological shocks; quests; treasure hunts; scavenger hunts; road trips; or any other such activities carried on outside or inside of the confines of the chapter house; kidnappings, whether by pledges, associate/ new members or active members; wearing of public apparel which is conspicuous and not normally in good taste; engaging in public stunts and buffoonery; morally degrading or humiliating games and activities; and any other such activities that are not consistent with academic achievement, fraternal law, ritual or policy, or the regulations and policies of the educational institution, or applicable state law. ("FIPG Risk Management," n.d.)

From the definition, the student affairs administrator can begin to get an idea of the types of hazing activities in which various student organizations have engaged. Nevertheless, many student organizations believe that they are involved in educating their incoming members and in doing so are not engaged in hazing. But as one can see, the above definition is quite comprehensive. Furthermore, as noted on page thirty-four of the FIPG manual, "THERE IS NO SUCH THING AS 'MINOR' OR 'HARMLESS' HAZING or 'hazing with a little 'h'" ("FIPG Risk Management," n.d.).

The FIPG manual also offers a series of questions on pages thirty-four and thirty-six with the caveat that if one can answer "no" to any of them, an activity would likely be considered hazing and hence should be avoided. Student affairs administrators working with student organizations would be well advised to share the FIPG manual, especially these questions, with the organizations' members. Examples of the questions posed are as follows.

- Is this activity an educational experience?
- Does this activity promote and conform to the ideal and values of the fraternity?
- Is it an activity that pledged and initiated members [in the case of Greek organizations] participate in together?
- Would you be willing to allow parents to witness this activity? A judge? The university president?
- Would you be able to defend it in a court of law?
- Does the activity risk emotional or physical abuse?
- Would you object to the activity being photographed for the school newspaper or filmed by the local TV news crew? ("FIPG Risk Management," n.d.)

Another excellent source for information about hazing is an organization known as StopHazing.org (www.stophazing.org). The site contains a wealth of information that would benefit student affairs administrators and student organizations of all types. In addition to including FIPG's definition of hazing, it also includes its own. According to its definition, "[h]azing refers to any activity expected of someone joining a group (or to maintain full status in a group) that humiliates, degrades or risks emotional and/or physical harm, regardless of the person's willingness to participate" ("Hazing Defined," n.d.).

The site also offers the following definition taken from page xxv of Hank Nuwer's 2002 book *Wrongs of Passage*. The definition was included in the 1999 Alfred University/NCAA survey of college athletes. There, hazing was defined as:

> . . . any activity expected of someone joining a group that humiliates, degrades, abuses, or endangers, regardless of the person's willingness to participate. This does not include activities such as rookies carrying the balls, team parties with community games, or going out with your teammates, unless an atmosphere of humiliation, degradation, abuse, or danger arises.
>
> Hazing is an activity that a high-status member orders other members to engage in or suggests that they engage in that in some way humbles a newcomer who lacks the power to resist, because he or she want [sic] to gain admission to a group. Hazing can be noncriminal, but it is nearly always against the rules of an institution, team, or Greek group. It can be criminal, which means that a state statute has been violated.

It is also worth pointing out the distinction between national fraternities and sororities and those that are "local," thus having no national affiliation. Because of the lack of national affiliation, a local fraternity or sorority would not be expected to adhere to the mission and purpose of such organizations as the NIC, NPC, and the NPHC, which take strong positions against hazing. In the case of local organizations, they would not have the benefit of information that national offices provide to their member fraternities and sororities, which could increase the possibility of local organizations engaging in hazing behaviors creating potentially serious risk and liability for their members, themselves, and their institution. Therefore, on campuses that have fraternities and sororities, student affairs administrators should be sure to know whether the organizations are "national" or "local."

In such cases, the student affairs administrator would likely be expected to spend more time educating the local organizations' members on the issue of hazing. In doing so, she may want to rely on such resources as those of FIRPG and StopHazing.org.

HAZING WITHIN VARIOUS TYPES OF STUDENT ORGANIZATIONS

Unfortunately, a wide range of student organizations engage in hazing activities and, therefore, their members can bring allegations of hazing before student affairs administrators. Such allegations must be aggressively addressed because of the potential risks to the students involved and also to the student affairs administrator and her institution. There are considerable risks to the administrator and her institution if the institution does not have polices in place that address hazing and if the administrator and the institution are found to have not taken appropriate action when allegations of hazing arose (Kaplin & Lee, 2009).

Student affairs administrators must also be attuned to the fact that, regardless of the organization, sometimes hazing is committed, not by current members of the organization, but by former members. One of the reasons that hazing has been such a longstanding problem on college and university campuses is the fact that former members—alumni—sometimes believe that, because a hazing ritual was a part of their becoming members, such behavior should be part of the current induction process. This attitude and the resulting behaviors can work against the anti-hazing efforts of student affairs administrators. Therefore, alumni of student organizations should also be included in the anti-hazing efforts in which student affairs administrators engage.

Before looking at some examples of the types of student organizations on college campuses that are capable of engaging in hazing, it is worth noting that hazing occurs in many other organizations not associated with colleges and universities. As noted on the StopHazing.org website, those other organizations can include student groups in high schools (which frequently involve athletic teams), as well as the military. Just as students bring other types of behaviors that they learned during their high school careers to campus, so, too, could they bring hazing behaviors. Films like *An Officer and a Gentleman* and many others portray what happens in boot camp when newly enlisted members of the armed forces go through "training." However, by the definitions provided earlier, such training activities clearly would be considered hazing.

As this book was being written, serious allegations of hazing also were reported in numerous sources of a more senior member of the Miami Dolphins, Richie Incognito, continuing to haze a player, Jonathan Martin, after his rookie season ("Former Dolphins: Incognito," n.d.). This implied that behavior one would consider hazing was accepted before that. As reported on November 8, 2013, at http://sportsillustrated.cnn.com/nfl/news/20131108/richie-incognito-jonathan-martin-hazing-code/index.html:

> The Miami Dolphins locker room had something like a code when it came to the jokes and pranks played on rookies. The guidelines were not written down, but like the rule that you don't hit your team's quarterback in practice, all the players knew them and were expected to abide by them.
>
> According to the code, training camp was a free-for-all. You could do almost anything to a rookie in training camp. Shave his head, take his car for a joy ride, throw his clothes in the cold pool, wrap athletic tape around the lock on his locker. All of that was allowed during training camp. But once the season started, it had to stop. That was the rule.
>
> One of the more striking aspects of the controversy swirling around Richie Incognito, the Dolphins veteran prankster, and Jonathan Martin, his frequent target, is that Incognito's treatment of Martin didn't stop.

Fraternities and Sororities

Greek organizations can be different from some other student organizations in that newly recruited members who are selected to become full or "active" members during a process of recruitment, historically referred to as "rush," have a distinctly different status from that of "active" members.

These newly recruited members generally are engaged in a period known as "new member education" for a period of weeks in order to fully understand and embrace the mission and values of the fraternity or sorority. During "rush," they were historically referred to as "pledges"—since they took a pledge to join the organization and achieve full or active member status—but more recently are referred to as associate members.

Most other student organizations do not make such a distinction. The fact that such a distinction exists in Greek organizations accentuates the status and power differences between full/active members and associate/pledge members. As noted on page thirty-five of FIPG's *Risk Management Manual*, "Hazing is an act of power and control over others" ("FIPG Risk Management," n.d.). All too often, those carrying out hazing activities claim that they once had been participants in the same types of activities and were not harmed. Therefore, the "tradition" of those types of activities is perpetuated from one generation of new members to another.

However, somewhat similar power differentiations can exist within other student organizations, even when the only status difference between a student who recently joined the organization and those who have been members for some time is the length of time that each has been affiliated with the organization. Therefore, a brief discussion follows about other types of student organizations that have been known to engage in hazing.

Sports Teams

One might say that a team is composed of individuals who rely on each other to accomplish a common task or goal. As with the members of any other group who have been together for a period of time, members of collegiate sports teams share common experiences and, as a result, develop a sense of camaraderie. In the previously cited Alfred University/NCAA study, the StopHazing.org website indicates that the study found that "approximately 80 percent of college athletes had been subjected to some form of hazing. Half were required to participate in drinking contests or alcohol related initiations while two-thirds were subjected to humiliating hazing" ("Hazing and Athletics," n.d.).

Cheer Squads

Cheer, pom-pom, and dance squads on college campuses have also been found to have engaged in hazing activities. In fact, as this book is being written, Towson State University received undesirable national media attention because of the one-year suspension of its national-championship cheer team for alleged hazing activities. (The team won the national championship in April of 2013.) On August 31, 2013, *The Christian Science Monitor* reported that, if the suspension is upheld upon appeal, the team will not be able to practice or perform at competitions (including defending its national championship) or university sporting events ("Towson University Hazing," n.d.).

Musical Organizations

Marching bands have also garnered undesirable headlines for their institutions because of alleged hazing activities. Here are a couple of examples of such alleged hazing infractions.

In November of 2011, a drum major at Florida A&M University (FAMU) died, allegedly as a result of being severely beaten in connection with a hazing activity. In May of 2013 thirteen people were charged in the incident. Hazing in Florida became a felony in 2005 after the death of a University of Miami student in 2001. Eleven of the thirteen in the FAMU case faced a felony charge of hazing resulting in a death, along with misdemeanor charges. Two others faced misdemeanor charges ("FAMU Hazing Update," n.d.).

Not quite a year after the tragedy at FAMU, the thirty-six member drum line known as the Marching Sound Machine at North Carolina Central University was suspended amid allegations of hazing ("NCCU Suspends Drum," n.d.). As in Florida and forty-two other states, hazing is a crime in North Carolina.

Other Student Organizations

The incidents referenced above received national attention. Unfortunately, in any given year, student affairs administrators will likely hear other stories about incidents of hazing. And while some receive national media attention, many, many others do not. Furthermore, the student affairs administrator should be cognizant of the fact that hazing can occur in any type of student organization and therefore should take any allegations of such behavior very seriously.

RISKS AND LIABILITY ASSOCIATED WITH HAZING

Risks to the Individual Being Hazed

The risks associated with being hazed fall broadly into two categories: those that are physical and those that are psychological/emotional.

While some of the physical, psychological, and emotional effects of hazing may be temporary, others may be long-lasting, affecting the victims' physical, social, emotional, and academic well-being. Such effects can be exacerbated if a victim is being treated for psychological or emotional issues prior to a hazing incident.

Examples of physical risks include sleep deprivation, which could result in other consequences; potentially serious injuries if the hazing activity involves beating someone or involves dangerous activities; alcohol poisoning from the over-consumption of alcohol; and even death, as noted in the alleged incident cited on the previous page.

Psychological risks are potentially more serious than some of the less severe physical risks, because those engaged in administering the hazing are not likely to be aware that the recipient has a psychological condition that could be exacerbated as a result of the hazing. For example, imagine what might happen to someone who is claustrophobic if the person is confined to a small space for a long period of time. Hazing activities could potentially trigger any number of psychological conditions, and those individuals affected could harm themselves or others.

Risks to Student Affairs Administrators and Their Institutions

Other chapters have addressed the importance of having appropriate policies and procedures in place that are designed to mitigate various types of risks and liabilities and implementing them when necessary. The same applies to the issue of hazing. First and foremost, institutions should have clear policies against hazing of any kind and assure that all student organizations are made aware of them in a variety of ways and at various times throughout the year. In states that also have laws against hazing, student affairs administrators should know what those laws are. In this way, the administrator may better understand her legal responsibility when an alleged hazing incident is brought to her attention. Additionally, the wording of the state law may help formulate the institution's policy to address hazing. Also, as is the case when any other alleged policy violations are brought to the student affairs administrator's attention, she should respond immediately.

Student affairs administrators must clearly understand that, as cited in the *FIPG Risk Management Manual*, there is no such thing as hazing with a small "h." Therefore, every alleged incident should be taken very seriously. It is also important to understand that different individuals are affected differently by an alleged hazing incident. Individuals involved in the same hazing incident are likely to respond differently to it. Some may not be affected at all and view it as simply a harmless incident that is a rite of passage for membership. Others who experience the same incident may be traumatized by it.

In addition to the individuals directly involved with an alleged hazing incident, there are others who will most likely share in its consequences: the parents of the students involved (on both sides of the incident); other students, faculty, and staff within the institution who may learn about the incident; members of the public if the incident receives media attention; and law enforcement authorities if hazing is in violation of the law. With all of these parties to consider—and most importantly for the health, safety, and welfare of the involved students—the student affairs administrator should certainly employ a comprehensive list of resources in addressing the incident. He should also remember that, whatever the outcome, he must adhere to privacy laws governing such matters.

CONCLUSION

Hazing is among the most serious, inappropriate behaviors in which members of student organizations can engage. It can result in serious physical and/or psychological consequences and, sadly, has resulted in the deaths of students from time to time. Consequently, student affairs administrators should be certain that their institutions have very clear policies that prohibit any form of hazing and that those policies are made known to students through a variety of means and at various times throughout the year. Furthermore, because hazing is a violation of the law in the vast majority of states, the student affairs administrator should know whether her state has such a law. Understanding the law will not only inform her legal obligations, but could also inform her institution's anti-hazing policy.

REFERENCES

FAMU Hazing Update: Two More Plead in Hazing Death of Drum Major Robert Champion. (n.d.). Retrieved from www.cbsnews.com/news/famu-hazing-update-two-more-plead-in-hazing-death-of-drum-major-robert-champion/

FIPG Risk Management Manual. (n.d.). Retrieved from http://cmssites.theginsystem.com/uploads/fipg/userfiles/FIPG_MANUAL.pdf

Former Dolphins: Incognito Violated Code by Continuing to Haze Martin. (n.d.). Retrieved from http://sportsillustrated.cnn.com/nfl/news/20131108/richie-incognito-jonathan-martin-hazing-code/index.html

Fraternal Information and Programming Group. (n.d.). Retrieved from www
.fipg.org

Hazing and Athletics. (n.d.). Retrieved from www.stophazing.org/athletic_hazing/
index.htm

Hazing Defined. (n.d.). Retrieved from www.stophazing.org/definition.html

Kaplin, W.A., & Lee, B.A. (2009). "Fraternities and Sororities." In W.A. Kaplin
& B.A. Lee. *A Legal Guide for Student Affairs Professionals* (4th ed.)
(pp. 538–548). San Francisco, CA: Jossey-Bass.

National Panhellenic Conference. (n.d.). Retrieved from www.npcwomen.org

National Pan-Hellenic Council, Incorporated. (n.d.). Retrieved from www
.nphchq.org

NCCU Suspends Drum Line for Hazing. (n.d.). Retrieved from www.newsobserver
.com/2012/09/13/2339547/nccu-suspends-drum-line-for-alleged.html

North-American Interfraternity Conference. (n.d.). Retrieved from www.nicindy.org

Nuwer, H. (2002). *Wrongs of Passage–99 Edition.* Bloomington, IN: Indiana
University Press.

State Anti-Hazing Laws. (n.d.). Retrieved from www.stophazing.org/laws.html

StopHazing.org: Educating to Eliminate Hazing. (n.d.). Retrieved from www
.stophazing.org

Towson University Hazing: Entire Cheerleading Team Suspended. (n.d.).
Retrieved from www.csmonitor.com/USA/Latest-News-Wires/2013/0831/
Towson-University-hazing-Entire-cheerleading-team-suspended

ADDITIONAL RESOURCES

Jones, R.L. (2010). *Black Haze: Violence, Sacrifice, and Manhood in Black
Greek-Letter Fraternities.* Albany, NY: SUNY Press.

Lipkins, S. (2006). *Preventing Hazing: How Parents, Teachers, and Coaches
Can Stop the Violence, Harassment and Humiliation.* Hoboken, NJ:
John Wiley & Sons.

CHAPTER 11

ALCOHOL AND DRUGS

INTRODUCTION

Many of the issues that student affairs administrators confront in the course of performing their duties do not originate on their campuses. This is especially true when it comes to addressing the use of alcohol and other drugs by students and even by employees whom the student affairs administrator might supervise. In the case of many students, patterns of use have been well developed prior to their arrival on campus (Wood, 2010).

This chapter reviews the issues associated with student alcohol and drug use and the duty of institutions to discourage irresponsible and/or illegal use of such substances and the risks associated with student misuse of them.

The first section of this chapter discusses what some of the underlying causes are for students' use of alcohol and/or drugs on campus, based on the behaviors they may have developed in high school and, sadly, in some cases, even before. The second section addresses the proactive, programmatic steps student affairs administrators should take (in keeping with their institutions' policies regarding these issues) aimed at informing students of the risks associated with the use of alcohol and/or drugs in order to reduce risks to students and the student affairs administrator. This section also addresses issues, such as room inspections and room searches in connection with suspected alcohol and/or drug policy violations in campus residential facilities. The third section offers a variety of measures that can be put in place in order to minimize risk when, in keeping with institutions' policies concerning alcohol, alcohol is authorized at various types of events.

THE PRECURSORS TO ALCOHOL AND DRUG USE ON COLLEGE CAMPUSES

Students bring many skills and behaviors with them when they begin their college careers. Some skills enable them to successfully participate in intercollegiate athletics, while others allow them to perform in theatrical productions or musical performances. Other skills and behaviors cause them to be actively involved in student governance roles or become active contributors as members of any number of clubs and organizations. However, in the case of many students, they also come to campus having had experience misusing alcohol and/or engaging in the illegal use of drugs—either illicit drugs or prescription drugs that were not prescribed for them.

One of the best sources for data about a wide range of characteristics and attitudes of entering college students can be found in the annual Freshman Survey conducted by the Higher Education Research Institute's Cooperative Institutional Research Program (CIRP.) The organization's website address is www.heri.ucla.edu/. As reported there, the 2012 CIRP Freshman Survey was based on responses from 192,912 freshmen who entered 283 four-year colleges and universities ("Higher Education Research," n.d.).

Given that the legal drinking age in the United States is twenty-one, the misuse of alcohol as discussed in this chapter refers to any use by someone under the age of twenty-one and use by someone twenty-one or older that results in inappropriate behavior. Understandably, many college students under the age of twenty-one wouldn't agree with this definition. Many believe that they should be able to consume alcohol as long as they are behaving responsibly when doing so. Unfortunately for those individuals, because the legal drinking age is twenty-one, the law would say that anyone who is under twenty-one and who consumes alcohol is not behaving responsibly.

Therefore, how might those under the age of twenty-one come to believe that they should be able to consume alcohol if they do so responsibly? Much of the research on this topic indicates that many young adults develop their attitudes and behaviors toward alcohol consumption—and the use of drugs—while still in high school, or even sooner (Wood, 2010). Once on campus, those attitudes and behaviors are influenced by the actual and perceived behaviors of others on campus.

One of the best sources of data for information about drug and alcohol use on college and university campuses is what is known as the Core

Institute at Southern Illinois University in Carbondale (http://core.siu .edu). As stated on the home page:

> The Core Institute is the largest national Alcohol and Other Drug (AOD) database about college student's [sic] drinking and drug use in the country. We offer a comprehensive range of cost-effective surveys that measure risky behaviors.
>
> The Core surveys are easy to use and will help any institution understand the drinking and drug norms of their college campus. Our surveys are the centerpiece for effective and data-driven interventions that address academic success and retention of today's college student. ("Core Institute," n.d.)

Among the data collected by the survey is the category of when the student first began to use alcohol and a list of many other substances. The possible answers begin with "under 10"—yes, under ten years of age—to "26+." Because a great amount of data are available on its website, readers who wish to examine the data further are encouraged to view the most recent (at the time this book was being written) national results from 2011, which can be found at http://core.siu.edu/_common/ documents/report11.pdf.

Another excellent source of information about the behaviors and characteristics of the students on a given campus in regard to these and other health-related issues is available from the National College Health Assessment (NCHA) available from the American College Health Association (ACHA) at www.acha-ncha.org/. This survey is broader than the CORE survey in that, in addition to collecting data on alcohol and other drug use, it also addresses sexual health, weight, nutrition, and exercise, mental health, and personal safety and violence ("American College Health," n.d.).

So what are the sources for these behaviors that some students develop long before coming to campus as freshmen? It is quite possible that student affairs administrators will recognize these from situations from their years in high school or before. First and foremost, there is a tremendous amount of peer pressure to want to be accepted and be seen as part of the "cool crowd" in school. While that can play out in many ways, for many young people it includes consuming alcohol.

Often, that peer pressure plays out at parties at which alcohol is present, either in someone's home, a club at which it is easy for those under twenty-one to consume alcohol, or at an outdoor gathering spot like a park or the beach. In the case of some parties at home, some parents have even been known to be involved in providing the alcohol out of a sense that they would rather have their under-age children and their friends consuming alcohol there, where they can "supervise" the activity, rather than have the consumption occur in an "unsupervised" manner elsewhere. In situations such as this, as with the case on campus in which someone of legal age provides alcohol to someone who isn't of legal age, many states have social host laws that make doing so a violation of the law. Therefore, student affairs administrators must be aware of such laws and communicate them to the students with whom they interact in an attempt to reduce risk to all involved.

Often, the use of illegal drugs (and especially prescription drugs not prescribed for the student) also begins at home before the student comes to campus. In many cases, drugs prescribed for someone else in the family, such as a sibling or parent, are consumed by the student for other than the drug's intended purpose. Additionally, some students may obtain prescription drugs from friends for whom they've been legally prescribed.

One of the most frequently misused drugs in this manner is Adderall, which was developed to be used by those with Attention Deficit Hyperactivity Disorder (ADHD) (Jacobs, 2005). Recently, it has been claimed by some athletes to be a performance-enhancer, while it also has received a great deal of attention from students because of claims that it enhances one's ability to study. As with the case of using alcohol before students arrive on campus, student affairs administrators should be conscious of the likelihood of illegal use of prescription drugs or the use of illegal drugs by students before arriving on campus, which would likely continue.

ADDRESSING ALCOHOL AND DRUG USE PROACTIVELY

Given the prevalence of the misuse of alcohol and the use of drugs in our society, the student affairs administrator must take real, meaningful steps to address those issues proactively from the very beginning of the academic year and continue to do so throughout the year. It is especially important to do so, as on a number of campuses relatively large numbers of students are on campus during times when classes are not in session, such as the time between semesters as well as during the summer.

The student affairs administrator would be well served by administering the Core Survey and or the National College Health Assessment survey on his campus so he has campus-specific data to compare with national data. Knowing what the behaviors and perceptions of the students are on one's campus could enable the student affairs administrator to design programs and services aimed specifically to address those behaviors.

In addition to the fact that addressing these issues proactively is the right thing to do, the federal government offers an important incentive in the form of the Drug Free Schools and Communities Act of 1986 and its amendments of 1989. The law applies to all institutions that receive federal financial assistance, which includes both federal student aid and research grants. To comply with the law, institutions must establish drug and alcohol abuse prevention programs for both students and employees.

As described on the website of the office of the General Counsel at the Catholic University of America (http://counsel.cua.edu/fedlaw/dfsca .cfm): "They [students and employees] must receive information annually that contain standards of conduct, a description of the various laws that apply in that jurisdiction regarding alcohol and drugs, a description of the various health risks of drug and alcohol abuse, a description of counseling and treatment programs that are available, and a statement on the sanctions the university will impose for a violation of the standards of conduct" ("The Drug-Free Schools," n.d.).

Also, according to the site, "The law also requires a biennial review of the program. Effective August 14, 2008, pursuant to amendments in the HEOA, any biennial review must include a determination of the number of drug and alcohol-related violations and fatalities that occur on the institution's campus or as part of the institution's activities and the number and type of sanctions imposed by the institution as a result of drug and alcohol-related violations and fatalities that occur on the institution's campus or as part of the institution's activities" ("The Drug-Free Schools," n.d.).

While the federal government historically has not paid much attention in the past to whether institutions met the requirements of this law, it has begun taking steps to do so. The reasons were addressed in an article in the June 1, 2007, issue of *The Chronicle of Higher Education* entitled "The Importance of Enforcing Alcohol Rules" by Stephen M. Guest. He noted that:

> The 1998 reauthorization of the act [Higher Education Act of 1965] included a "sense of Congress," an advisory that urges institutions to provide students with "maximum opportunities" to "live in an alcohol-free environment" and apply a "zero tolerance" policy for the illegal consumption of alcohol—as well as vigorous enforcement of sanctions for those in violation. Congress expressed renewed interest in the issue in the recently enacted STOP (Sober Truth on Preventing Underage Drinking Act) legislation by including a similar statement. (Guest, 2007)

Therefore, student affairs administrators would be well served—as would their institutions—if they made compliance with this law the foundation for their proactive, programmatic efforts.

Other information that student affairs administrators would do well to incorporate into their proactive programmatic efforts to reduce risk and liability is that regarding local and state laws. For example, most states have laws that make it an offense for someone of legal age to provide alcohol to someone who is not. That not only includes someone who would sell the alcohol to the underage person directly, but also one who buys it legally and then gives it to the person who is not at least twenty-one. Similarly, many states have laws that make it illegal to knowingly provide alcohol to someone (even if he is of legal age) if the person appears to be intoxicated.

As this book is being written, the laws in a number of states have changed regarding the medical and even recreational use of marijuana. In fact, on January 1, 2014, *The Denver Post* reported that the first licenses (for a total of thirty-seven stores) for dispensing marijuana for recreational use to anyone twenty-one years of age or older were issued in Denver, Colorado (Ingold, 2014). However, the conundrum for student affairs administrators in Colorado (and other states where the use of medical marijuana has been approved for sale) is that marijuana is illegal under federal law, which includes the Drug Free Schools and Communities Act.

Therefore, at least until legal cases provide guidance, one might expect that marijuana purchased through these legal outlets could still be illegal to use on a college or university campus. Naturally, this will have ramifications for the development of policies associated with marijuana use on campuses in those states. Consequently, student affairs administrators will have to be vigilant in staying up-to-date with this rapidly evolving area of law and, hence, institutional policy-making and the associated risks and liability.

One of the areas in which addressing the misuse of alcohol and the use of drugs is often problematic and therefore presents a range of risks to student affairs administrators is that of campus housing facilities. The situation may vary somewhat based on whether an institution is public or private. However, even most private institutions respect students' right of privacy in what is essentially their home. Consequently, student affairs administrators may be challenged and be exposed to significant liability if they are involved in what is determined to be an unauthorized or illegal search of one's premises.

On the other hand, campus housing officials often schedule safety inspections and/or are called upon to address a situation in a student's residence brought about by a complaint or by becoming aware of a student's inappropriate behavior. In those cases, the student affairs administrator might become aware of a violation of the institution's policies and/or the law. If such were the case because the violation was in plain view and not found as a result of a search, the potential risk of liability would be significantly reduced.

While student affairs administrators may be focused on addressing these issues as they pertain to students, they should know that most institutions have a number of other activities and venues at which the consumption of alcohol occurs. These include such things as faculty and staff events and those for trustees and donors, as well as having alcohol available at the institutions' athletic events, both in the events' venues and often at tailgate activities outside of them. Student affairs administrators should make a point of knowing whether the provisions of their institutions' alcohol policy for those events are different from those for events that are primarily designed for students. To the extent that differences exist, the possibility for risk and liability could increase if the appropriate policy provisions are not followed.

While the vast majority of programmatic initiatives address the need to comply with the law that has set the minimum legal drinking age at twenty-one, in the last few years another effort has begun whose goal is to engage in a vigorous discussion about the effects of the twenty-one-year-old drinking age, citing binge drinking that occurs and the ethical issues associated with using fake IDs to access alcohol prior to being twenty-one years old.

The Amethyst Initiative and its members who have agreed to support the effort are virtually all college and university presidents or chancellors. The organization's website address is www.theamethystinitiative.org. In September 2013, it noted that 136 such individuals had signed the statement encouraging such a discussion. According to the information on the website, those in support of the initiative do not believe that current measures (including and, especially, the legal drinking age of twenty-one) are reducing the negative consequences of underage and inappropriate alcohol consumption and believe more would be gained by encouraging moderation and responsibility ("Amethyst Initiative: Rethinking," n.d.).

However, others vehemently disagree. William DeJong summarized that position in an August 27, 2008, article in *The Chronicle of Higher Education* entitled "The Age-21 Law Saves Lives; College Leaders Should Focus Instead on Prevention Strategies." He cited evidence to support that claim and specifically challenged the signatories of the Amethyst Initiative to "serve their students better by working with the current law and devising evidence-based prevention strategies that are being used successfully at other institutions" (DeJong, 2008).

Whatever the nature and type of the proactive programmatic efforts in which student affairs administrators are engaged, the following principles should be taken into account in order to reduce risk and potential liability. First, information should be provided early in the students' experience at the institution. Second, in keeping with the notion of a "teachable moment," the information should be provided at various times throughout the year. Third, a variety of media and approaches should be utilized, since some means of communication are more effective with some individuals than others. Fourth, it is important to provide the information to the entire student body. Why? Based on the Core Survey data, the misuse of alcohol and the use of drugs are prevalent across the entire student body on most campuses. Therefore, it would be inadvisable to target specific subpopulations of students. Finally, if the information is to be heard, it is important that the communication occur in such a way so as to "meet students where they are," both intellectually and emotionally.

MINIMIZING RISK WHEN ALCOHOL IS APPROVED TO BE CONSUMED AT STUDENT EVENTS

Many campuses do not ban the use of alcohol. When alcohol is permitted at student functions, there are generally policies and procedures in place that enable student affairs administrators and others to take steps to minimize the risks associated with the consumption of alcohol. Generally speaking, those policies cover three stages of such events; pre-event planning and registration, procedures to be followed during the event, and post-event evaluation. Each of these will be discussed here. However, what follows are general statements about what policies and procedures one might expect to find on many campuses. Consequently, the student affairs administrator would be well advised to become very familiar with the specific policies and procedures on her own campus.

Pre-Event Planning and Registration

The following are among the important steps to be taken during this stage of the process in order to increase the likelihood of a successful event, that is, one which does not have any alcohol policy violations. It's also important to note that these steps should apply whether the event is held in a campus facility (including fraternity and sorority houses) or at a location off campus.

1. All student organizations that wish to have an event at which alcohol is available should be required to have some of their members (ideally, officers) participate in a training program offered by the institution, often led by student affairs administrators. The program should be designed to familiarize the students with the institution's policies and procedures concerning such events, in addition to the hosts' responsibilities based on local laws involving the distribution of alcohol.

2. The institution should have, and the host organization should complete, an event registration form. Such forms generally should provide a thorough description of the event, including its location, duration, theme, what will be available in terms of non-alcoholic beverages and food (not potato chips and popcorn) that will be served, and the type of supervision provided.

   It also usually indicates how the alcohol will be made available: sold, distributed by licensed bartenders, or whether students will bring their own. In the latter case, many organizations set a limit on the number of containers (usually cans) that one will be able to consume during the event. The form also describes the measures that will be taken to assure that only those of legal age consume alcohol.

   On many campuses, campus security or campus police officers are required to be present whenever alcohol is served at an event. Also, on many campuses, the organization's advisor must approve the event by signing the form and being present during the event.

3. The institution usually requires that the form be submitted to the appropriate office(s) for approval far enough in advance of the proposed event so that any deficiencies or insufficient information can be corrected by the sponsoring student organization before the form is approved—or the request denied.

4. In order to minimize issues related to crowd control, many institutions do not permit organizations to plan events that offer an open invitation to the campus community or beyond. Instead, the number of guests might be based on a ratio to the number of members in the sponsoring organization or the size of the location where the event is held.

   Failure to take the appropriate steps during this stage of the process can set the stage for serious risks and liability for those involved, including the student affairs administrator, if problems arise at the event associated with the misuse of alcohol.

Procedures During the Event

Without over-simplifying what occurs during a student organization event at which alcohol is available, the overall goal and focus should be to comply with the terms and conditions for holding the event, as indicated on the event registration form. However, one should be prepared for that not to be the case and have plans in place that can be quickly implemented should problems arise. Those plans typically include calling on those present who are designated to supervise the event (including campus safety personnel) to intervene as needed, in addition to having plans in place and predetermined communication strategies for calling upon others in the community to assist.

Post-Event Assessment

Following all student organization events, especially those at which alcohol was present, the appropriate student affairs staff members (and perhaps others) should do an evaluation of the event to determine whether any changes need to be made in policies and/or procedures based on what occurred. Additionally, in the unfortunate event that problems occurred to the extent that some participants and/or members of the host student organization were charged with violating institutional policies or procedures or laws during the event, the appropriate disciplinary process should be initiated.

CONCLUSION

The misuse of alcohol and prescription drugs and the use of illegal drugs by college students continue to be among the most difficult issues that student affairs administrators address. The other factor that makes these substances so troubling is the potential harm that can be done as a result of their use. Because of that, student affairs administrators must be extremely conscious of the measures they should employ within the scope of their duty to care for students under their supervision, balanced by the responsibility that students have to care for themselves. When there are disagreements about where one of those responsibilities ends and the other begins, room is created for potentially significant liability for student affairs administrators.

REFERENCES

American College Health Association National College Health Assessment. (n.d.). Retrieved from www.acha-ncha.org/

Amethyst Initiative: Rethinking the Drinking Age. (n.d.). Retrieved from www
    .theamethystinitiative.org/

Core Institute. (n.d.). Retrieved from http://core.siu.edu/

DeJong, W. (2008, August 27). "The Age-21 Law Saves Lives; College
    Leaders Should Focus Instead on Prevention Strategies." *The Chronicle
    of Higher Education.* Retrieved from http://chronicle.com/article/
    The-Age-21-Law-Saves-Lives-/114568/

Guest, S. (2007, June 1). "The Importance of Enforcing Alcohol Rules." *The
    Chronicle of Higher Education.* Retrieved from http://chronicle.com/
    article/The-Importance-of-Enforcing/9526/

Higher Education Research Institute. (n.d.). Retrieved from www.heri.ucla.edu/

Ingold, J. (2014, January 1). "World's First Legal Recreational Marijuana Sales Begin
    in Colorado." *The Denver Post.* Retrieved from www.denverpost.com/news/
    ci_24828236/worlds-first-legal-recreational-marijuana-sales-begin-colorado

Jacobs, A. (2005, July 31). "The Adderall Advantage." *The New York Times.*
    Retrieved from www.nytimes.com/2005/07/31/education/edlife/jacobs31
    .html?pagewanted=all&_r=0

The Drug-Free Schools and Communities Act Amendments of 1989. (n.d.).
    Retrieved from http://counsel.cua.edu/fedlaw/dfsca.cfm

Wood, M. (2010, 07). Teens Drink More During Summer Before College, Study
    Finds. Retrieved from www.sciencedaily.com/releases/2010/07/
    100707152209.htm

ADDITIONAL RESOURCES

An example of a national program that provides general training for those who supervise events at which alcohol is present is the TIPS program. Its website address is www.gettips.com, which notes the following: "TIPS® (Training for Intervention ProcedureS) is the global leader in education and training for the responsible service, sale, and consumption of alcohol. Proven effective by third-party studies, TIPS is a skills-based training program that is designed to prevent intoxication, underage drinking, and drunk driving."

A source of education about the use of alcohol and marijuana are the e CHECKUP TO GO (eCHUG) (for alcohol) program and the e CHECKUP TO GO (eTOKE) (for marijuana) at San Diego State University. The programs' website address is www.echeckuptogo.com.

CHAPTER 12

COUNSELING AND HELPING SERVICES

INTRODUCTION

Counseling and helping students and staff are core activities in the professional lives of student affairs staff members. Licensed professional counselors are familiar with their exposure to liability and the protections afforded them through licensure, but this chapter will address the risks associated with counseling and helping students by those student affairs staff members who are not licensed. Licensure requirements vary by state, but those who become licensed are well aware of the limits to their exposure for liability. Therefore, those who are not licensed need to become informed about ways in which their helping students can present risk. It is quite normal for many residence life staff, student activities personnel, and those working in Greek life to help students through personal difficulties and normal challenges associated with their lives as students. In those areas of their work and in almost every other area, giving personal support to students is natural and normal, but it is not without risk.

COLLEGE STUDENT MENTAL HEALTH PROBLEMS

When student affairs staff members encounter students who are deeply in distress or have high levels of need, the most important thing is to get those students to the appropriate resource, on or off campus, where properly prepared counselors or other professionals can give assistance. The various types of mental health problems faced by students should be understood, so the appropriate referral can be made. It is essential for student affairs staff to know when such a referral is called for. Professional therapists and psychiatrists have training and skills that prepare them for responding to the most complex and difficult of emotional challenges. Student affairs administrators who are not trained must recognize the importance of a referral to a professional better equipped to respond to a student in difficulty.

Pressure and Stress

At many times during their college experience, students can feel overwhelmed by pressure and exhibit stress (Kadison & DiGeronimo, 2004, pp. 7–16). Naturally, students often feel pressure due to the academic rigors of college. Many students arrive in college with high hopes and ambitious aspirations. When their actual performances in the classroom do not make those aspirations seem likely, it can be very stressful. The reframing of career and academic aspirations can be challenging and disappointing, and students experiencing those challenges may need help. Additionally, experiencing peer academic competition can be unsettling and stressful.

A central concern for many new students is the dynamic nature of their personal relationships. Some students find new challenges in their relationships with their parents and other family members. Students who attend colleges that are far from their homes may experience serious bouts of homesickness, and, for some, their parents and siblings may also struggle with the separation, making it even more challenging for the student. Social relationships with student peers can also present challenges for individual students, particularly younger students. Finding friends and partners through social encounters on or off campus or social networking sites can be a difficult and stressful experience, often filled with disappointment and hurt feelings.

The wise and alert student affairs administrator is sensitive to the signs of stress and distress in the students she serves, particularly, in those she knows best. Talking with students about their feelings and frustrations is natural for those who work closely with them, and, when students acknowledge their distress, a referral for counseling is natural. Observing the signs of student distress and failing to act appropriately can create risk for those working in student affairs. When a student harms himself or others or suffers loss in some fashion, the administrator who saw evidence of the distress and failed to act can be exposed to legal liability, as well as public embarrassment.

Finances

Many students experience financial hardship while attending college. Sometimes, that is due to changing financial circumstances, either their own of those of their families. It may also be due to poor decision making about purchases and unwise use of credit. Irrespective of the cause, students who are worried about whether they can pay their bills can become very distressed and overwhelmed, if they do not see a way out of their difficulty. Student affairs staff members need to be approachable by students and seen as helpful problem solvers in order for this issue to come to their attention. Many students are uncomfortable discussing personal finances, and often do so with only those with whom they have close, helping relationships. This is particularly the case when the difficulty is the result of bad choices the student has made. Those choices may have been unnecessary and wasteful purchases, excessive generosity and gift giving, or gambling online (a real problem on college campuses, but one that is very hard to find evidence of). Helping students in those circumstances is natural for student affairs staff; they should be handled with sensitivity and care.

Some students in financial difficulty decide to address the problem by seeking employment. The student who works, particularly off campus, may be taking on a time commitment that interferes with success in college. Student affairs staff members may see the evidence of an over-commitment of time and may be able to conclude that it is, at its heart, a financial issue. Many students need to work to support themselves or their families, so their balancing those pressures with the duties associated with academic performance can be quite difficult and stressful.

Responsible student affairs administrators should be alert to the signs of financial distress in students. Knowing or even suspecting that a student is in distress due to financial concerns is a call to action. Helping the student navigate possible solutions is appropriate and necessary. The helping referral for a student who is distressed over such matters might be the office of financial aid, an on-campus employment agency or department, the counseling center, or another source.

Social Isolation

Some students struggle making friends. It may be due to their natural shyness or to opportunities being limited by other obligations and roles. A student who lives at home and has an off-campus job may have fewer chances to make new friends than a student who lives on campus. Even those who live in college housing can distance themselves from their peers. The students who routinely take their meals away from the dining hall or those who live on campus but take most coursework online may be less likely to interact in healthy ways with their peers. Students who take courses or have majors in disciplines that require a lot of solitary work and little group work can find themselves isolated from peers.

Respecting the privacy of isolated/disengaged students, student affairs staff members can make the effort to meet them and try to build relationships with them in order to help them feel a connection to the institution or to their peers.

Crises

A crisis can take many forms and affect the lives of students in ways that are distressing and stressful. Experiencing a crime, either directly or indirectly, can be a stressor. When a student is victimized by crime, there is confusion and emotional duress in the aftermath. Violent crime, in particular, can be traumatic for quite some time after the event. Highly publicized incidents of crime affecting others can also be very distracting and disconcerting for students; they may feel unsafe or insecure in their surroundings.

A natural disaster affecting the college campus is another form of crisis that can be distressing for students. Hurricanes, floods, earthquakes, or blizzards can each create circumstances that disrupt campus operations and make students accommodate to unsettling or insecure conditions.

Crises of a personal nature can cause duress for students. A death or serious illness in the family can be difficult for a college student to manage. The divorce of a student's parents can be equally unsettling.

Student affairs administrators must be sensitive to the emotional reactions of college students to crisis events in their lives. Administrators must give support and make accommodations in the transactions between colleges and students to make coping with the circumstances feasible for students. Failing to do so can create risk of legal liability and public embarrassment.

Substances

Student misuse or abuse of alcohol is a significant problem in American higher education (Kadison & DiGeronimo, 2004, pp. 112–118). There are clear risks associated with student alcohol use, and one of them is the emotional consequence of drinking on the life of the student. Promiscuous and unwanted sexual behavior, academic failure, the loss of or damage to peer relationships, and property damage or injury are among the possible consequences for the individual student. Alcohol is the substance of choice for many students, but there are other substances with which students might experiment. The college years are a time of testing and experimenting, and alert student affairs administrators should be sensitive to the signals of alcohol and drug misuse and its consequences and intervene with care to help students manage the circumstances in which they find themselves.

Depression

College students are susceptible to depression for many of the reasons described previously. Academic struggles and problems with relationships may be principle among the causes for depression, and there may be a family history of clinical depression. Depression is treatable, and student affairs administrators should be alert to its signals. The emotional challenges of college life can be draining for students, and they may on occasion feel overwhelmed. Ignoring the signs of depression or failing to respond appropriately can result in very serious consequences for the student and others and a significant exposure to risk or legal liability for the administrator.

Eating Disorders

Some students struggle with eating disorders. There are always underlying causes: stress, image issues, or insecurity. Student affairs administrators should be sensitive to the signals of the disorders. Concerned students might report their observations of a student with symptoms of an eating disorder. It may be uncommon for a student affairs staff member to have direct observation of an eating disorder, but when peers report their concerns about student behavior in this regard, it is very important to make a swift and effective response.

Gambling

Gambling is, in many ways, a hidden phenomenon. This is particularly the case with online gambling. The result of student gambling can be excessive debt, which can produce a myriad of other conditions, including depression. However, student affairs may not realize that a particular student has a gambling problem, and his or her peers may not either. Evidence of such a problem may come too late for others to be helpful. When students ask for help or give signs of difficulty in this area, it is important to make a timely response, but it could be that the best approach to this issue is a program of teaching and building awareness of the risks.

Bullying

The phenomenon of bullying is quite present in higher education (Pavela, 2012). Many times, it takes the form of cyberbullying, using social networking sites to insult or abuse peers. The victims of cyberbullying can be devastated by the mean behavior of their peers. One of the challenges for the student affairs staff member is the extent to which cyberbullying can remain silent and not be discernable by others. Campaigns to stop it and to report when it is happening may have some effect, but victims need support and assistance to navigate their way to emotional health.

ACADEMIC ADVISING

Many student affairs divisions include offices that provide students with academic advice. Academic advisors must take care to stay within the parameters of their jobs. Students may raise delicate personal or emotional concerns in advising sessions, and advisors must be careful to not engage students in personal counseling for which they are not trained. For example, advisors who attempt to give students psychological advice may be assuming risk at a higher level than is advisable.

Academic advisors also have to be careful to give accurate advice. If students act on wrongful advice and take courses that are not necessary or fail to take courses that they need to complete degree programs, the advisor may be exposing the institution to risk. Advisors must also take care to avoid giving advice that results in students taking courses that are beyond their capacity. The resulting negative academic consequence can result in unwelcome risk.

Academic advisors must also be sensitive to their obligations relative to the confidentiality of academic information to which they are privy. The release of a student's confidential academic information to an unauthorized party exposes the institution to risk.

SPECIAL POPULATIONS AND DIVERSITY ISSUES

Those who help, counsel, and advise students must be sensitive to the diverse ways in which those whom they serve differ from one another. Counselors and advisors might be inclined to treat their clients in ways that are identical, or at least equal. But differences between people call for different kinds of help and support.

Age is an important consideration in helping students. The student who is under eighteen, for example, may have her parents involved in a helping circumstance, or at least may have some rights or restrictions related to state law and psychological licensure regarding the treatment of minors. The Family Educational Rights and Privacy Act (FERPA) is clear on this matter. FERPA rights transfer from the family to the student when the student enrolls in college, irrespective of age. However, the alert student affairs professional is sensitive to state law regarding the treatment of minors.

Similarly, counselors and advisors should be sensitive to the rights of older persons. The Age Discrimination Act of 1975 prohibits discrimination against older persons, specifically persons who are older than forty. An older student who is discouraged by an advisor or counselor from pursuing a certain discipline or career may have a cause of action of age discrimination.

Race and ethnicity impact the counseling and helping relationships that student affairs professionals have with students. Different cultures have varying norms regarding disclosure and seeking assistance, and those who are in helping relationships with students should be sensitive to those differences. Treating an Asian student in a counseling session the same way as a student from the Bronx in New York City may create a difficult situation for the Asian student and expose the counselor to some risk.

Sexual orientation is another consideration around which an advising or counseling relationship might vary. Counselors and advisors have to be aware of the possibility that students they are helping may be of a sexual orientation that is not obvious. A student's disclosure of his or her sexual orientation can ready a counselor to be sensitive to this circumstance. When students do not disclose their sexual orientation, the counselor or advisor should refrain from making assumptions in order to avoid the risk associated with a presumption that is inaccurate.

Many students with disabilities who are attending institutions of higher education have conditions that are apparent or obvious. Counselors and advisors must remain sensitive to their needs and ensure that they are appropriately accommodated, including in the referral process. A large population of students with learning disabilities have conditions that are generally not visible or apparent to others. Thus, advisors need to be sensitive to the possibility of a student client having a learning disability, but the advisor should not ask the question and the student might not volunteer the information. The advisor can ask whether the student has ever been evaluated for a learning disability and, if not, recommend an evaluation.

A student with an emotional disability may present to an advisor or a counselor. A mental health condition such as this may be apparent to the trained professional counselor, but less so to the academic advisor. Being sensitive and unobtrusive is essential in these situations, and a caring, warm approach to set the student at ease may be the easiest way to avoid risk and build trust so the student can disclose any condition that should be accommodated.

CONCLUSION

Those who guide, counsel, and advise students have to be sensitive to the trust that students place in their hands. To dedicated counselors and advisors, giving advice and support to students that is helpful and supportive is an essential aspect of their work. However, in their interactions with students, they must take care to avoid risks of negligence that may be associated with common mental health problems of students or to the differences in the diverse populations they serve. The mitigation of risk has to do with protecting students who are experiencing emotional difficulties from harm and ensuring that they receive the help and support that they need.

REFERENCES

Kadison, R., & DiGeronimo, T.F. (2004). *College of the Overwhelmed* (pp. 7–16, 112–118). San Francisco, CA: Jossey-Bass.

Pavela, G. (2012, March 30). *The Pavela Report*. St. Johns, FL: College Administration Publications.

ADDITIONAL RESOURCES

Benton, S.A., & Benton, S.L. (2006). *College Student Mental Health: Effective Services and Strategies Across Campus*. Washington, DC: NASPA: Student Affairs Administrators in Higher Education.

Cintron, R., Weathers, E.T., & Garlough, C. (Eds.). (2007). *College Student Death: Guidelines for a Caring Campus*. Lanham, MD: American College Personnel Association: University Press of America.

Sandeen, A., & Barr, M.J. (2006). "Who Has Responsibility for the Lives of Students?" In A. Sandeen & M.J. Barr, *Critical Issues for Student Affairs*. San Francisco, CA: Jossey-Bass.

CHAPTER 13

PROVIDING A SAFE ENVIRONMENT

INTRODUCTION

Large numbers of college and university campuses are readily accessible—not only to their students and employees, but also to literally anyone who chooses to come onto the campus and into many of its facilities. It is the rare campus that is designed in such a way that this is not the case. Urban institutions that are surrounded and crisscrossed by public streets are the most accessible to just about anyone.

While such a configuration has many benefits, it also presents serious issues related to risk and liability for campus administrators, including student affairs administrators who are obligated—by their institutions' policies and procedures and by various laws—to make reasonable efforts to provide a safe environment for all who are on their campuses' grounds and in their facilities. As is sometimes the case, some individuals come onto a campus with the sole intent of violating the law in one way or another.

Because of the potentially serious risks that can occur in connection with a campus' environment, the focus of this chapter is on the challenges that colleges and universities face related to property ownership and facility care (including academic facilities, housing facilities, and venues designed for public gatherings, such as arenas and stadiums). The chapter also addresses the duty—and legal requirement—of institutions to protect and/or warn students about the risks associated with assaults and other potentially violent crimes.

The first section of the chapter addresses the federal requirements with which all institutions must comply in regard to these issues. Some of the material described was also covered in Chapter Six. The second section addresses facility-related issues for the various types of facilities. The final section of the chapter addresses the issues related to the steps that institutions take to proactively protect and warn members of the campus community about the fact that assaults and other potentially violent/criminal activities can occur on or near the campus.

FEDERAL REQUIREMENTS FOR COLLEGES AND UNIVERSITIES

The Higher Education Opportunity Act of 2008

The Higher Education Opportunity Act (HEOA) of 2008 reauthorized the Higher Education Act of 1965 as amended ("Higher Education Opportunity," n.d.). It applies to all institutions of higher education that receive federal financial assistance. Consequently, noncompliance could cause an institution to lose its eligibility for receiving federal financial aid for its students. Needless to say, that would be devastating to most institutions. The full text of the Act can be found at the following website: http://www2.ed.gov/policy/highered/leg/hea08/index.htmll.

The document containing the full content of the Act on this site is over four hundred pages and addresses many aspects of higher education. Two of the topics addressed that relate to the issues addressed in Chapter Three require that: (a) institutions include in their biennial review of their drug and alcohol policies the number of drug- and alcohol-related violations and fatalities that occur on campus and as part of the institution's activities along with the number and type of sanctions imposed and (b) upon enrollment, provide students with information about the consequences of a drug conviction on their Title IV financial aid. Further, if a student is convicted for a drug offense, the institution must notify him of the loss of his eligibility for federal financial assistance and how he may regain that eligibility.

The following are other provisions of the Act that address issues with which student affairs administrators are involved:

○ It added several crimes to the list of crimes that must be reported as hate crimes and that must be reported according to type of prejudice.

○ It requires institutions to provide, in their annual Clery Act (security report), a statement of current campus policies that address immediate emergency response and evacuation procedures.

○ It requires that, upon request, institutions disclose to any alleged victim of a crime of violence or non-forcible sex act the results of the conduct proceedings against the alleged perpetrator.

○ It requires that institutions develop a missing student notification policy and procedures for on-campus residents that allows students to designate a confidential contact to be notified if they are determined to be missing for more than twenty-four hours. The institution must also notify students under eighteen years of age that their parents will be notified if they are missing for more than twenty-four hours, along with letting them know that local law enforcement will be notified no later than twenty-four hours after a student is determined to be missing.

○ It requires that institutions with on-campus housing facilities publish an annual fire safety report and keep a log in which all fires in on-campus student housing that occur throughout the year are recorded. The log must include the nature of the fire, date, time, and general location.

The Jeanne Clery Act

According to Wikipedia:

> The Jeanne Clery Disclosure of Campus Security Policy and Campus Crime Statistics Act or Clery Act is a federal statute. It requires all colleges and universities that participate in federal financial aid programs to keep and disclose information about crime on and near their respective campuses. Compliance is monitored by the United States Department of Education, which can impose civil penalties, up to $35,000 per violation, against institutions for each infraction and can suspend institutions from participating in federal student financial aid programs.

The law is named for Jeanne Clery, a nineteen-year-old Lehigh University freshman who was raped and murdered in her campus residence hall in 1986. The backlash against unreported crimes on numerous campuses across the country led to the Jeanne Clery Disclosure of Campus Security Policy and Campus Crime Statistics Act. The Clery Act, signed in 1990, was originally known as the Crime Awareness and Campus Security Act.

The best source of information about the Clery Act can be found on the website of the Clery Center for Security on Campus, http://clerycenter. org/summary-jeanne-clery-act.

On September 6, 2013, the site noted the following:

> The Jeanne Clery Disclosure of Campus Security Policy and Campus Crime Statistics Act (20 USC § 1092(f)) is the landmark federal law, originally known as the Campus Security Act, that requires colleges and universities across the United States to disclose information about crime on and around their campuses. The law is tied to an institution's participation in federal student financial aid programs and it applies to most institutions of higher education both public and private. The Act is enforced by the United States Department of Education.
>
> The law was amended in 1992 to add a requirement that schools afford the victims of campus sexual assault certain basic rights, and was amended again in 1998 to expand the reporting requirements. The 1998 amendments also formally named the law in memory of Jeanne Clery. Subsequent amendments in 2000 and 2008 added provisions dealing with registered sex offender notification and campus emergency response. The 2008 amendments also added a provision to protect crime victims, "whistleblowers," and others from retaliation. ("Summary of the. . .", n.d.)

It also noted the following as the key provisions of the law with which institutions must comply in order for enrolled an student to continue to receive federal financial aid. The reader will note that what follows is quite an extensive list. This is all the more reason why one must pay particular attention to these reporting requirements in order to avoid the possibility of an institution's federal aid being jeopardized. It requires the cooperation of many departments both within Student Affairs and across one's campus to do so.

- Publish an Annual Security Report (ASR) by October 1, documenting three calendar years' of select campus crime statistics, including security policies and procedures and information on the basic rights guaranteed victims of sexual assault. The law requires that schools make the report available to all current students and employees, and prospective students and employees must be notified of its existence and given a copy upon request.
- Have a public crime log. Institutions with a police or security department are required to maintain a public crime log documenting the "nature, date, time, and general location of each crime" and its disposition, if known. Incidents must be entered into the log within two business days. The log should be accessible to the public during normal business hours; remain open for sixty days;

and, subsequently, be made available within two business days upon request.

○ Disclose crime statistics for incidents that occur on campus, in unobstructed public areas immediately adjacent to or running through the campus, and at certain non-campus facilities, including Greek housing and remote classrooms. The statistics must be gathered from campus police or security, local law enforcement, and other school officials who have "significant responsibility for student and campus activities." The Clery Act requires reporting of crimes in seven major categories, some with significant subcategories and conditions:

- Criminal Homicide
  - Murder and Non-Negligent Manslaughter
  - Negligent Manslaughter
- Sex Offenses
  - Forcible
  - Non-Forcible
- Robbery
- Aggravated Assault
- Burglary
- Motor Vehicle Theft
- Arson

○ Schools are also required to report statistics for the following categories of arrests or referrals for campus disciplinary action (if an arrest was not made):

- Liquor Law Violations
- Drug Law Violations
- Illegal Weapons Possession

○ Hate crimes must be reported by category of prejudice, including race, gender, religion, sexual orientation, ethnicity, and disability.

○ Statistics are also required for four additional crime categories if the crime committed is classified as a hate crime:

- Larceny/Theft
- Simple Assault
- Intimidation
- Destruction/Damage/Vandalism of Property

○ Issue timely warnings about Clery Act crimes that pose a serious or ongoing threat to students and employees. Institutions must provide timely warnings in a manner likely to reach all members of the campus community.

Schools must also:

○ Devise an emergency response, notification, and testing policy. Institutions are required to inform the campus community about a "significant emergency or dangerous situation involving an immediate threat to the health or safety of students or employees occurring on the campus." An emergency response expands the definition of timely warning, as it includes Clery Act crimes and other types of emergencies (such as a fire or infectious disease outbreak).

○ Compile and report fire data to the federal government and publish an annual fire safety report. Similar to the ASR and the current crime log, institutions with on-campus housing must report fires that occur in on-campus housing, generate both an annual fire report, and maintain a fire log that is accessible to the public.

○ Enact policies and procedures to handle reports of missing students.

From the foregoing list of requirements, student affairs administrators can clearly see how much specific and detailed information is expected to be compiled and communicated as a result of these provisions of the HEOA and the Clery Act. Failure to do so not only could put students and others at serious risk, but could also create significant liability for the administrator who doesn't comply with the legislation and for his institution. Therefore, student affairs administrators would be well advised to assess the extent to which their campuses are in compliance with the HEOA and the Clery Act.

Department of Education's Dear Colleague Letter Regarding Sexual Violence

This letter was issued on April 4, 2011, and brought new requirements to colleges and universities that receive federal financial aid. The letter was issued in response to the increasing number of acts of sexual violence that were occurring on college campuses across the country and that, in far too many cases, were not being reported. As stated in the letter found at

the following website (http://www2.ed.gov/about/offices/list/ocr/letters/
colleague-201104.pdf):

> Title IX of the Education Amendments of 1972 (Title IX), 20 U.S.C.
> §§ 1681 et seq., and its implementing regulations, 34 C.F.R. Part 106,
> prohibit discrimination on the basis of sex in education programs or
> activities operated by recipients of Federal financial assistance. Sexual
> harassment of students, which includes acts of sexual violence, is a
> form of sex discrimination prohibited by Title IX. In order to assist
> recipients, which include school districts, colleges, and universities
> (hereinafter "schools" or "recipients"), in meeting these obligations,
> this letter: 1) explains that the requirements of Title IX pertaining to
> sexual harassment also cover sexual violence, and lays out the specific
> Title IX requirements applicable to sexual violence. 2) Sexual violence,
> as that term is used in this letter, refers to physical sexual acts perpe-
> trated against a person's will or where a person is incapable of giving
> consent due to the victim's use of drugs or alcohol. An individual also
> may be unable to give consent due to an intellectual or other disability.
> A number of different acts fall into the category of sexual violence,
> including rape, sexual assault, sexual battery, and sexual coercion. All
> such acts of sexual violence are forms of sexual harassment covered
> under Title IX. ("Dear Colleague," 2011)

The letter requires that institutions put in place many specific procedures that address sexual violence, with the failure to do so creating the
possibility of the loss of the institution's ability to receive federal financial
assistance for its students. These include: designating primary, and in some
cases secondary, Title IX coordinators; resolving complaints in a timely
manner, specified as generally no more than sixty days; respecting a com-
plainant's request for confidentiality, but weighing that against the need to
proceed regardless out of concern for the well-being of others; publishing
grievance procedures and making them known to students and parents;
notifying both parties of the outcome of the complaint; and taking proactive measures to address the issue with students through various programmatic initiatives. The letter even specifies what some of those could be.

Department of Justice's Title II Regulations Regarding Direct Threat in Relation to the Americans with Disabilities Act (ADA) and Section 504 of the Rehabilitation Act

Prior to the publication of this regulation, many institutions had policies
and procedures that enabled them to take disciplinary action (including

separating a student from the institution involuntarily) if the student was found to be a direct threat to others OR to himself. This regulation indicates that institutions should omit any references to direct threats to self.

This naturally caused most institutions with such policies to wonder how to address students who might be seen as a direct threat to themselves. Many professional associations including Student Affairs Administrators in Higher Education (NASPA), have made efforts to clarify the issue (Grace, 2014). It is anticipated that, following the publication of this book, there could be further clarification regarding this issue of threat to self or others that will provide further guidance to student affairs administrators and others on college campuses.

Local and State Statutes

If the above-mentioned federal laws weren't enough to require a student affairs administrator's time and attention, local and state laws may also be in place that would impose additional requirements and potential risks of liability on the administrator and her institution. Sources that would be beneficial in determining whether such laws apply would be the institution's office of general counsel or other legal counsel available to the institution, along with the institution's office of campus safety or police department.

REDUCING RISKS ASSOCIATED WITH THE USE OF CAMPUS FACILITIES

Non-Academic Facilities

By and large, student affairs administrators are responsible for non-academic facilities on their campuses. Many of those involve campus housing facilities (including fraternities and sororities), student unions, and recreation facilities. From what has been discussed in the previous section, one can see the variety of issues that can occur in such facilities that require the administrator's careful and ongoing attention in order to reduce risk to students who reside there.

Other risks, however, are associated with the fact that the institution owns, operates, and is expected to maintain those facilities. While the following list may not be exhaustive, it provides examples of the potential risks that fall into this category that the student affairs administrator must also address:

- Assuring that doors function properly, especially if they are equipped with systems that limit access to certain areas of the facilities

○ Assuring that fire alarm systems and fire extinguishers are in proper working order

○ Assuring that elevators are working properly and inspected as required

○ Assuring that HVAC systems are routinely inspected and are working properly to avoid, among other things, possible exposure to carbon monoxide gas

○ Inspecting for and reporting any possible asbestos that may be in a state that could allow it to become airborne

○ Assuring that recreational fields and indoor facilities are appropriately maintained and that recreational equipment is in proper working order

○ Assuring that exterior lighting and any emergency call stations are working properly

○ Assuring that sidewalks, stairways, and parking lots are maintained properly, especially during winter storms, to avoid falls

Academic Facilities and Facilities Designated for Public Gatherings

With the possible exception of student unions, student affairs administrators are not usually responsible for these types of facilities. Nevertheless, there are many occasions for which the student affairs administrator will find herself utilizing such facilities. When doing so, she should be equally as cognizant of the issues in those facilities that could create risks for students as she is in those facilities she supervises. Obviously, should concerns be identified, the administrator should bring the issue to the attention of those responsible for addressing it as quickly as possible, again, to reduce risk to the students present and to the institution.

REDUCING RISKS ASSOCIATED WITH ASSAULTS AND OTHER VIOLENT ACTS

The Role and Responsibility of Campus Police/Safety/Security Officers

Up to this point, the focus in this chapter has been on the role and responsibilities of student affairs administrators in addressing these issues. However, student affairs administrators have many partners on their campuses to assist them in these efforts. Among the most important of those are the individuals who serve as campus security, safety, or police officers. Generally, police officers have the power to arrest someone, whereas campus safety or security officers do not. However, all are on the front line, working proactively to help the student affairs administrator and the institution minimize risk and liability in connection with the issues identified in this chapter.

These colleagues also keep up-to-date through membership in professional associations that are accompanied by publications and websites that support those efforts. One of those websites is www .campussafetymagazine.com. It is mentioned here because student affairs administrators could also gain some valuable information from this site in regard to reducing risk and liability.

For example, when viewed on September 6, 2013, clicking on the "University Security" tab brought up the following topics pertinent to the discussion in this chapter: Clery Act; Active Shooters; Police; Sexual Assaults; and Weapons ("Campus Safety," n.d.).

The Role and Responsibilities of Other Administrators

Just as student affairs administrators will find themselves utilizing facilities for which they are not responsible—and possibly being exposed to risks while doing so—others on the campus, including faculty, staff, other administrators, and students, can find themselves in situations in which risks present themselves. Therefore, just as the need for partnering with campus security personnel seems obvious, student affairs administrators must build relationships with others on campus if the effort to minimize risks and reduce liability is to be truly comprehensive.

CONCLUSION

Federal laws and regulations, along with local laws and institutional policies and procedures, provide the framework within which student affairs administrators function in regard to many of their duties and responsibilities—especially those addressed in this chapter. The issues addressed in this chapter are, arguably, among the most critical, not only because of the risks they pose to students and the institution, but also because of the significant liability to which the student affairs administrator and his institution would be exposed if the issues were found not to have been addressed properly.

Therefore, it is imperative that the student affairs administrator be aware of the laws, policies, and regulations that address these issues.

Additionally, the administrator should build relationships with others at her institution (including campus safety/security personnel, physical plant personnel, other staff and faculty, and, of course, students) who also play a vital role in reducing the types of risks addressed here.

REFERENCES

Campus Safety. (n.d.). www.campussafetymagazine.com/

Clery Act. In *Wikipedia.* Retrieved from http://en.wikipedia.org/wiki/Clery_Act

Dear Colleague. (2011, April 4). Retrieved from http://www2.ed.gov/about/offices/list/ocr/letters/colleague-201104.pdf

Grace, T. (2014, 01 29). *Self-Endangering Students: The Public Policy Conundrum.* Retrieved from www.naspa.org/rpi/posts/self-endangering-students-the-public-policy-conundrum

Higher Education Opportunity Act—2008. (n.d.). Retrieved from http://www2.ed.gov/policy/highered/leg/hea08/index.html

Summary of the Jeanne Clery Act. (n.d.). Retrieved from http://clerycenter.org/summary-jeanne-clery-act

ADDITIONAL RESOURCES

Lake, P.F. (2011). "Managing the Institution of Higher Education Environment. Part I: Safety, Risk Management, Wellness and Security." In P.F. Lake (Ed.), *Foundations of Higher Education Law & Policy* (pp. 91–178). Washington, DC: NASPA: Student Affairs Administrators in Higher Education.

Pavela, G. (2013, March 22). "University Threat Assessment Passes Legal Test." *The Pavela Report, 18*(8). St. Johns, FL: College Administration Publications.

Sandeen, A., & Barr, M.J. (2006). "Who Has Responsibility for the Lives of Students?" In A. Sandeen & M.J. Barr, *Critical Issues for Student Affairs.* San Francisco, CA: Jossey-Bass.

PART FIVE

CONTRACTS

The five chapters in this part of the book present the exposure to risk faced by student affairs administrators in the context of the contracts between institutions and students, as well as contract issues with employees. Chapter Fourteen describes the issues associated with the off-campus behavior of students and the risk management implications. Chapter Fifteen presents the strategies for managing contracts for events and activities and managing the associated risk. Chapter Sixteen reviews the contract issues associated with hiring and supervising employees in student affairs, including the special issues involving student employees. Chapter Seventeen describes the management of risk connected to staff development and training. Chapter Eighteen details the challenges of managing risk that is connected to student conduct systems and practices.

CHAPTER 14

OFF-CAMPUS INCIDENTS AND BEHAVIOR

Student affairs professionals have clear responsibility for supervising and responding to the behavior of students that occurs on campus. Their oversight of residence halls, student unions, campus recreation, and other spaces and facilities clearly obligates them with duty for conduct in those places. Their obligations for student organizations also create duty for them regarding the conduct and activities of those organizations on campus. This chapter will explore the responsibilities of student affairs staff members for the activity and conduct of students when not on campus and the risks that are associated.

CODES OF CONDUCT

The institution's code of conduct sets the parameters for its expectations of students and their organizations. It may also establish the terms under which the institution makes a response to students for their activities when not on campus.

The code of conduct may very specifically establish the authority of the institution regarding the off-campus behavior of students and student organizations. If an institution wishes to assume the ability to respond to such behavior, it is best for that to be clear in the code of conduct. Then, as a matter of contract, the institution can reserve the authority. The way to frame that standard is around what the institution may do, not necessarily what it will do, or is obligated to do. If the code establishes authority, it should also establish the conditions under which it reserves the right to respond to off-campus behavior.

CRIMINAL PROCEEDINGS AND STUDENT CONDUCT PROCEEDINGS

One of the reasons that students and their families become confused about student accountability for off-campus behavior relates to the difference between student conduct proceedings and criminal proceedings. In Chapter Eighteen, we discuss more thoroughly the distinctions between the educational purposes of student conduct proceedings in higher education and the process employed in criminal law. Those distinctions become most evident when students face criminal charges for off-campus behavior and are also called to account for their conduct by the institution. It can be quite confusing to students and their families when findings and outcomes of a criminal proceeding are different from those of a student conduct process. For example, the differences in standards for outcomes of the respective proceedings can easily produce different results. In a criminal process, the standard of proof is "beyond a reasonable doubt," which is a very high standard. In a campus judicial proceeding, the standard is "a reasonable person's conclusion," a substantially lower standard. For those reasons, a student may be found not guilty in a criminal process, but held responsible and receive a disciplinary sanction in a campus judicial process. There are many other ways in which the processes and standards are different, and they are discussed in more detail in Chapter Eighteen. In any event, those differences often present themselves as students are held accountable for their behavior off-campus.

TYPES OF OFF-CAMPUS ACTIVITIES

Fraternities

Greek letter organizations often sponsor activities away from the campus environment. They may do so without the knowledge of campus officials or the presence of chapter advisors. The activities can present risks for the institution, whether they are aware of them or not.

Social functions. Off-campus fraternity parties can present serious consequences for students involved, the national fraternity, and the institution of higher education. The risk of disruption in the community, property damage, disturbance of the peace, and other inappropriate behaviors or violations of the law and institutional regulations can be substantial. Students might think that their behavior off campus insulates them from the consequences of institutional action, but, if the institution reserves for itself the right to respond to conduct off campus and institutional officials learn of the behavior, disciplinary action may follow. If college officials are unaware of the social function, they are still vulnerable to a claim that they failed to adequately supervise the fraternity chapter.

Hazing. In addition to social functions that occur off campus, fraternities may engage in hazing activity. Although hazing is discussed in detail in Chapter Ten, we raise it here because it often occurs off campus. Fraternity social functions may be more likely to draw the attention of college officials, because they are more likely to involve guests other than fraternity members. One of the challenges associated with hazing is that it often occurs in secret and at times and in places about which college officials do not know. It is quite common for hazing to occur at off-campus locations. There is risk in that behavior, of course, because students subjected to hazing can suffer emotional or physical consequences. As we pointed out earlier, institutions have the responsibility to educate fraternity members about the risks of hazing and to regulate against it.

Property ownership. On some campuses, fraternities have residential and social facilities located on college-owned property at their disposal. This creates a quasi-campus situation, if the institution owns the land while the fraternity owns the building. The property lease arrangement should be understood by institutional officials in order to be clear about their responsibility and their authority regarding the fraternity house.

Alcohol. Fraternities commonly have alcohol available at their off-campus social functions. We describe the risks associated with student alcohol use in Chapter Eleven, but it merits discussion here, also, because it may be more likely to occur off campus than on campus. If alcohol is available at fraternity social functions, the risk would be for students who are not of legal age to consume alcohol or have access to it. Underage drinking, when it is called to the attention of local police, can result in consequences for the young people involved, the fraternity chapter, and the institution, if it failed to regulate against underage drinking or to supervise the event.

Student Trips

Many student groups travel to events or activities off campus. For example, campus-based affiliates of national organizations might travel to regional or national conferences sponsored by the larger group. Such organizations might be academic honorary societies, politically affiliated organizations, or groups organized around social issues. The student groups that organize such trips are the responsibility of the institution, and usually of student affairs professionals. They are often funded through university resources, a situation that further commits student affairs administrators to oversight and supervision. When such student travel is arranged through commercial entities, the transportation aspect of risk is generally transferred to those entities. When transportation is provided by the institution, the risk assumed for travel is greater. Irrespective of transportation, the behavior of students while away from campus presents some risk to the institution. Engaging students about to travel on behalf of the institution in discussions about their responsibilities and the expectations that the institution has is sound practice by student affairs professionals.

Club Sports

Some student organizations are organized around sports activities. Some are highly physical, and often take place away from campus. Clubs organized around risky behavior that occurs in places distant from campus can present unwelcome risk for the institution (Kaplin & Lee, 2009, pp. 119, 120, 437, 438). Activities such as skydiving, scuba, and downhill skiing present, by themselves, substantial risk. When they occur in places far away from campus, the institution is exposed to risk. That risk can be modified if participating students execute a waiver of liability or secure appropriate insurance.

Study Abroad

Student affairs staff may serve as sponsors or supervisors for organized trips to foreign countries. There can be substantial risk associated with such trips, either drawn from hazards of life in the host country or from conduct by students who believe they are not accountable to the institution. Ignorance of the culture or the laws of the host country further exposes students to the challenges of risky behavior. The informed student affairs administrator will be familiar with the country being visited, will orient students making the trip, and will provide supervision and oversight as appropriate.

Service Trips

Student affairs staff members who coordinate and manage service trips for students need to be sensitive to several issues associated with risk management. Principle among those issues is the fact that the service trips during spring break or summer sessions are often to locations that have elements of safety risk. For example, trips to inner-city, high-need areas may involve challenges associated with keeping students safe, particularly when the students involved are naïve or inexperienced regarding urban environments and safe practices. The orientation of students who participate must include preparation for managing their behavior in the environment into which they are headed.

Social Functions

Student organizations other than fraternities often sponsor social events off campus. A campus programming board that sponsors a fall semiformal at an area hotel, for example, might expose the institution to elements of risk. Other special events, such as boat cruises or bus rides to athletic contests, involve extra risk if there is alcohol involved; but even when there is no alcohol, the supervision of students and how they interact with the environment and with each other is an essential duty of the responsible student affairs administrator.

OTHER CHALLENGES

Retrieving Information

It can be challenging for student affairs administrators who are not in attendance at off-campus events and activities to gather facts about reports they receive of problematical behavior. Individual students may have conflicting observations, and coming to a clear understanding of what actually happened can be quite difficult. Sometimes, media reports can be accessed, but media outlets might resist becoming sources for institutional action. Reports from observers can conflict with each other or with student accounts. As challenging as it can be to gather information about activities involving students that occur off campus, gathering facts about what occurred may be substantially easier than gathering accurate information about the identities of students who were allegedly involved. Such incidents may involve risk of liability, but also risk of a public relations or community relations consequence.

Local Community Relations

Institutions that are located in or near residential communities have particular challenges regarding student interactions with the local community, especially if there are students living in that community. Students who move off campus to escape campus residences and their regulations may engage in behavior that is troubling to the permanent residents of the neighborhood. Institutions in such circumstances need to engage their students and prepare them for the expectations of the local community. This responsibility typically falls on student affairs staff members. It is also advisable to have a designated contact person for neighbors who wish to communicate with the institution about matters of concern.

CONCLUSION

The risks associated with student behavior in off-campus settings can be substantial. It is important for student affairs staff to stay informed about what activities are occurring in off-campus property and where the responsibility for supervision or regulation lies. To mitigate risk regarding off campus activities, the responsible student affairs administrator should consider whether attending the function would be the best way to ensure that students who are attending engage in safe and healthy behavior. The staff member should help to prepare and educate student leaders who are organizing the activity, to improve the chances of a risk-free event. The staff member and participating students should also be alert to how the event or activity might affect those who live or work close to the location of the event. These steps can modify or mitigate risk for this collection of challenging activities and events.

REFERENCE

Kaplin, W.A., & Lee, B.A. (2009). *A Legal Guide for Student Affairs Professionals* (4th ed.) (pp. 119, 120, 437, 438). San Francisco, CA: Jossey-Bass.

CHAPTER 15

CONTRACT MANAGEMENT

"Will I breach the contract if. . ."

INTRODUCTION

Often, answering questions that begin this way can require an understanding of the most up-to-date legal information and the nuances that center upon contract management and negotiations. Student organizations that are a part of an institution's Student Activities Office and ultimately housed within a Division of Student Affairs are continually plagued with challenges in this arena. In particular, events that include performers, such as speakers, disc jockeys, lecturers, or entertainers (bands, dance troupes, singers, etc.), who are being paid require a fully executed contract. How does a program or event translate into a binding contract without extending risk to the university? Student activities contracts are of great importance and magnitude and require knowledge of contract law and superior negotiation skills. Unfortunately, new student affairs professionals and student leaders are often left at the helm to make decisions without the proper training and guidance. This chapter was written to help professionals in college union/student activities understand what they need to know about the ever-changing world of contract law and student activities. In this chapter, we will examine the reasons that contracts are needed, the core elements of a contract, common uses for contracts in student activities, negotiating and executing a contract, and the pitfalls to contract negotiation.

OVERVIEW OF CONTRACT LAW

A contract is a binding agreement between two parties, entered into voluntarily, and seeking to give something in exchange for something else (Lake, 2011, pp. 83–88). For example, a commercial contract indicates an exchange of goods or services for a fixed price; for example, an apartment lease indicates an exchange of space and maintenance for the payment of rent. Student organizations regularly enter into contracts for such things as speakers or performers, lecturers, apparel sales, car or bus rentals, and facilities rentals.

A contract should be used any time there is a need for a clear understanding of responsibility, that is, any time a student organization is paying for a person's services or providing travel, lodging, or meals for a performer/speaker, or any time any duties are being performed in exchange for payment. In the event that the party being invited to campus will not be paid, but will be performing on university property, then a contract may still be required to clearly define the agreement to comply with institutional policies, as well as to document any insurance requirements or special conditions of the agreement. In summary, a contract should be used when there is expected performance of duties by one entity in exchange for consideration (payment or the opportunity to perform) by another entity. When a student organization is giving or receiving services in exchange for anything of value, a written agreement can serve to protect the interests of both the organization and the university.

GOVERNING LAW

Courts within the United States often render legal opinions that are not based on statues, administrative laws and regulations, or constitutional provisions. In contract interpretation and breach of contract disputes, the prevailing law is often judicial holdings the courts have created themselves. This is known in the American judicial system as *common law*. Common law is judge-made law that does not originate from statutes, ordinances, or administrative rules and regulations. Contract interpretation and contract disputes are governed by common law and vary from state to state. Because of this, it is critically important for new campus activities professionals and student organization representatives to draft and interpret contract language in accordance with the laws of the institution's respective state. If a contract is written subject to another state's laws, the contract must be changed, and it is highly recommended that one contact legal counsel to provide guidance in this area.

STANDARD CONTRACT PROVISIONS

Contracts can be simple or complex and legalistic; yet, they are comprised of standard terminology and clauses that are included in a majority of student activities contracts. It is imperative that new campus activities professionals or student organization representatives understand commonly used terminology and contract provisions. A sample of terms commonly used is provided below. If a campus student activities office regularly brings events to campus, then campus activities professionals and advisors and student organization representatives should become familiar with these terms. If language in a contract is difficult to understand or unfamiliar, the responsible student affairs staff member should contact an attorney.

For example, many artists have "agents," a person who has the power to make commitments on behalf of the artist. A "block price" is the discounted amount the organization may pay for an artist when the artist has several performances in the area within the span of a few days. A "contract rider" is an attachment to the contract. It may contain requests of the artist for hospitality or equipment needs. "Fully executed" contracts are those that have been signed by both the artist/agent or artist representative and the organization representative authorized to execute an agreement.

In addition to standard contract terminology, a contract should contain certain basic information necessary to understand the intent of the parties. If this information is missing, the campus activities professional or student organization representative is wise to seek the advice and guidance of a supervisor or an attorney. The contract provisions outlined within this chapter are not an exhaustive list, as every contract is unique to the specific event hosted and the parties who are privy to the contract. The following is meant to serve as a guide for those who are in the practice of reviewing and/or executing contracts on behalf of a student activities office or student organization.

A contract should have a description of the parties in the contract, the date of the contract and of the event, and a general overview of the goods or service being contracted. A contract should include a statement of the contract duration, clarifying how long the document will be valid, and also a list of definitions of words or expressions found in the remainder of the contract.

The contract should include specific descriptions of each party's obligations and responsibilities as a result of the contract and detail any relevant operative provisions, such as applicable warranties or exclusions.

Often, this section will appear as a disclaimer or have other limiting language that may give one party advantage over the other. A contract should include a list of enforcement provisions to cover any "what if" situations, such as a party failing to fulfill its obligations, dispute resolution plans, and unforeseen circumstances affecting the terms of the contract. The contract should conclude with a closing section that indicates the agreement of both parties to the terms of the contract.

WRITTEN CONTRACTS VERSUS OTHER CONTRACT FORMS

In a previous paragraph, we listed commonly used terminology and standard contractual provisions used in most student activities contracts. However, the most important concept in contract law is having the agreement in writing and signed by all parties involved. Courts will generally treat a written contract signed by both parties as the final written expression of the parties. However, the word "contract" is not necessary for an agreement to be a contract. For example, an agreement negotiated by an exchange of letters can be a contract. A document called a "memorandum of understanding" or "memorandum of agreement" is a contract. Contracts vary in their complexity based on the nature of the goods or services or the monetary value of the contract. Even an oral exchange of terms can be a contract, but it is not the best form for contractual arrangements. If there is any doubt about whether an agreement is a contract, the student affairs staff member should contact a supervisor or an attorney.

AGREEMENT ON CONTRACT TERMS

With respect to a contract dispute, courts will examine the original intent of both parties and the terms listed in the final, signed version of the contract. It is, therefore, important to ensure full agreement about all terms listed in the contract and any additional terms, such as those in an addendum. Student affairs staff members should maintain open communication with the other party as they review the contract and make any changes, and indicate any additional terms on the final document before signing it.

VALIDITY OF THE CONTRACT

A key component of contract validity is the authority of the signing party to contract on behalf of the organization or institution. Therefore, the campus activities professional signing the contract should indicate in writing that he has the permission and authority to act on behalf of the organization. Contracts will likely not be valid if they involve any illegal activity or break the law themselves. For instance, the student affairs staff member's capacity to enter into a contract will be affected if he or she is under duress, intoxicated, or coerced in any way. Another factor to consider is the age of the signing party, as contracts signed by minors (under the age of eighteen) may not be enforceable.

FAIRNESS OF THE CONTRACT

When a contract is extremely one-sided in that one party holds heavy responsibility, while the other guarantees nothing, courts may declare the document "unconscionable." For instance, one party may be sophisticated in writing contracts and include language that waives all liability on its part and requires the other party to pay the costs of any contract dispute. The student affairs staff member should look closely for such language in reviewing a contract, and seek assistance from a supervisor or an attorney if there are any questions or concerns about the operative provisions.

UNIVERSITY ORGANIZATIONS AND STUDENT ACTIVITIES CONTRACTS

Organizations registered and recognized by an institution are entitled to several rights and privileges, including the use of the university name, logo, and symbols and the use of procedures to request funding. However, with this privilege also comes responsibility, and advisors to student organizations must realize that there is a fine balance in the relationship between a student organization and the university.

On the one hand, a student organization representative's behavior and decisions reflect on the university. To that extent, it is vitally important that the student representative conduct himself and the organization's affairs in an appropriate manner. However, it should be clear that, while an organization's conduct can reflect on the institution, a student representative should not represent to third parties in contract formations or other business dealings that he is representing the university. Student organizations are student groups recognized by the institution, but the student representative is usually neither an employee nor a designated person authorized to enter into binding contracts on behalf of the institution. Again, it is a fine line in the balance of responsibilities.

When a student organization is negotiating with third parties and vendors while using the institution's name, we recommend avoiding any possible misperception regarding the organization's authority to act (either with direct or apparent authority). Language that makes this clear can help avoid any possible links between the organization's activity and the institution. Again, the organization's ability to use the institution's name, logo, and so forth does not make the student delegate a representative of the university. It simply allows the organization to use some of the privileges of being a recognized student organization at its respective institution.

If a contract signed by a student leader does not sufficiently make clear that the student does not represent or obligate the institution, then the vendor or third party might believe that the university will take responsibility if the student organization fails in its obligation. This type of scenario is definitely avoidable if enforced by the campus activities professional staff member who is advising the student organization. Therefore, it is advisable that student organizations include language in their contracts that makes it clear that someone's ability to enter into an agreement or contract is a function of his role as a student leader in the group, and not as a representative of the institution.

This section has provided a basic overview to the contracting process for a recognized student organization. Clearly, it is in the best interest of student representatives and campus activities professionals to read contracts carefully and submit the contract for review prior to execution. This allows the institution to assure no obligations are being made in the name of the university and avoids foreseeable risk and harm to the institution.

INDEPENDENT ORGANIZATIONS AND STUDENT ACTIVITIES CONTRACTS

Independent organizations, such as unrecognized student clubs or independent fraternities or sororities, may wish to seek independent legal advice prior to entering into a contractual agreement on behalf of their organizations. The independent organization, and not the institution, is party to, and bound by, the agreement. While professional staff members working in the student activities office cannot offer legal advice, it is generally acceptable for administrators to consult with independent organizations and offer recommendations relative to acceptable contract terminology and provisions.

CONTRACT REVIEW PROTOCOLS

At many institutions, recognized student organizations are required to submit activities and event contracts for review by campus activities professionals prior to execution. In addition, campus activities professionals should establish contract review protocols for student organizations. That can have the effect of ensuring consistency among student organizations and protecting student representatives from irresponsibly contracting for an event or activity. Such contract review protocols provide a check and balance to ward off potential risk.

Contract review protocols may vary from institution to institution based on the event type and/or activity. However, at a minimum, student affairs staff members should convene an event and contracts meeting with representatives from student organizations as part of their training and orientation. Additionally, if a contract involves a major band or performer, world-renowned speakers or lecturers, it is advisable for student affairs staff members to hold an event and contract review meeting at least six months in advance of the event.

COMMON TYPES OF EVENT CONTRACTS

Events that include performers, such as speakers, disc jockeys, lecturers, or entertainers (bands, dance troupes, singers, etc.) who are being paid should require a fully executed contract and rider. Three types of contracts are commonly used by institutions of higher education: performers receiving payment, free performance, and lectures. In addition, some institutions require an institutional rider for all performers or lecturers who provide their own contracts. When an artist does not have a contract, independent and university organizations can draft a contract and send it to an artist or her agent for review. These types of contracts can be considered "standard engagement agreements" and should be developed by the institution's attorney.

PRACTICAL TIPS FOR CONTRACT NEGOTIATIONS

Before making an offer to an artist, the student leader or campus activities professional should consider working closely with an attorney to adhere to university and department procedures related to negotiating contracts. If the department has implemented contract review protocols, then the student representative or campus activities professional should complete all necessary forms to comply with the contract negotiation process. Additionally, it may be prudent to develop a budget and secure adequate funding for all aspects of the event prior to entering into a contract. Furthermore, all co-sponsorships for the event/activity should be identified in writing, which will eliminate ambiguity relative to fiduciary responsibility for all parties. Finally, the student representative or campus activities professional should schedule a meeting with the appropriate supervisor prior to negotiating an offer to ensure the elements of a contract are understandable.

PITFALLS OF CONTRACT NEGOTIATIONS

Contract negotiations can be difficult and can compromise the institution of student affairs professionals. In this section, we will identify some common aspects of contract discussions that can present challenges.

Hold Harmless/Indemnification Clauses

Lawsuits are a common occurrence in our litigious society. An effective way for third parties and vendors to limit their liability is to specify their responsibility in a contractual relationship. Risk can be transferred contractually by including "hold harmless" clauses in agreements. In a hold harmless agreement, one party agrees to protect or "indemnify" another from claims brought by a third party for financial loss or damage. A good example in the student affairs arena is when a world-renowned performer (band or singer) contracts to perform at the university and a portion of the performance includes pyrotechnics. To protect himself, the performer may request the student organization to sign a hold harmless agreement. The agreement would indemnify the performer if any problems were to arise from the use of pyrotechnics (for example, the pyrotechnics set a fire on the football field). In a hold harmless agreement, the party that has assumed the liability is responsible for all financial loss. Some hold harmless clauses are very broad. Surprisingly, they may include liability, even if the indemnified company was solely responsible for the damage. On the other hand, a contractual liability insurance policy can protect the person or organization assuming the risk, but may not cover all aspects of liability.

In some states, many proposed contracts seek to have a university assume all responsibility for any liability arising out of the contract or products of the contract. Some states do not permit this assumption of liability because the state and the public university are self-insured only for acts and omissions of its own employees and agents. It cannot assume responsibility for acts and omissions of others. In these circumstances, the representatives of institutions must delete contractual clauses requiring indemnification of the other party to the contract. An attorney can assist in redrafting these clauses.

Binding Mandatory Arbitration

When a third party or vendor includes a binding mandatory arbitration (BMA) clause, it means that any contractual disputes that arise must be decided by a private legal system. Typically, an arbitrator, a neutral third party with experience in contract law, is summonsed to act as a "private judge" to settle the dispute. While binding mandatory arbitration is hailed in the legal system as an innovative alternative dispute resolution strategy, many higher education institutions will not allow campus activities professionals or student representatives to sign contractual agreements with BMA clauses.

The problems with BMA clauses include that they limit dispute resolution options and that they may not follow clear and consistent rules. For example, an arbitrator may not be required to follow procedures that allow a party to request information from the other. A BMA may also involve significant expenses, even costs to simply initiate the arbitration process.

Prior to extending an offer to a third party or vendor, the student representative or campus activities professional should inquire whether the third party or vendor requires that a binding mandatory arbitration clause be incorporated in the activities/events contract. If the third party or vendor requires such an agreement, then it would be prudent for a student organization or campus activities professional to refuse to contract with the vendor.

Breach of Contract and Attorney Fees Awards

In a breach of contract lawsuit, courts generally do not make the losing party pay for the winning party's attorney fees. However, there are exceptions. A third party or vendor, in a breach of contract, may be able to recover reasonable attorney's fees from the student organization or institution, in addition to the other damages that the court will award, if the activities contract provided for such an award or there is a state statute. Thus, it is incumbent upon campus activities professionals and student representatives to read the activities contract carefully and verify that this type of provision is not included in the activities contract.

In some states, attorney fees may be mandated by statute, meaning that they are automatically awarded to the prevailing party according to the law. An automatic award of attorney fees and costs is typically set forth when the winning party prevails in court and is awarded damages for the breach, presents evidence that the fees incurred in the case were reasonable, and satisfies any requirements that the court may have for how this evidence is to be presented. Alert student affairs professional staff members will know whether the state in which they are employed has enacted a law for an automatic award of attorney fees and costs in breach of contract situations.

Personal Liability on Behalf of the Signer

To determine whether a campus activities professional or student representative who signs a contract is personally liable, courts consider the written instrument in its entirety. To avoid personal liability, those signing legal instruments on behalf of their organization or institution should unambiguously demonstrate that their signatures are made in a representative capacity only. This should be done by clearly manifesting in the body of the instrument, and in each signature field, that the commitment tendered is that of the organization or institution, not the individual signer. From an institutional perspective, the potential for personal liability on behalf of the signer shows why it is critically important for the institution to establish who can sign a student organization or institutional contract.

CONCLUSION

In this chapter we discussed the principles associated with negotiating contracts for an original activity or performance. We presented some key terms in contract design and the issues of contract validity and fairness. We described how contracts should be crafted and reviewed and presented the ethical issues associated with contract matters. We gave some practical tips for contract negotiations and discussed the risks.

The informed student affairs administrator must understand contract design issues and the risks associated with contracts that may be poorly or incompletely configured. The value of seeking counsel on such matters is obvious.

REFERENCE

Lake, P.F. (2011). *Foundations of Higher Education Law & Policy: Basic Legal Rules, Concepts, and Principles for Student Affairs* (pp. 83–88). Washington, DC: NASPA: Student Affairs Administrators in Higher Education.

CHAPTER 16

EMPLOYMENT ISSUES

INTRODUCTION

Student affairs administrators, even those in their first, entry-level positions, are likely to find themselves in the position of a supervisor. As a supervisor, there are many employment-related issues associated with supervising others that create numerous risks and liability if not addressed properly. The administrator might supervise a variety of student employees, such as resident assistants, and those who work in the administrator's office.

Likewise, the administrator could find herself supervising other employees of the institution, who may be hourly employees or administrative (exempt) employees. Each of these categories presents its own unique employment issues that could create risk and liability. The type of liability to which a student affairs administrator can be exposed is related to each of three broad stages of the employee/supervisor relationship, as discussed in this chapter.

Therefore, this chapter addresses the risks that are present in connection with one's role as a supervisor of both student employees and other employees of the institution. It is organized so as to follow three broad stages of the employee/supervisor relationship. Unless specifically noted, the issues identified apply to one's role as a supervisor of both student employees and other employees of the institution.

The first section addresses the issues, risks, and liability associated with the search and selection process. The second addresses the issues, risks, and liability associated with the relationship between the student affairs administrator as supervisor and the employee as each goes about discharging his or her responsibilities. The third addresses the issues, risks, and liability associated with the relationship between the student affairs administrator and the employee during the time that the employee separates from the institution; either voluntarily or at the decision of the supervisor.

Finally, it should be noted that the purpose of this chapter is not to enable the student affairs administrator to be a human resources professional or replace the need for the administrator to work closely with the human resource professionals on his campus on all employment-related issues. All institutions have personnel policies and procedures that address the three types of employment issues discussed in this chapter, and the student affairs administrator would be well advised to become familiar with those and consult with the human resource professionals at his institution on employment-related matters.

ISSUES ASSOCIATED WITH THE SEARCH AND SELECTION PROCESS

Position Descriptions

Arguably the description for any position could be considered the cornerstone for the search and selection process. At a minimum, it contains the duties associated with the position, although there is often reference to the fact that other appropriate duties may be assigned. Additionally, it contains the required and, sometimes, preferred qualifications associated with one who would be appointed to the position. Often, it also describes the general working conditions in which the student affairs administrator would find herself, for example, an office environment with minimal need to lift heavy objects but sometimes finding it necessary to work outside of the typical work day, including nights and weekends.

Understanding what the working conditions are is important because some candidates may have a disability that would inhibit them from performing the duties of the position without a reasonable accommodation being provided. Therefore, by knowing these, a candidate would be in a position to request such an accommodation.

The student affairs administrator's risk potential begins with and continues throughout the stages of employment issues discussed in this chapter. Why? That is because hiring someone without the designated qualifications could lead to actions by others who felt that they were better qualified. Also, once in the position, the qualified incumbent may have a basis for taking action if he feels that he is routinely being required to do things that are considerably outside of the scope of the job's duties and responsibilities or if the working conditions are not in keeping with those described in the position description.

Searches: Preparation and Procedures

At some point in time—and likely early in a student affairs administrator's career—she will be responsible for conducting a search to fill a position, whether for a student employee or for an hourly or administrative (exempt) employee. While the position description is the starting point for the search process, many other elements must also be addressed, each of which, if not done in accordance with her institution's personnel policies and procedures, creates the opportunity for risk and liability as a result of some potential candidates being excluded from the applicant pool for reasons that, if known to those individuals, could result in a challenge that could disrupt the hiring process or, worse, cause the process to be restarted once someone was hired.

The search process begins with determining where and how the notice of the vacancy and the desire to fill it will be communicated to prospective candidates. In the case of student employees, such notices are, by definition, communicated to students enrolled in the institution. Such positions as resident assistants and students serving as admission office tour guides and student staff in the student union and recreation facilities come to mind. In the case of making the vacancy known to prospective candidates for hourly or administrative positions, some institutions require that the notice first be posted internally, while others have no such requirement. The student affairs administrator should be sure to know what his institution's policy is on this point.

When the position is posted outside of the institution, the administrator must determine where it will be posted. That may include local and national print publications, as well as electronic postings on various organizational websites that prospective candidates for such positions would be expected to monitor. For student affairs positions, some of the more common websites that contain job postings are those of ACPA, ACUHO-I, NASPA, *The Chronicle of Higher Education,* and *Inside Higher Ed.*

The cost of placing the position announcement can become a factor, so that should be weighed (in consultation with the institution's human resources staff) to balance that cost against attempting to assure that a notice reaches the widest audience of prospective candidates possible. With that in mind, the announcement should contain the position title, basic duties, minimum and desired qualifications, the materials to be submitted to be considered a candidate, the date by which they are due, and the expected starting date. In some cases, it is advisable to indicate the salary for the position in the announcement. In other cases, the administrator may discuss that with the candidates who are formally interviewed for the position.

The advisability of addressing this issue before bringing candidates to campus for the interview process is obvious. It lets candidates know what the compensation is for a position and, if it is not in keeping with a candidate's expectations, it saves the candidate and the institution the time and expense of bringing someone to campus to be interviewed who would not be able to accept the position based on the level of compensation. Finally, because cost can be a deciding factor in how much to include in the announcement, often a link to more information on the institution's website about the position and the application process is included.

Affirmative Action and Equal Employment Opportunity

The position announcement should also address the fact that the institution follows and is in compliance with Affirmative Action and Equal Employment Opportunity laws and guidelines. Affirmative Action is a federal policy that seeks to redress past discrimination and avoid future discrimination through active measures to ensure equal opportunity, especially in education and employment (*Wikipedia*). Since the emphasis is on equal *opportunity*, Affirmative Action does not involve the use of quotas—which would, in fact, be illegal.

According to the website of the U.S. Equal Employment Opportunity Commission (www.eeoc.gov), equal employment opportunity laws make it illegal to discriminate against a job applicant or an employee on the basis of the person's race, color, religion, sex (including pregnancy), national origin, age (forty or older), disability, or genetic information ("U.S. Equal Employment," n.d.). It is also advisable for the announcement to reference the institution's policy on non-discrimination since some institutions only include those categories required by law, while others are broader. Failure to adhere to these policies in the search and selection process is one of the surest ways to create a legal challenge resulting in potentially serious risk and liability for the student affairs administrator. Addressing these important issues can also have a bearing on where the position announcement is placed.

The Search Committee and the Screening and Interview Process

A search committee will likely have to be created for virtually any position, along with establishing the process for screening application materials and conducting interviews. In some cases, the student affairs administrator who will supervise the person ultimately selected may desire to serve on the committee, and perhaps even chair the committee. In other cases, the administrator may wish to instead have the committee recommend some number of qualified candidates who would be interviewed by the administrator in order to make a selection. Because this process can vary widely, here again, the institution's human resources staff can offer valuable information, including providing guidance about who should be on the search committee.

Screening of the application materials can take many forms. For example, all members of the search committee may read all of the materials of all of the applicants, or that process may be divided among the committee members. Similarly, once some number of candidates has been identified as those to be interviewed, that process can vary widely from institution to institution and according to the type of position being filled.

A key part of the screening process is checking references that applicants are usually asked to provide. This part of the screening process presents its own unique liability issues. In some cases, references listed by the applicant are reluctant to provide any negative information (if any exists) out of a concern that the applicant will find out about it and, especially if the applicant isn't offered the position, may seek legal action against the reference. In some cases, the hiring institution may seek reference information from people not listed by the applicant as a result of someone on the selection committee knowing someone at the applicant's institution. Here again, based on the type of information provided, this could create liability issues for the hiring institution and the person who provided the information. Because of that, many human resource professionals recommend only providing the basic employment information regarding an individual, such as the position held, the date of hire, and the date of departure—if not currently employed.

Again, the advice of the institution's human resources staff is invaluable. The most important consideration, however, to avoid risk and the potential liability of a challenge to the search and selection process is to be sure that the same process and procedures are followed for all of the applicants.

The Offer of Appointment

At some point, the search process will conclude with the administrator making an offer of appointment to one of the candidates. While that may initially be discussed verbally, it should always be followed up in writing. Depending on the institution's policies, such a written offer may come from the student affairs administrator who led the search and who will supervise the employee or from a member of the human resources staff. More and more frequently, institutions are indicating to candidates that the offer is contingent on conducting a background check that results in nothing that would cause the offer to be rescinded. The offer of appointment can also vary from a letter that states the terms and conditions of the offer to a more formal contract. Paying careful attention to these critical elements of the search and selection can help avoid risks and liability that could arise later.

Finally, many institutions have a period of ninety days or so in which the newly appointed employee is considered to be in a probationary status. Generally, this means that if something were to occur that would be cause to terminate the employee, it could be done with relatively limited justification. However, if an institution has such a policy, once the employee has gone past the probationary period, the same institutional policies regarding the employee's employment status apply, just as they would to other employees who have been at the institution for many more years.

ISSUES ASSOCIATED WITH THE SUPERVISOR-EMPLOYEE RELATIONSHIP

As with the search and selection process, the student affairs administrator must know his institution's policies regarding the relationship between himself and those he supervises and to consult with the institution's human resources staff as needed. Within that overall framework, the following are some particular areas that could create risk and liability within the supervisor-employee relationship.

Working Conditions

The student affairs administrator who supervises employees should be mindful of the employees' working conditions and be sure to address legitimate concerns raised by the employees regarding changes in those conditions, especially those that create an unsafe or unhealthy work environment. Among the obvious things that come to mind are such things as exposed asbestos (or what one perceives to be exposed asbestos), which should be promptly evaluated by those trained to do so; failure of the heating or cooling system that could create an unhealthy environment; and the presence of mold in the building's HVAC system or elsewhere that could be harmful to an employee's health. There could be other, less obvious changes in one's working conditions that, if legitimate and unaddressed, could result in potential liability for the student affairs administrator.

Another aspect to one's working conditions involves the hours one is expected to work. Student employees generally work fewer than thirty hours a week (and often much less than that) and receive no benefits like those associated with full-time employees of the institution. However, for some student employees such as resident assistants, job duties cannot be confined to only "working" during certain times or for a certain number of hours per week as they are expected to address issues that arise whenever and however often they occur. In such cases, institutions vary their methods of compensation from keeping track of resident assistants' hours worked and paying them accordingly to providing a stipend (often in the form of covering the resident assistant's room and board costs) in exchange for the duties that the resident assistant performs. Here again, it is crucial for the student affairs administrator to know and comply with her institution's policies for student employees in order to reduce risk and liability.

Full-time employees, on the other hand, generally fall into one of two categories: exempt or non-exempt. Exempt employees are those administrative and professional staff (like student affairs administrators) who are *exempt* from wage and hour laws that require one to receive overtime pay when one works (generally) more than forty hours per week. Similarly, by definition, non-exempt employees are those employees (those paid hourly) who are *not exempt* from the wage and hour laws and who therefore must receive overtime pay when they work either more than eight hours a day and/or more than forty hours per week.

Finally, on many campuses, some segment of the employee population (if not all employees) are represented by labor unions. In those cases, the working conditions of those employees are often defined by the terms of the contract between the union and the institution. Being aware of those terms in such cases is critically important in order for the student affairs administrator to avoid risk and potential litigation.

The Relationship Between the Supervisor and Employee Both At and Away From the Workplace

This aspect of the various employment issues a student affairs administrator is likely to face is arguably the most complex and likely to create the potential for risk and liability. The best advice that can be given is that, at all times, the supervisor should conduct himself in a manner that conveys that the relationship between him and the employees he supervises is strictly professional. However, student affairs administrators and the employees they supervise do not live in an ideal world. As a result (and one might say from a positive perspective), the administrator might find himself attracted to an employee and have a desire to establish a personal relationship. On the other hand (and one might say from a negative perspective), administrators have been known to engage in behavior toward employees that is intimidating and demeaning and even violates various laws when it rises to the level of harassment, discrimination, and sexual violence. This would expose the administrator and the institution to civil and even criminal liability, as well as potentially serious public relations consequences.

Any and all of those types of situations between a student affairs administrator and the employees he supervises creates potentially significant risk and liability for the administrator and for his institution. Therefore, the administrator should have a thorough understanding of his institution's policies regarding these matters and adhere to them very carefully in order to reduce the risk and associated liability of doing otherwise.

Performance Appraisals and Disciplinary Action

Another critical institutional personnel policy with which the student affairs administrator should be thoroughly familiar is that addressing performance evaluations/appraisals and the process to be followed if disciplinary action needs to be taken in connection with that process. These can vary from one institution to another, so careful attention should be paid to what they are at one's institution.

Specifically, many institutions require that a formal performance evaluation or appraisal be done annually. In such cases, the appraisal often forms the basis for consideration for an increase in compensation. Therefore, it is very important that the process be followed according to the institution's policies in order to avoid the risk of a challenge of, for example, favoritism or discrimination. By its definition, an annual performance evaluation is summative. It evaluates an employee's performance over the previous year. However, to be helpful to the employee and to reduce risk to the student affairs administrator who supervises the employee and conducts the performance appraisal, the administrator would be well advised to offer formative evaluation to the employee in the form of feedback throughout the year. Put simply, the employee should not be surprised by the information contained in the annual performance review but instead see it as reaffirmation of what has been communicated (verbally and in writing) at various times throughout the year.

Among the communications that might occur during the year are those that are disciplinary in nature. These can cover a broad range, from verbal suggestions and warnings to more formal actions like written reprimands and, in some cases, based on the nature of the employee's behavior, immediate termination from the institution. One will be exposed to significant risk and liability if one does not strictly adhere to the institution's disciplinary process, which in some cases requires different steps for exempt and non-exempt employees and also if the employee in question is a member of a labor union. Here again, and as with any other employment related issue, the student affairs administrator should seek the advice and counsel of the human resources staff at her institution to avoid creating significant risk and liability to herself and her institution.

ISSUES ASSOCIATED WITH AN EMPLOYEE'S SEPARATION FROM THE INSTITUTION

Except in the rarest of circumstances, an employee will not work his entire career at the institution that offered him his first position. Therefore, during the course of one's career, one should expect to leave one institution in order to accept a position at another, until the person decides to retire. Retirement has its own unique set of separation issues that are not addressed here.

Separating from an institution can either be initiated by the employee or by the institution. Needless to say, the former is far more preferable than the latter, from the standpoint of minimizing risk and liability on the part of the employee's supervisor and institution. However, in both cases, the person who supervises the employee who is leaving needs to be aware of the steps to be taken to reduce risk and liability.

When the separation is initiated by the employee, the following are among the things that must be considered and addressed, either by the student affairs administrator or by the institution's human resources office:

- o Does the employee have unused vacation or sick leave for which the employee is entitled to be paid?
- o Is the employee in a category of employee who is entitled to severance pay?
- o Can the employee request and expect to receive a letter of reference/recommendation from the administrator who is the employee's supervisor?

Understandably, the potential for risk and liability to the student affairs administrator is much less when a separation is initiated by the employee than when it is initiated by the institution. Even when it is initiated by the institution, some actions create a greater likelihood for risk and liability than others. For example, an institution may decide to reduce the size of its workforce in order to reduce expenses and maintain a balanced budget. If such a process is handled equitably and fairly, the potential for risk and legal challenges will be minimized.

On the other hand, the potential for risk and legal challenges is significantly greater if the employee is separated "for cause" relating to behavior that is unacceptable because it violates institutional policies or for failure to adequately perform the duties associated with the employee's position. In such situations, one can readily see the importance of having adhered to all of the relevant personnel policies referenced earlier in this chapter in order to be in a position to successfully defend against a challenge that an employee might bring for wrongful termination.

Whatever the circumstances under which an employee leaves an institution, the student affairs administrator would be well advised to make every effort to maintain the dignity of the employee and, especially when the separation is institutionally initiated, to not discuss the circumstances with those who don't have a legitimate need to know.

CONCLUSION

Student affairs administrators are expected to address a wide range of employment related issues. These involve both student employees and other full-time employees of the institution. It is incumbent upon the administrator to be fully informed of the institution's personnel policies and procedures but, more importantly, to rely on the human resources professionals at the institution in order to minimize risk and liability associated with addressing employment related issues inappropriately.

REFERENCES

Affirmative Action. In *Wikipedia*. Retrieved from http://en.wikipedia.org/wiki/Affirmative_action

U.S. Equal Employment Opportunity Commission. (n.d.). Retrieved from www.eeoc.gov/eeoc/index.cfm

ADDITIONAL RESOURCES

College and University Professional Association for Human Resources. www
    .cupahr.org/

Kaplin, W.A., & Lee, B.A. (2007). "The College and Its Employees." In
    W.A. Kaplin & B.A. Lee, *The Law of Higher Education* (4th ed.)
    (pp. 142–240). San Francisco, CA: Jossey-Bass.

Society for Human Resource Management www.shrm.org

WEBSITES FOR POSTING POSITIONS

ACPA: College Student Educators International: http://www2.myacpa.org/

Association of College and University Housing Officers–International:
www.acuho-i.org

NASPA: Student Affairs Administrators in Higher Education: www
.naspa.org/

The Chronicle of Higher Education: http://chronicle.com

Inside Higher Ed: http://careers.insidehighered.com/

CHAPTER 17

STAFF DEVELOPMENT AND TRAINING

INTRODUCTION

This chapter focuses on the strategies that professionals who work in student affairs can employ in staff development and training in order to best manage or avoid risk. In Chapter Sixteen, we detailed the risks associated with hiring and supervising staff. This chapter expands on those principles by detailing the essential issues associated with giving staff the training, knowledge, and skills necessary to be effective in their jobs. Embedded in the staff training duty is the common law notion of *respondeat superior,* or the responsibility of the employer for the actions of employees. Supervisors of employees and the institutions that employ them can be held accountable for their actions, so it is prudent to engage in employee training and development.

Student affairs staff have a number of unique responsibilities that call for specialized training and preparation. Therefore, a staff development and training program sponsored specifically for student affairs staff is necessary for any general orientation and training program provided by the human resources department of an institution.

GENERAL ISSUES

This section describes staff development and training topics that should be included for student affairs staff members who have responsibilities related to the training. Of course, the various chapters of this book point toward other topics that are relevant in staff training. Staff members who are responsible for working directly with student organizations and who give oversight to student events should be familiar with the matters discussed in Chapter Nine in Part Four on Tort Issues. Staff members with duty associated with contracts—those negotiating contracts with students and those with employees—should be briefed on the principles in Chapter Fifteen on Contract Management. Most staff should be introduced to the issues we present in Part Two on the U.S. Constitution and Part Three on the Regulatory Challenges presented by government and outside agencies.

Sexual Harassment

Sexual harassment presents a substantial training responsibility in student affairs. Student affairs staff members develop relationships with students and employees, and close relationships can expose employees to circumstances that risk sexual harassment charges. Sexual harassment is defined in two basic forms: hostile workplace and *quid pro quo* (Kaplin & Lee, 2009, pp. 410, 411). The hostile workplace form of sexual harassment is when unwelcome sexual advances, requests for sexual favors, or other verbal or physical conduct of a sexual nature has the effect of interfering with an individual's work performance or creates an intimidating or hostile working environment. The quid pro quo form of sexual harassment is when the individual's submission to or rejection of unwelcomed sexual advances is used as a basis for employment decisions affecting the individual.

Training employees on sexual harassment is an essential component in any defense of a charge against the institution for indifference to the matter, and it should have the effect of reducing the likelihood of sexually harassing behavior by employees. Employees should learn about the forms of sexual harassment and the behaviors that could lead to charges of harassment. A training program should include aspects that lead to preventing sexual harassment in the workplace and also ensure that employees understand their rights as potential victims of sexual harassment. Telling employees what they should do if they feel they have been subjected to sexual harassment is an essential aspect of a training program. The supervisory relationship must be protected from harassing behaviors, because a key element in any harassment charge is when there is a differential in power or authority.

Because of the unique nature of student affairs work and the quality of relationships that professionals develop with students, a training program on sexual harassment should include a component on staff member/student relationships. The close, helping relationship that a student affairs staff member can have with a student should not be permitted to develop into one that is perceived as harassing. In this respect, student affairs staff must be trained to recognize their obligations to have only appropriate relationships with students. As, presumably, the more mature party in any relationship with a student, the student affairs staff member must act appropriately at all times.

Another important element of a staff training program is associated with addressing consensual relationships in the workplace or with students. It is best if the institution has a clear and unambiguous policy associated with consensual relationships and for that policy to be described in some detail. Even if there is no formal institutional policy, the risks associated with such relationships can be described in a training session.

A training program on sexual harassment and consensual relationships can be part of the orientation of new staff. That is good practice, because it can be systematic. However, the institution should concern itself for the education and training of continuing staff members. Material covered should include steps to avoid claims of a hostile workplace, the significant risks and ethical problems associated with *quid pro quo* circumstances, and the problems that can arise in consensual relationships with students or other staff members. Best practice is to do what is possible to train every employee. Whether the institution makes in-person training or electronic, online training available to its employees, a commitment to educating employees on this subject is essential.

OSHA and Employee Safety

The Occupational Safety and Health Administration (OSHA) establishes standards for the training of employees regarding workplace safety and health (http://counsel.cua.edu/fedlaw/Osha.cfm). In general, the human resources department assumes responsibility for training associated with workplace safety and health. Obviously, employees who work in offices have some risk associated with their exposure to hazardous materials, that is, the chemicals associated with the machines and technology in offices. They should be trained on how to avoid risk. Custodial personnel who work with chemicals and cleaning agents must adhere to standards for safe interaction with those materials. Fire protection and access to first aid equipment are part of OSHA standards. Additionally, employees must know to use respiratory protection when mold and mildew are in buildings.

The student affairs administration may supplement training provided by human resources by addressing issues specific to student affairs work. Staff members who work in campus recreation may need training

associated with exercise equipment, swimming pools, and materials associated with outdoor recreation. Employees who work in student health
might need training associated with medical supplies and sharp equipment and its disposal. Student affairs staff employed in campus activities may benefit from training on the equipment and materials associated
with fairs and carnivals that vendors may bring to campus for sponsored
activities.

Staff members should also be trained to be alert and to report potentially hazardous conditions on campus property, for example, slippery
surfaces, loose pavement, broken handrails, and so forth. Training staff is
an essential step in making a campus safer and managing the risks associated with property ownership and the workplace.

Discriminatory Practices

Student affairs supervisors should train their staff in practices and statements that might be considered discriminatory. All staff members should
be trained to be sensitive to diversity and individual differences. Humor
that others might consider discriminatory and offensive must be discouraged and confronted. The broad range of human characteristics that
should be shielded from discrimination is typically mentioned in institutional policy. Staff members should necessarily be trained on those
policies; however, student affairs professionals and student staff need to
be sensitized in as broad a range of possibilities as possible. No person
should ever feel discriminated against by a person employed in student
affairs, even if there are no legal consequences, ethical risks, or problems
associated with the image of a student affairs unit.

Clarifying Expectations

Staff members working within student affairs should be fully trained on
the scope and limits of their authority and responsibilities. Their duties
should be clearly articulated in position descriptions. All staff should
know when they are authorized to act independently and when they
should seek the support of their supervisor. This is often a matter of judgment, but a good training program can help staff members discern the
extent of their authority to independently make decisions.

All staff should receive training on the nature and quality of relationships with students whom they serve. For example, all employees should
understand what is expected of them regarding social interactions with
students. Training should outline the risks associated with socializing

with students. Additionally, all student affairs staff should understand their responsibilities related to protecting confidential information. It can be difficult to recover from an incident when sensitive, confidential information is inappropriately shared. Good training and clear expectations can help student affairs supervisors avoid such issues.

Supervising Student Employees

It is common for student affairs divisions to employ large numbers of students. Students who are given authority over their peers must be trained to understand the risks associated with their access to information about other students and their responsibility to manage that information with maturity and professionalism. Student employees cannot be treated the same as professional or full-time staff. They should be protected from access to information that they have no need to know, and they should be thoroughly trained on the scope of their responsibilities and their limits. They should be helped to understand the importance of their work, that serving students is noble and honorable, and that the information about their peers must be protected from release or distribution.

Minors on Campus

Student affairs administrators need to be sensitive to the presence of minors on campus. They come to campus for school tours, for summer camps, for visits with their older siblings, and for other reasons. Minors are a protected class, in the eyes of the law, and society exacts a higher burden for their care and safety. It is essential that student affairs staff members be aware when minors are on campus, in residence halls and athletic facilities and student union buildings, and they must take precautions to ensure that the young people are safe and supervised well and that they are treated with care and caution. All staff should be trained on these matters and should be prepared to respond appropriately on behalf of minors and their employing institutions.

Record-Keeping, Documentation of Expectations

Staff orientation and training should not be the only place in which expectations and scope of authority are clarified for student affairs employees. Material that is relevant and important should be in writing and given out to all employees. Job descriptions are useful tools for establishing responsibility and expectations, as are employee manuals and handbooks. Student affairs supervisors should be sensitive to which training matters should be in writing and which subjects can be covered through discussion and conversation.

PROFESSIONAL ASSOCIATIONS

Not all professional staff development and training takes place on campus. Many professional development opportunities are presented by student affairs professional associations. Quite a few of these associations have sophisticated professional development offerings. Large generalist associations, like the National Association of Student Personnel Administrators (NASPA) and the American College Personnel Association (ACPA), serve a wide range of professional development interests of student affairs administrators. Some associations serve the special needs of student affairs and other staff working at specific types of institutions, such as The Association of Public Land-Grant Universities (APLU), the Commission on Independent Colleges and Universities (CICU), the Association of Catholic Colleges and Universities (ACCU), the related Association for Student Affairs at Catholic Colleges and Universities (ASACCU), and The Jesuit Association of Student Personnel Administrators (JASPA). Additionally, a number of professional associations serve the interests of those student affairs administrators working in particular functional areas, such as the Association of College and University Housing Officers–International (ACUHO-I), the National Association of Campus Activities (NACA), and the National Orientation Directors Association (NODA).

Student affairs staff members should recognize the value of these associations in the professional development of employees. Staff should try to attend professional conferences, either national or regional, because it is a good way to stay current in the field and understand what best practices are. Involvement in professional associations also gives student affairs staff the opportunity to establish a network of colleagues, who can be excellent resources in developing programs or in giving advice on managing difficult situations.

Most professional associations produce literature about issues that are current in the field and research that informs practice. A good resource for self-assessment is the ACPA/NASPA Professional Competency Areas for Student Affairs Practitioners, a set of ten areas of competency for student affairs work and the behaviors that indicate competence at one of three particular levels. Even if an employee cannot attend a national conference, staying abreast of the field by reading journal articles relevant to

the work is a good way to stay professionally sharp. An even more pow-
erful way to engage the profession is to write for professional journals,
either by describing innovative programs or discussing research findings
that would be useful to other professionals. Contributing to the profession by generating scholarship is sound practice that has the additional
effect of modeling behavior that is expected of teaching faculty. Making
such a connection to faculty colleagues is beneficial to the student affairs
professional.

Limited institutional resources may make membership in a wide variety of professional associations difficult. That leaves the individual staff
member with a choice to self-fund membership or not to join. Many professionals recognize the value of paying membership dues out of pocket.

CONCLUSION

Preparing individual student affairs staff members for working in the field
is a shared responsibility. Institutions have the duty to give staff members the knowledge and skills that they need to be successful. Supervisors
should be alert to training and staff development opportunities, and
they should encourage their employees to take advantage of what they
can. The individual staff member bears responsibility, also. Those who
work in student affairs must recognize their obligation to stay prepared
and updated on issues in the field and those practices that lead to success.

A strong program of professional development that delivers information and enhances skill development in a timely way is an essential
step toward the management of risk. The question of timeliness should
be evaluated carefully. Some information needed for success in student
affairs work should be covered early in the tenure of a staff member.
Other information and skill development can be part of an extended
professional development program that occurs over a longer period of
time. Supervisors must recognize what is essential early and what can be
covered over the course of the academic year.

REFERENCES

Kaplin, W.A., & Lee, B.A. (2009). *A Legal Guide for Student Affairs
     Professionals* (4th ed.) (pp. 410–411). San Francisco, CA: Jossey-Bass.
Office of General Counsel, Catholic University of America. (n.d.). *Occupational
     Safety and Health Act of 1970*. Retrieved at http://counsel.cua.edu/fedlaw/
     Osha.cfm

ADDITIONAL RESOURCE

Pavela, G. (2008, March 14). "Defining the Scope of Workplace 'Hostile Environment' Sexual Harassment and Retaliation." *The Pavela Report*, *13*(9). St. Johns, FL: College Administration Publications.

CHAPTER 18

STUDENT DISCIPLINE SYSTEMS

INTRODUCTION

From the earliest days of the evolution of the student affairs profession, institutional leaders expected those working in student affairs to function as student conduct administrators. Deans of students functioned as helpers and advisors to students, but they were principally disciplinarians. The conduct function acquired more importance in the 1960s in response to student unrest and protests, and courts began to give more attention to the process and outcomes of student conduct proceedings. With guidance from the judicial system, the nature of the student judicial process became more refined.

DUE PROCESS

Procedural due process as it applies to various property matters is described in Chapter Five, and it is also a key element in the management of student conduct. Due process has the effect of helping to control the quality of outcomes in student conduct proceedings. It improves the chances of appropriate outcomes in student conduct matters, and it makes the administrators of conduct systems accountable. When due process is followed carefully, it reduces the risk of an external review of the student conduct system.

The Fifth Amendment to the U.S. Constitution is the source for the due process requirement. The relevant section of the Fifth Amendment indicates that "No person shall be... deprived of life, liberty, or property, without due process of law." Student conduct systems do not address matters of life or liberty, but they very much address issues of property. A college education is considered property, as are a tuition payment, a residence hall room, and various other matters that may enter into play in a student conduct proceeding.

Because public institutions act as government, they are obligated to conform to the Fifth Amendment. The principle elements of due process in the conduct proceedings at public institutions are the requirements (1) to provide notice of conduct charges and the grounds for those charges and (2) to provide a hearing where the student charged can respond and provide explanation. In reality, most public institutions outline student conduct proceedings in much more detail, with more far-reaching rights afforded to students in institutional codes of conduct. Based on the described institutional code of conduct, due process becomes more a matter of contract law than constitutional law. In private higher education, where the Constitution has a more limited effect, contract law is almost entirely the legal basis for due process (Kaplin & Lee, 2009, pp. 470–474). Therefore, process for the management of student conduct that is published in the code of conduct or the student handbook obligates the private institution.

Student conduct matters are addressed in student affairs departments other than those principally responsible for addressing student rule violations. Campus recreation officials might exercise sanctions against students for their misuse of facilities or for misconduct during intramural sports competitions. Residence hall staff may also initiate charges against students for residence hall rule violations. Students may be sanctioned for their misuse of institutional technology. Some of these matters may be routinely referred to the office that manages responses to allegations against students, but some institutions may permit the originating department to manage the case. The essential issue is that student rights are protected and institutional policies for due process are followed, whether a matter is addressed by residence hall staff members, those who work in campus recreation, or any other department.

CODES OF CONDUCT

The code of conduct that is published by the institution normally has four elements. First, it describes the standards or rules that students are expected to follow. It details that failing to conform to published rules can result in disciplinary charges. Next, it describes in detail the procedures for addressing alleged violations of rules; what rights are afforded to students who stand charged with infractions; and what obligations the institution has in the process. Finally, the code describes the sanctions or outcomes that are possible in a student conduct matter (Kaplin & Lee, 2009, pp. 443–446).

Although the elements described are included in most institutional codes of conduct, such codes can vary significantly. Some codes require that a student be informed of evidence brought against her. Some codes permit the assistance of an attorney or allow the student to question witnesses; others do not permit either. These variations in codes of conduct are evidence of the range of cultures that exist at various institutions of higher education.

Challenges to codes of conduct in the public sector of higher education are usually related to their alleged vagueness or their breadth. Challenges to codes in the private sector often raise concerns associated with the basic principles of fairness. Most importantly, student affairs professionals should follow their institutions' established procedures and avoid arbitrary and capricious decisions. When the procedures for conduct matters that are published in the code of conduct are not followed, the institution is exposed to risk—despite good intentions or perceived greater good.

CRITICAL ISSUES IN STUDENT CONDUCT MATTERS

This section will explore a set of specific issues in the management of student conduct systems. Student affairs administrators who are responsible for addressing student conduct may be faced with all of these issues or a select few.

Sanctions and Property Rights

The Fifth Amendment to the Constitution ensures that the people will not risk the loss of their property without due process of law. Some sanctions in conduct systems can involve the property of students, but many sanctions have no relationship at all to property. A warning or admonition to not violate rules in the future does not seem to have a connection to property and, by Constitutional standard, may not require a formal process. Of course, sanctions involving suspension or expulsion from college are clearly involving property. Most institutions provide the same process for addressing student conduct, irrespective of the significance of the violation or the severity of the sanctions, and it seems to be a logical practice. Some advocate, however, for different, more informal, procedures when the sanctions have no relationship to property. The informed student affairs administrator knows which approach to use in specific cases and what published procedures permit.

It is common for sanctions for offenses to be designed to relate to the offense and provide a learning opportunity for the student. Removal from residence halls may result from misconduct in that setting. An alcohol or drug violation may result in a letter to the parents of the student. A student who violates a rule at a campus event may be restricted from attending activities in the future. These creative approaches may be good practice as educational tools, but, again, conforming to established rules of procedure is of utmost importance.

Regulations and the Freedom of Speech

Some institutions have regulated against certain forms of speech. In an effort to foster civility and enhance community, student affairs professionals may support rules that regulate against speech that is inflammatory or demeaning. There is risk associated with that practice, as it could be interpreted as giving an undue burden to the speaker or the speech is protected by the First Amendment.

Special Nature of Victims' Rights

The informed student affairs administrator is familiar with the rights of victims in student conduct proceedings. Their access to outcomes and their ability to participate in the proceeding is fully protected. Student conduct administrators should be sensitive to the rights of victims and ensure that the process protects them.

Medical or Psychiatric Dismissals

Some institutions have designed special procedures when it is believed that a student's behavior is related to a psychological condition or a disability. Those procedures can divert a case from the student conduct process if the student lacks the capacity to respond or if the student did not know how wrong the conduct was at the time of the offense. Those procedures can involve substantial risk, particularly if there is a perception of a violation of due process or of the Americans with Disabilities Act.

The Role of Counsel

Since many students facing conduct charges may also be responding to criminal charges, they are often accompanied by counsel. In the code of conduct, the institution should make clear whether a student charged with a rule violation can be accompanied by an attorney and what role the attorney can play in the process. A code might indicate that the student can have an advisor in the process, leaving unstated whether the advisor can be a lawyer. Absent specification, an attorney probably can be party to the process. The code might permit an attorney to join a student as an observer and have a limited role as an advisor, not a participant in the process. The student affairs administrator should know what the code permits as far as active participation by an attorney and follow that standard.

Double Jeopardy

Some people become confused around the subject of double jeopardy in student conduct proceedings. If a student is arrested and subjected to the criminal process, some believe that a student conduct proceeding puts the student in double jeopardy. Some might even argue that a student conduct proceeding is double jeopardy if the student, for example, has already been disciplined by a coach through his role as a student athlete. Neither is true. The Fifth Amendment to the U.S. Constitution protects people from being tried twice in a criminal court for criminal acts. The simple fact is that a single act by a student may result in multiple consequences, due to multiple relationships the student has, from a relationship with the university, to one with a sports team, to one with family, to one with the larger community. Student affairs administrators should be alert to this distinction.

Media Interest

At times, local media outlets may be interested in the outcomes of student conduct proceedings. Student affairs administrators may be asked to disclose the outcome of conduct proceedings when, for example, the student has also been arrested and charged criminally. The results of a student conduct process are protected by the Family Educational Rights and Privacy Act (FERPA), as discussed in Chapter Six, and should not be disclosed to the media (Kaplin & Lee, 2009, pp. 270–278). If the student wishes to disclose the outcome of a conduct case, she is generally free to do so.

Negotiated Withdrawal

An institution may negotiate a withdrawal from classes with the student who is facing conduct charges, and a suspension from classes is a likely outcome. This is a way of circumventing a conduct proceeding and leaves the case in a pending review status. This may seem like an efficient way to manage misconduct, but a student affairs administrator should take care to avoid pressuring a student to accept an outcome that is not in his or her best interests.

Appeals

The code of conduct should define the nature and framework of any appeal or review of a student conduct process. The code might provide for a single review of conduct proceeding, or it may offer several steps. The code may also have a distinct appeal process for cases involving suspension or expulsion from classes. The most important thing for a student affairs administrator is to carefully follow the process as defined in the code.

Review of Prior Conduct

A student conduct office may have responsibility for reviewing the records of candidates for admission who have experienced previous poor conduct matters. The prior conduct matter may be associated with criminal behavior or an encounter with an educational institution. Not all institutions have a process for managing these cases, but, when such a process exists, it should be followed diligently. Making a decision that a candidate for admission is not suitable for the environment of the institution should follow a reasonable and fair process, and it should be managed by persons with experience in reviewing conduct matters.

ACADEMIC MISCONDUCT

Student violations of standards of academic integrity are far too common in American higher education, and there are many reasons for the condition (Pavela, 2013). Responding to charges of academic misconduct is usually not the purview of student affairs staff. The consequence for violations is, logically, an academic one, so the initial review of allegations commonly starts with the involved faculty member. If the matter is not resolved at that level, the case may be reviewed by an academic administrator or a panel or students or students and administrators. The process is typically rather decentralized, at least at larger institutions, and record-keeping is often not unified. That can leave the institution vulnerable to recidivism or repeat offenses.

Since the management of academic misconduct is usually not the responsibility of student affairs personnel, we will not go into depth in discussion of it. However, student affairs staff are often called into discussions about process and procedures and can be helpful in arranging a reasonable process that satisfies due process and gives the best chance of a fair outcome to these kinds of cases.

STUDENT CONDUCT MANAGEMENT AND CRIMINAL LAW PROCEEDINGS

Purpose Differences

Student affairs administrators can help students, families, and the institutional community understand the distinctions between the management of student conduct and the legal proceedings for handling criminal behavior. There is some risk when a student conduct proceeding mirrors the criminal process in its language and standards. An aspect of that risk is associated with subjecting a student to an adversarial process. The purpose of a student conduct proceeding is, fundamentally, educational. The purpose of the criminal process is the protection of society and the punishment of behavior that jeopardizes society.

Terminology

The language of a student conduct process should be distinct from the language of the criminal law process. In the criminal courts, the accused experiences a trial and may be found guilty. The student conduct process does not normally involve an event that would be called a "trial." It does not typically conclude that a student is "guilty." It would not result in a student being given a "sentence." These distinctions are important, because clarity in the differences between the student conduct process and the criminal process can be embedded in the terminology. Student affairs administrators can support that by using the appropriate terminology and correcting those who do not.

Standards of Evidence

In a criminal trial, a person is found guilty only when the standard of proof of "beyond a reasonable doubt" is met. That is a very high standard, as it should be. In a student conduct proceeding, the standard for holding a student responsible is a "reasonable person" test. In other words, if the conduct process concludes that a student most likely committed the alleged offense, the standard is met; that is a much lower standard than "beyond a reasonable doubt." The rules of evidence in a criminal court do not allow circumstantial evidence or hearsay testimony. Most codes of conduct and conduct proceedings do not prohibit such evidence and are more casual in nature. One can see, because of these distinctions, how the outcome of a case in a criminal court might be very different from the same case being managed at a college conduct proceeding.

Confidentiality

A final source of distinction between criminal proceedings and a student conduct process is related to their relative openness. The process of the criminal legal system is open to the public, beginning with the arrest, which would commonly appear in the local media. The outcome of a trial is generally open to the public, and transcripts of court proceedings can be made public. None of this is true regarding a student conduct process, which is confidential and closed to the public. Student affairs administrators must be sensitive to this distinction and represent it to their constituents.

CONCLUSION

Several functional areas within student affairs may have responsibility for addressing student conduct and managing discipline systems. The student conduct office is naturally the core office for general student conduct matters, but authority may be delegated to residence hall professionals to address conduct issues in housing. Student activities staff may have responsibility for managing allegations of misconduct against student organizations, and staff members in Greek life may have the duty for responding to charges against fraternities and sororities. No matter how far the authority for responding to student conduct charges is spread, all staff members who have the responsibility must manage the discipline systems consistently and exactly as the process is described in the code of conduct in order to manage the associated risks.

The best rule of thumb is to have procedures and standards that are readily understood and clear—and then to follow them carefully. Standards should be designed that are readily available, and they should be reviewed and adjusted as needed on a regular basis. Student affairs staff will be seen as the campus experts on student behavior, and they need to be very well informed about the process and ensure that it is focused on student learning and the protection of the institutional community.

REFERENCES

Kaplin, W.A., & Lee, B.A. (2009). *A Legal Guide for Student Affairs Professionals* (4th ed.) (pp. 270–278, 443–446, 470–474). San Francisco, CA: Jossey-Bass.

Pavela, G. (2013, March 15). *The Pavela Report, 18*(7). St. Johns, FL: College Administration Publications.

ADDITIONAL RESOURCES

Kaplin, W.A., & Lee, B.A. (2007). "The Disciplinary Processs." In W.A. Kaplin & B.A. Lee, *The Law of Higher Education*(4th ed.) (pp. 441–477). San Francisco, CA: Jossey-Bass.

Pavela, G. (2010, October 1). "Judicial Review of 'Arbitrary and Capricious' Disciplinary Decision Making." *The Pavela Report. 15*(29). St. Johns, FL: College Administration Publications.

PART SIX

RESOURCE PROTECTION

The four chapters in this section present the exposure to risk faced by student affairs administrators regarding the resources for which they are responsible. Chapter Nineteen addresses the risks associated with information technology and the ways in which student affairs administrators who have responsibility for information technology can best manage those risks. Chapter Twenty describes the risk management issues that are associated with facilities and property for which student affairs personnel have supervisory duty. Chapter Twenty-One presents the risk issues that involve fiscal resources, including cash and its management. Chapter Twenty-Two reviews the risk issues that result from natural disasters and emergencies and how student affairs staff can best manage those risks.

CHAPTER 19

INFORMATION TECHNOLOGY

DATA PROTECTION

INTRODUCTION

It is not much of an overstatement to say that the area of an institution that provides the most significant opportunities for risks to occur is that of information technology (IT) and data management/protection. One just needs to reflect for a minute on the incredible number of functions that are performed through the use of technology. Here is just a sampling: emails sent and received, some of which have sensitive information attached to them or malware embedded in them; financial transactions for the institution and for individual students; grade reports; records maintained by any number of offices, with some of the most sensitive being those maintained by the counseling center or health center; and the list could go on and on.

This chapter describes the increasingly complex issues related to information technology and the related complexities of what is required to protect an institution's IT infrastructure and the data and information contained within it.

Many of the issues discussed in this chapter were identified as the top ten IT issues in 2013 in a story published on June 3, 2013, in EDUCAUSE Review online (Grajek, 2013). More will be said about EDUCAUSE (www .educause.edu) later. These issues included: "leveraging the wireless and device explosion on campus"; "supporting the trends toward IT consumerization and bring-your-own-device"; and "facilitating a better understanding of information security and finding appropriate balance between infrastructure openness and security" (Grajek, 2013).

The first section of this chapter offers a brief look at the ever-evolving nature of information technology and what has to be taken into account to keep an institution's IT network as up-to-date as possible. In doing so, an institution's chief information officer (CIO) and others also have to make every effort to assure that additional upgrades and enhancements that offer more and better services to the institution do not also create new and additional security vulnerabilities.

The next section will describe the importance of establishing an institution's information security system and provide examples of several institutions that have done a very comprehensive job of doing so. The final section will describe a five-factor framework for evaluating an institution's IT vulnerability and identifying and understanding the risks involved in order to engage in risk management and mitigation. While the processes that are addressed in these two sections are very complex and involve the entire institution, they can be summarized as encompassing three important elements: preparation; detection and analysis; and containment, eradication, and recovery.

After reading the previous paragraph, the student affairs professional may think: "I'm not in my institution's IT department. That's their problem, not mine." However, that would be a naïve view of one's responsibility for taking steps to reduce risk within student affairs in regard to one's IT infrastructure. With that in mind, some of what follows may initially appear to be better suited to IT professionals, rather than student affairs administrators. However, the hope is that this information will (a) help student affairs administrators better understand the nature, complexities, vulnerabilities, and risks associated with a campus' IT infrastructure and (b) therefore enable student affairs administrators to more effectively communicate with their IT colleagues. In doing so, the preparation, detection, analysis, containment, eradication, and recovery mentioned above can be more effectively carried out.

IT'S ELEVEN O'CLOCK: DO YOU KNOW WHERE YOUR DATA ARE AND WHO IS TRYING TO GAIN ACCESS?

Almost daily, there are media reports about data and information that have been compromised by hackers from almost anywhere in the world whose goal is to circumvent an organization's IT security measures in order to gain access to what is intended to be protected information.

Some of these attacks are primarily aimed at creating an annoyance, while others are aimed at obtaining certain information that will be used to commit very serious crimes.

While unrelated to higher education, the following headline and story appeared in *The New York Times* on May 9, 2013: "In Hours, Thieves Took $45 Million in A.T.M. Scheme" (Santora, 2013). The story indicated that those involved were in two dozen countries and that "In New York City alone, the thieves responsible for the A.T.M. withdrawals struck 2,904 machines over 10 hours on Feb. 19, withdrawing $2.4 million." As more and more legitimate ways are created for those with authorization to access information, those means of access create additional opportunities for others to gain unauthorized access.

What follows are a few examples of the different ways that data are available and, hence, vulnerable to unauthorized access. However, consider this: because it takes several months from the time the first draft of a book is written to when it is published, we suspect that some of the examples presented here may seem out-of-date at the time the reader is reading this, and others will likely have occurred that are not included here. This merely emphasizes the fact that increased reliance on and use of technology creates ever-increasing ways for the data associated with it to be compromised.

On many campuses, the days of connecting one's desktop computer to a wire to be on the institution's server are rapidly disappearing or are already gone. More and more campuses tout the fact that most, if not all, of the campus offers wireless access. In fact, according to EDUCAUSE's Core Data Service, in 2012, "47 percent of responding institutions reported that a majority of campus open areas were covered by wireless network access" ("Educause Core Data," n.d.). If that is the case, imagine the level of connectivity inside most campus buildings!

As wired networks provide security measures to ensure accessibility to only those authorized users, so, too, do wireless networks. However, most CIOs would agree that securing wireless networks is more difficult because individuals are using an ever-increasing number of devices to access the network wirelessly. Thus, as each has unique characteristics that enable connection to the network, each also has unique security requirements.

The issue of securing wireless networks goes beyond different brands of laptop computers or differences between PCs and Macs. The landscape is further complicated by the increasing variety and use of tablets and by the growing number and capabilities of smart phones. Just think about what consumers are seeing—virtually everywhere—about the growing number of features and capabilities of smart phones alone and why we should buy one rather than another.

Colleges and their CIOs are responding to this increasingly complex issue by developing Bring-Your-Own-Device (BYOD) policies. For example, the University of Virginia's BYOD policy states: "The purpose of this policy is to clearly define requirements for owners and overseers of University of Virginia network-connected devices to close security gaps" ("Security of network," n.d.).

In fact, the reader may want to explore the University of Virginia's overall Information Policy in greater detail at www.virginia/edu/informationpolicy. It provides an example that is quite comprehensive and addresses such topics as a security risk management program, data protection policies, administrative data access, and the electronic storage of highly sensitive data, among others. Another example of a comprehensive institutional approach is that of Cornell University. See www.it.cornell.edu.

As more and more devices become available and more students own the "latest and greatest" devices, colleges and universities have had to consider developing BYOD policies and keep their IT departments ahead of the curve to assure that data that are accessible through these devices remain secure. While there are any number of things that might cause a student affairs administrator to awaken in the middle of the night, these concerns are certainly among those that cause CIOs to do so!

But this is not just an issue for CIOs. Student affairs administrators are likely to find themselves in conversations about what type of technology should be available on their campuses. For example, some institutions provide laptop computers to all entering students. In those cases, conversations about which make it should be, what type of software should be loaded, and what type of software and/or applications students can add, along with many other considerations, should include input from student affairs professionals. Similarly, when student housing facilities are built or renovated, decisions have to be made about whether the facilities should be wired or wireless and whether telephone and cable lines should be provided. All of these factors impact the quality of student life on campus and should include knowledgeable input from student affairs professionals about the benefits of such amenities as well as the risks they present.

A FIVE-FACTOR FRAMEWORK FOR EVALUATING AN INSTITUTION'S IT VULNERABILITY AND ASSESSING AND ADDRESSING RISKS

This section draws heavily from the resources available at EDUCAUSE (www.educause.edu), which describes itself on its home page as "a nonprofit association whose mission is to advance higher education through the use of information technology" ("Educause," n.d.). The reader needs to spend only a few minutes on the website to realize what an understatement that is. EDUCAUSE is arguably the most comprehensive organization for all things IT related to colleges and universities, both through its own website content and the hundreds upon hundreds of links to others that it contains.

The reader is referred to the Toolkits page of EDUCAUSE's Higher Education Information Security Council (HEISC) section (https://wiki .internet2.edu/confluence/display/itsg2/Toolkits) to see a brief example of available resources ("Educause Internet 2," n.d.). HEISC's Information Security Governance Assessment Tool for Higher Education at www .educause.edu/library/resources/information-security-governance-assessment-tool is another great resource for gaining an understanding of an institution's potential IT vulnerability ("Educause Internet 2," n.d.).

Again, while the information found at these locations is primarily aimed at IT professionals at colleges and universities, it also is very useful to student affairs professionals, who need to understand the risks and vulnerabilities that technology in the areas for which they are responsible presents. Familiarity also greatly enhances student affairs administrators' ability to "talk the talk" of their campus IT colleagues. This can go a long way toward improving the collaboration needed to identify, minimize, and mitigate risks associated with data and technology for which the student affairs administrator is responsible.

The five-factor framework that follows is based on a similar model by HEISC. It can be found in more detail at https://wiki.internet2.edu/ confluence/pages/viewpage.action?pageId=7503935.

1. What Data Are in My Area of the Institution and Where Are They Located?

One cannot determine vulnerability and risk unless one can answer this question. A quick brainstorming session among student affairs colleagues would likely identify numerous types of data that should be protected. Foremost are those that are protected by the Family Educational Rights and Privacy Act (FERPA.) These include disciplinary records, grades, records in the institution's counseling and health centers (with the latter also protected by the Health Insurance Portability and Accountability Act (HIPAA) of 1996; records associated with requests for reasonable accommodations under the Americans with Disabilities Act (ADA); records associated with student concerns that might be created as a result of retention initiatives, such as those created through a product known as MAP Works (www.webebi.com/mapworks); or those that may be created by groups of institutional representatives that are referred to generically as threat assessment or students of concern teams.

The over-arching factor in addressing this component of the five-factor framework is the need to protect personally identifiable student data to which many student affairs professionals have access for perfectly appropriate and legitimate reasons. However, measures need to be in place to assure that only those within the institution who have a legitimate education-related reason can have access to such information. While the days of using Social Security numbers as student ID numbers or in connection with posting grades on a faculty member's door are now ancient history in higher education, that information can be associated with an individual student in a number of ways. Therefore, steps must be taken to assure that does not occur.

Once the types of data have been identified, the whereabouts of the data must be addressed. For example, it is likely that some data that need to be protected are in the form of paper records. One would be wise to consolidate those to as few locations as possible and be certain of the security measures in place to assure access to only those at the institution who have a legitimate education-related reason.

One must also be certain to address this question with reference to data that are stored electronically. Specifically, one would need to know the location of all of the computers in his area of responsibility that contain sensitive data. However, that is just the tip of the iceberg because data that need to be protected can easily be moved from an institution's desktop computers to any number of other devices in a matter of seconds with a few keystrokes.

Consider the following scenarios. An employee wants to take work home in order to meet a deadline. In order to do that, files with personally identifiable data that are protected behind the institution's firewall are moved to the person's laptop, emailed to the person's home email address, or transferred to a thumb drive to be taken home. One can simply use one's imagination to create a series of "what ifs" in connection with the data that were transferred. Among them are the thumb drive is lost and then found by someone who should not have the data; the laptop is left in a car briefly during a quick stop at a convenience store on the way home and is stolen; or the data are transferred to one's home computer, which is hacked.

Personally identifiable and sensitive student information and/or data held by third parties afford a critical vulnerability. This can occur in numerous ways, most commonly by merchants and business that regularly do business with an institution. Student affairs departments, through the institution's business office, may choose to create blanket purchase orders to facilitate purchases throughout the year. Working with third-party providers of student health insurance, perhaps more than any other third-party provider, impacts the work of student affairs administrators. It does not take much to imagine the type of personally identifiable information that is collected in connection with providing the insurance coverage and, hence, the need to ensure that it is protected. If one's institution has this type of relationship, one would be well advised to ask for a copy of the third-party provider's data protection and security policy.

2. How Sensitive Are the Data in My Area of the Institution?

Reference has been made to "sensitive data," but one might argue that some data are more sensitive than others. A starting point would be identifying the data one's institution considers to be sensitive. A corollary to this inquiry is determining whether one's institution has a data privacy and security policy, such as the one in place at the University of Virginia described above. As noted previously, certain laws and government regulations (FERPA, HIPAA, and ADA) specify what data need to be protected and describe the legal consequences of failing to do so. Other sensitive data may need to be protected because of the provisions of a grant or a contract in place with a particular department within the institution.

3. Who Has Access to and Is Responsible for the Security of Data in My Part of the Institution?

A variety of people within a student affairs administrator's area of responsibility will likely have access to data that should be protected. Therefore, the student affairs administrator should take steps to assure that those individuals understand the institutional, governmental, and legal requirements for protecting the data. It is best to know what training is offered to new employees by the institution's IT and/or HR department. If the institution's IT and/or HR department have policies in place that address these issues, the student affairs administrator should take steps to assure that her staff members have read and understand the policies, document that fact, and repeat the process periodically. Other means of providing training regarding data security include attending programs at local, regional and national professional association meetings and, increasingly, by means of webinars that numerous companies and professional associations offer.

The student affairs administrator should also recognize that he is not the only person at the institution who has a responsibility to address the issue of data protection. Therefore, he should not hesitate to seek advice and support from others. Naturally, the institution's IT professionals are valuable resources, as are the institution's general counsel and chief financial officer.

4. Do I Really Need to Keep All of These Data and, If So, for How Long, and How Do I Get Rid of It?

One should first examine the necessity of keeping a particular type of data. The more places that the same data are located, the more chances there are for it to be compromised. So to reduce departmental as well as personal risk, one should give careful thought to what data one keeps in what form.

If the data originate with the student affairs administrator, the administrator should probably keep the data. However, there may be situations when such data should be sent elsewhere in the institution for storage. If the data do not originate with the student affairs administrator, one has to carefully consider whether or not to keep it because of the potential for inappropriate access. In fact, it is probably best to take the position that, for data that does not originate with the student affairs administrator, one should not keep it unless someone else in authority can make a compelling case to do so. Simply put, it is a very straightforward risk-benefit analysis: Does the benefit of keeping the data outweigh the risk of it being accessed inappropriately, especially if the data can be readily accessed from another department or office?

Recognizing that there will be some quantity of data that require oversight and storage, the student affairs administrator must consider how long the data should be kept and what the procedures are for disposing of it in a secure manner. Many institutions have document/data retention policies that define how long records (data)—paper or electronic—are to be maintained. In some cases, the period of time is defined by law or by terms of a contract or grant.

Once it has been determined that data can be disposed of, do so in a secure manner to avoid the possibility of any sensitive and/or personally identifiable information falling into the possession of someone who should not have it. Ideally, an institution's IT department will have policies that also address these issues.

5. What If Sensitive or Personally Identifiable Data Is Obtained by Someone Who Should Not Have It?

Even with all of the precautions and steps that an institution might take to protect data from being accessed inappropriately, it is best to presume that at some point in time a breach is going to occur. Therefore, policies and procedures must be in place that address this eventuality.

Whether the data are stored on paper or electronically, one needs to know how to recognize when the data have been compromised. A breach of either means of stored data may not be obvious. Therefore, a system that periodically examines both means should be in place. The institution's IT staff are most helpful in determining how to identify electronic breaches within the network. However, breaches that result from electronic files being removed from campus are more difficult to discover. Hence, the student affairs administrator must understand her institution's policies and procedures for addressing the misappropriation of data and whom to notify.

CONCLUSION

Based on the content of this chapter, one might feel overwhelmed by the depth and breadth of issues associated with IT security and data protection. Contributing to this is the fact that, as technology evolves, so do its associated risks. However, one should not be deterred from persevering to protect sensitive data, especially personally identifiable student data, from those who do not have legitimate access to it. In doing so, it is wise to realize that those with access to such data need appropriate training to help avoid some of the more common causes of inappropriate data access. Beyond appropriate training, institutions should have adequate policies in place, be certain their employees are aware of them, and strictly enforce them.

REFERENCES

Educause. (n.d.). Retrieved from www.educause.edu/

Educause Core Data Service. (n.d.). Retrieved from www.educause.edu/
    research-and-publications/research/core-data-service

Educause Internet 2 Higher Education Information Security Council Tool Kits.
    (n.d.). Retrieved from https://wiki.internet2.edu/confluence/display/itsg2/
    Toolkits

*Educause Internet 2 Information Security Governance Assessment
    Tool.* (n.d.). Retrieved from www.educause.edu/library/resources/
    information-security-governance-assessment-tool

Grajek, S. (2013). "Top Ten IT issues, 2013: Welcome to the Connected Age." *Educause Review Online*. Retrieved from www.educause.edu/ero/article/top-ten-it-issues-2013-welcome-connected-age

Santora, M. (2013, May 9). "In Hours, Thieves Took $45 Million in A.T.M. Scheme." *The New York Times*. Retrieved from www.nytimes .com/2013/05/10/nyregion/eight-charged-in-45-million-global-cyber-bank-thefts.html?_r=0

Security of Network Devices. (n.d.). Retrieved from www.virginia.edu/informationpolicy/netdevices/

ADDITIONAL RESOURCE

Kaplin, W.A., & Lee, B.A. (2007). "Campus Computer Networks." In W.A. Kaplin & B.A. Lee, *The Law of Higher Education* (4th ed.) (pp. 371–379). San Francisco, CA: Jossey-Bass.

CHAPTER 20

FACILITIES

INTRODUCTION

A college or university campus is a community because of the people who occupy it and the interactions that occur among them. This is the case whether the campus consists largely of residential students or is primarily attended by commuter students. In both cases, however, the individuals and their interactions take place in the campus's facilities, including classroom buildings, labs, libraries, residence halls and apartments, arenas, stadiums, fraternity and sorority houses, and outdoor facilities such as recreation fields and swimming pools.

In addition to the members of the campus community who use the institution's facilities, hundreds if not thousands of others can be expected to access an institution's facilities during the year. These can include invited guests to events such as lectures, concerts, theatrical performances, sporting events, summer sports and/or academic camps, as well as members of the public who simply come onto the campus to do nothing more than buy something to eat or drink in the student union.

Based on what has just been described, one can imagine the risks that are present in connection with the care and protection of institutional facilities and property. Therefore, this chapter will address the issues, concepts, and principles designed to help reduce risk and the likelihood of incurring liability as a result of the use of an institution's facilities and property by individuals.

On most campuses, these are addressed by a wide range of individuals, including student affairs administrators in a variety of areas such as housing, student activities/student union, Greek life, and so forth. They are also addressed by those responsible for the day-to-day management of academic buildings and athletic facilities. Campus safety or security officers are also involved in monitoring the use of an institution's facilities and intervening when a problem develops.

However, generally speaking, the overall responsibility for an institution's facilities and property falls to what is commonly known as the physical plant department. As is the case with most professions, there is a professional association for physical plant administrators that provides a wealth of information and guidance for the care and protection of an institution's facilities and property, the Association of Physical Plant Administrators, whose web address is www.appa.org.

This organization has a framework for facilities management (divided into four core areas). Two of those areas have direct implications for issues of risk that involve student affairs administrators, which form the basis for the two primary sections in this chapter. The organization's remaining two core areas have a less direct relationship to student affairs administrators, but will be addressed briefly since student affairs administrators need to be aware of them, too ("APPA Four Core," n.d.).

The reader will recall from the previous chapter that the information provided may have been seen as being more appropriate for IT professionals than for those in student affairs. However, becoming familiar with the issue of data management enables student affairs administrators to be more effective in addressing those issues and working effectively with their IT colleagues. The same can be said regarding the role that student affairs administrators have in reducing risk and liability in connection with facilities and being able to converse effectively with their physical plant colleagues.

As one reads through this chapter with an eye toward the role proactive planning plays in reducing risks, one might expect to read about the role that physical plant personnel, student affairs administrators, and others play in anticipating and planning for threats to the overall physical environment of the campus, whether natural disasters or threats from individuals. However, this topic, while related to what is presented here, is sufficiently important that it will be addressed separately in Chapter Twenty-Two.

The first section of this chapter addresses general administration and management. The next addresses operations and maintenance. This aspect of the care and protection of facilities and property presents the greatest risk potential for student affairs administrators based on their typical duties and responsibilities. The final section focuses on energy, utilities, and environmental awareness/stewardship, along with planning, design, and construction. Each of these areas presents a range of risks and potential liabilities with which student affairs administrators should be familiar, even though they are not as directly involved.

GENERAL ADMINISTRATION AND MANAGEMENT

As with any other well-run program or department within a college or university, the general administration and management of a physical plant will assure that its staff (and the impact that the department has on other areas of the institution) is meeting the institution's needs, which, of course, include minimizing risks associated with those who use the institution's facilities and property. A key element is being proactive and planning for the unexpected. For student affairs administrators, the key to reducing risks in their areas of responsibility when it comes to facilities and property is to have a clear understanding of the role and responsibilities of the staff of the physical plant department and, more importantly, to know the proper procedures to follow should a potential risk related to the facilities or property come to their attention.

Understanding the role and responsibilities of an institution's physical plant department's staff begins with knowing where the department is in the overall organizational structure. This is critical because that organizational alignment can potentially help or hinder the staff's ability to fulfill their responsibilities.

While the organizational structure of colleges and universities varies widely, it would be rare to find student affairs administrators and physical plant administrators within the same chain of command. On the other hand, it would not be as unusual to find the physical plant and safety and security personnel in a close reporting relationship. Because it's likely that student affairs staff and physical plant staff have different reporting channels, establishing cooperative and collaborative working relationships and effective communications channels is critical for both areas to be able to work together to maintain high-quality facilities and identify and mitigate risks. This is true for staff at all levels in both areas.

For entry-level student affairs administrators such as resident directors, such relationships begin with the physical plant staff in their buildings, such as housekeeping staff, maintenance personnel, and custodians. The relationships extend outside of one's building to staff members who maintain the grounds. Such relationships are very important when a student affairs administrator identifies a risk that needs to be addressed by physical plant staff.

An effective physical plant department begins with having the appropriate level of human and physical resources to effectively fulfill its responsibilities. That said, it's fair to say that no program believes that it has all of the resources it needs. That's not based on being unrealistic or greedy. Instead, it's based on a desire to always do a little more, to strive to be a little better, and to keep up with the constantly changing environment of higher education in order to provide the best experience possible for students.

Fortunately, the Association of Physical Plant Administrators has developed standards for the appropriate level of staffing, as well as the cost per square foot of facilities (Bigger, 2011). While all institutions certainly don't meet those standards, they provide a benchmark. Being familiar with such standards as a student affairs administrator can help strengthen bonds with staff in the physical plant department.

Effective student affairs administrators plan for the unexpected so that, when something occurs, they can respond quickly to minimize the negative impact. Often, costs are involved (sometimes significant costs) to address the problem. Consequently, a student affairs administrator must know whether the financial resources to address the problem are there or elsewhere. Wherever the financial resources are, decisions have to be made based on the risk potential associated with the problem as to how—and how quickly—to address it. In such situations, positive relationships between student affairs and physical plant staff are most important.

Another potential area of risk involves those times when work is being done in one's facility by outside contractors hired for anything from a minor project to a major renovation, or even new construction. These situations can bring a number of individuals to one's campus about whom virtually nothing is known. Presuming that such individuals are on campus under the auspices of the physical plant department, the student affairs administrator should make a point of knowing whether steps have been taken to assure that the individuals employed by the contractor do not pose a threat to the campus community. For example, it would be important to know what the contractor's hiring policies are, especially in relation to conducting background checks to determine whether any of those working for the contractor have a criminal record that would indicate that they might pose a threat to the campus community.

OPERATIONS AND MAINTENANCE

The day-to-day and long-term operation and maintenance of an institution's facilities and property arguably present the greatest potential for risks to occur. The list of potential risks could go on for pages, but some that immediately come to mind include slips and falls due to wet floors or icy sidewalks; locks that fail on doors that allow entry of unauthorized persons; failure of heating systems during the winter, resulting in freezing and bursting water lines that damage facilities and personal property; improper cleaning or ventilation that allows harmful mold to grow; improper cleaning of dining facilities that leads to food-borne illness; and on and on.

To address these and other issues, a well-run physical plant department should have a comprehensive schedule of routine maintenance and housekeeping for both facilities and grounds. A student affairs administrator should make it a point to know what these schedules are so that, if something is unaddressed, he can take steps to be sure that it is.

Separate and apart from any schedule that the physical plant department has for the campus's facilities and grounds, a student affairs administrator should assure that something similar is in place for the facilities and grounds for which she has direct responsibility. Here are but a couple of examples:

1. Procedures to be followed by resident directors and resident assistants, especially when they are "on duty" for their facility and for those who oversee student unions. These would include periodic checking of exterior doors to be sure they're not propped open and that locks are working as they should; detecting the odor of natural gas; addressing improperly stored bicycles or scooters that are found to be blocking stairways or building exits; and so on.

2. Procedures to be followed by those who operate recreational facilities, especially a swimming pool. These would include those steps mentioned above, along with addressing the issues associated with maintaining proper water quality in the pool to avoid illness. The procedure for a pool should include policies regarding hours of operation, not swimming alone, and what is and is not permitted in the pool area. Often institutions prohibit glassware and alcohol, for obvious reasons.

Just as the potential for risks can occur as a result of those employed by contractors, as mentioned earlier, the same potential for risk exists in relation to those employed by one's institution. In an effort to minimize risks associated with individuals who have a criminal record that would indicate that they might pose a threat to the campus community, the student affairs administrator should know what his institution's policies are regarding background checks for potential employees. An added dimension to this is the fact that many institutions outsource a variety of services, including those that involve the care and protection of their facilities and property. In such cases, the student affairs administrator should be cognizant of the outsourced company's hiring policies, including those regarding background checks.

One area that is outsourced on many campuses that merits mention because of the extent to which students are involved and the risks associated with it is an institution's food service program. Such a program (particularly the dining venue(s) for residential students) is almost always closely aligned with the campus's housing program which, on many campuses, is led by student affairs administrators. In addition to the residential dining venue(s), retail dining operations in student unions, arenas, and stadiums also are included.

Whether operated by one's institution or outsourced, student affairs administrators should be familiar with the dining program's policies and procedures and work closely with those involved in the program to minimize risks. Risks that one would likely find associated with an institution's dining program include the following, some of which are more under the control of the student affairs administrator to correct than others: slips and falls due to water or food on the floor; broken glassware; and, perhaps the most serious, improperly prepared or stored food that could result in a food-borne illness.

Those aspects of a dining program generally are the responsibility of the food service program's administrators. However, the student affairs administrators who work closely with those individuals have an opportunity, on virtually a daily basis, to assure that measures are in place to minimize risk and to bring issues to the attention of dining personnel. One particular food service area in which student affairs administrators are often involved is working with students who have dietary restrictions for medical, religious, or cultural reasons.

Of those, medical issues pose the greatest risk of liability because a variety of medical conditions can pose serious harm to a student if restricted food and/or certain ingredients are consumed. This issue can be further complicated for the following reasons: First, like any special condition, the student has to make it known to someone (often a student affairs administrator) and request an accommodation. In addressing the matter, the student affairs administrator can serve as a liaison between the student and dining services to see whether the student's need can be met through offerings within the dining program or whether the student's condition justifies a release from it.

This situation can be compounded further if the student can show that the dietary restriction is related to a disability. In such cases, the Americans with Disabilities Act (ADA) would come into play in addition to the institution's dining policies. For the student affairs administrator, it's important to involve any and all appropriate staff to ensure that the response is appropriate to reduce the chances that the student would experience a negative medical episode.

Even with all of the proactive steps student affairs administrators and others take to reduce risk in connection with the day-to-day operation, use, and maintenance of their campus facilities, accidents can occur, some of which, unfortunately, result in the death of an individual. In such cases, the aftermath of determining what happened, whether it could have been avoided, and who might bear responsibility can extend over a long period of time—often years. Not only is that costly and time-consuming to those involved, but it also impacts the reputation of the institution negatively, which can last long after the resolution of the matter. Obviously, then, it makes sense to do as much as possible to anticipate risks and take all reasonable steps to avoid them.

ENERGY, UTILITIES, ENVIRONMENTAL AWARENESS/STEWARDSHIP, AND PLANNING, DESIGN, AND CONSTRUCTION

The potential risks associated with these aspects of an institution's facilities and property are not as likely to impact student affairs administrators as those in the previous sections. Nevertheless, it's important to be familiar with them, because the student affairs administrator has an opportunity to strengthen her relationship with her physical plant colleagues in this way.

Here are just a few things about which the student affairs administrator should be aware in regard to energy, utilities, and environmental awareness/stewardship. Arguably the latter, commonly referred to as "sustainability," has generated the most attention in recent years among not only physical plant administrators but also students and student affairs administrators. For example, more and more campuses provide recycling opportunities, but depending on what those are, where they're located, and how they're managed, certain risks can be present that need to be addressed.

Campuses also use a variety of sources of energy to heat and cool their facilities. While those are outside the purview of the student affairs administrator, they should be generally known and understood in order to work with students to take precautionary steps to minimize risk.

Risks are also associated with the planning, design, and construction of campus facilities, for which student affairs administrators must work closely with physical plant staff to reduce risk. One potential long-term risk associated with building a new facility, such as a new residence hall, which would likely involve student affairs administrators, involves the ongoing cost of operating the facility in addition to having funds available for the repair and renovation of it. Some institutions require that any new building have a maintenance endowment created for it beyond the cost of construction. That amount might be in the range of 10 or 15 percent of the cost of construction.

The idea is to allow the endowment to grow (as any other endowment the institution has does) during the early years of the building's operation when repairs and maintenance are minimal in order to use the earnings from the endowment to address those issues later on. This may not seem like a concern for a student affairs administrator. But let us stay with the residence hall example to see how it could be. Without such an endowment, those repair costs might have to come from the administrator's housing budget. If funds weren't available, the condition of the facility could decline, increasing the likelihood of risks occurring. If funds could be found, they might have to be shifted from other critical areas, possibly creating risks there.

Another more immediate source of risk associated with constructing a facility on campus has to do with the active construction site itself. It's not too hard to imagine the types of risks to which individuals would be exposed were they to gain access to it inappropriately. Again, while this issue is not likely to fall within a student affairs administrator's direct area of responsibility, he has an opportunity to work proactively with students and collaboratively with his physical plant colleagues to minimize such risks.

CONCLUSION

Because the facilities and property of campuses tend to be easily accessible to members of the institution as well as members of the general public, there is the potential for a wide variety of risks. Such risks can result in minor consequences to others that are potentially very serious, even to the point of threatening the well-being of the institution. Also, while some of those risks fall within the scope of responsibility of the student affairs administrator, others fall under the purview of those directly responsible for the operation and maintenance of the institution's physical plant, including its buildings and grounds. Wherever the responsibility falls, student affairs administrators have a very important role to play when it comes to identifying and mitigating risks associated with their institutions' facilities and property.

REFERENCES

APPA Four Core Areas. (n.d.). Retrieved from www.appa.org/FourCore/index.cfm

Bigger, A. (2011, July 8). "APPA's New Operational Guidelines for Educational Facilities." *Facilities Manager,* (n.d.). Retrieved from www.appa.org/files/FMArticles/TrilogyIntroduction2.pdf

ADDITIONAL RESOURCE

Price, J. (Ed). (2003, Spring). "Planning and Achieving Successful Student Affairs Facilities Projects." *New Directions for Student Services,* (101). San Francisco, CA: Jossey-Bass.

CHAPTER 21

MONEY MANAGEMENT PRACTICES

INTRODUCTION

When asking why someone decided on student affairs as a profession, often one hears about the person's desire to have a positive impact on the lives of young adults. Contributing to their education and development through out-of-class programs and activities is often mentioned. Of course, student affairs administrators must have the necessary human and financial resources to accomplish those goals. Just as student affairs programs are diverse, so are the ways in which financial resources are generated, managed, and disbursed.

This chapter describes the challenges and risks associated with the fiduciary care of fiscal resources, including attention to cash transactions managed by student affairs professionals through the various budgets they oversee. Numerous departments within an institution receive funds and have the same issues to address. Two prominent examples of such departments are athletics and fund-raising/advancement. However, those areas will not be addressed in this chapter, although much of the information discussed here would be applicable.

The improper handling of an institution's funds not only exposes the student affairs professional to personal liability, but also to the possibility of prosecution for fraud, embezzlement, or other crimes. Word to the wise: to avoid problems, the student affairs professional should learn her institution's financial policies and access the staff in the business and purchasing offices for good advice on all things related to handling the institution's funds.

The first section of this chapter provides an overview of the types of fiscal resources for which a student affairs professional is likely to be responsible. The second section provides examples of how different types of funds could be handled. The third section addresses what the student affairs administrator can do to minimize risk and liability.

TYPES OF FISCAL RESOURCES FOR WHICH ONE MAY BE RESPONSIBLE

Departmental Budgets

Every student affairs administrator has institutional funds allocated to her in the form of a departmental budget. Because these budgets are the most common means of having fiduciary responsibility and because institutions handle these budgets in different ways, this topic is covered first. While how one's budget is developed will not be addressed here, it is important to understand how that process works in order to provide appropriate input. Briefly, one should know whether the budget is developed annually or biannually and whether it is zero-based (meaning every expense line begins at zero so that justification is needed for the new, proposed amount) or starts with the allocation from the previous fiscal year.

Departmental budgets provide financial support for the vast majority of a student affairs administrator's expenditures and thus offer the greatest degree of potential risk and liability. Such budgets provide support for supplies and equipment, travel and entertainment, telecommunication services, professional services, and many other expenditures.

Student Organization Budgets

In some form, virtually all student organizations have funds for which the organizations' members are responsible. The funds may come from a variety of sources. For example, the institution may allocate an amount to each organization or to an overall student government association, which then makes allocations to officially recognized student organizations. Alternatively, funds may come from payment of a student activity fee assessed on all students, or funding can be from a combination of these sources.

Some student government organizations are quasi-independent of the institution, while others are not. These distinctions can determine the level of supervision and nature of the fiduciary responsibility the student affairs administrator has over the organization's budget, so it is advisable to have a clear understanding of the organization's relationship with the institution. Whatever the organization's alignment with the institution, the funds are generally seen as the institution's funds once collected and, hence, subject to the same fiduciary polices as other institutional funds. Also, virtually all student governments and organizations have an employee of the institution (often a student affairs administrator) who serves as the organization's advisor. In such a role the person accepts responsibility for the proper fiduciary management of any funds.

Funds Received from Third Parties (Including Vendors) as a Result of Contractual Relationships

Colleges and universities enter into contractual arrangements with third-party providers who offer a wide range of services to the institution. Food service programs, bookstore operations, and maintenance of facilities and grounds are among the most common of these arrangements. Other common types of contracts involve vendors who provide vending machine services throughout the institution and those who provide concession services at an institution's arena and stadium venues. Often, the contract spells out that a certain percentage of money collected will be provided to the institution as part of the contract.

In the case of a food service program, for example, the provider may commit to a certain amount each year to support the ongoing maintenance and upkeep of the institution's dining facilities. Such arrangements require the institution's representative—often a student affairs administrator—to handle such funds appropriately. Another common example is a company that provides vending machine service. Modern machines accept cash, credit cards, and funds that reside in a student's institutional account accessible through an ID card. In exchange for the service, the institution generally receives a commission based on sales.

In the case of contracts with third parties, it is not uncommon for a third-party representative to want to express appreciation for the opportunity to conduct business at the institution. However, how such appreciation is expressed could create the appearance of being inappropriate or, in some cases, even in violation of the institution's policies. For example, an invitation to lunch (for which the representative pays) or a modest gift during the holiday season may be acceptable. However, a weekend trip or tickets to major sporting events, such as the NCAA Final Four basketball tournament or the Super Bowl, may be highly unacceptable or, in the case of some public institutions, a violation of the law.

Therefore, the student affairs administrator should have a very clear understanding of what her institution's policies (and state laws, in the case of public institutions) are regarding such gifts. The staff members in the institution's purchasing and/or business offices would be appropriate to consult on this topic. However, when in doubt, one should err on the conservative side and decline any type of gift that may give the appearance of being inappropriate.

Funds Collected Through Ticket Sales for a Wide Variety of Events

Institutions collect (and many student affairs administrators are responsible for) funds from the sale of tickets for concerts, speakers, musical or theatrical performances, and, in some cases, athletic events. Such funds can be paid by credit card, in person, online, and in cash. In many cases, additional funds are also collected at such events in the form of sales at concession stands. Hence, it doesn't take much of an imagination to see how important it is to properly handle such funds in order to reduce risk and potential liability for oneself and the institution.

Petty Cash Funds

Within each of the categories above, not only is one likely to receive cash, but one often is also responsible for maintaining a "petty cash fund." This is cash (the upper limit of which is often set by the institution's business office) for which the student affairs administrator is responsible and has the authority to access within guidelines set by the institution. Most institutions also require that records be kept of funds going into and out of one's petty cash fund, and it may be officially audited annually. Consequently, keeping accurate records, including receipts for all transactions, is critical.

Naturally, were an unauthorized person to gain access to the cash and spend it inappropriately, it could be very difficult to determine who did so and, more importantly, the student affairs administrator likely would be held accountable. Worse, depending on the nature of the inappropriate use of the cash, the student affairs administrator might be believed to be guilty of the abuse. Unless absolutely necessary, the student affairs administrator may want to avoid using petty cash funds. However, if such a fund is needed, the administrator should work closely with the institution's business office to have appropriate safeguards and procedures in place.

Funds Received from Fundraising Events

Often student organizations engage in fundraising activities. On many campuses, Greek organizations commit themselves to support local or national charitable organizations. To raise funds, they conduct a variety of events that result in other members of the campus community, especially other students, making cash contributions. Other student organizations may seek to raise funds to support local charitable organizations, such as a local food bank or Habitat for Humanity or Big Brothers Big Sisters, among many others. One can see how critical it is for the funds to be appropriately handled and accounted for so that they are received by the designated organization. To help assure that and to provide appropriate backup information for auditing purposes, it is recommended that the funds be received into (and disbursed to the designated organization from) the student organization's institutional account.

HOW THE TYPES OF FUNDS ARE HANDLED

Departmental Budgets

These budgets cover many of a student affairs administrator's expenditures. Therefore, there are many opportunities for risk if they are not managed properly. Among the things to be considered are the following. First, are the budgets zeroed out at the end of the fiscal year or do they carry over from one year to the next? Being zeroed out means that any funds not spent by the end of the fiscal year revert back to the general budget of the institution. At some institutions, an administrator has responsibility for both types of budgets, so it is important to know which category one's budgetary expenditures fall into.

Second, one's institution probably has a date near the end of the fiscal year by which all purchases need to be made so that the budget can be closed out properly in preparation for the annual audit. Beyond that, if what is purchased will be used in the upcoming fiscal year, the business office may not allow the expenditure to come out of the current year's budget, but instead allocate it to the upcoming year's budget.

Third, institutions usually have well-defined policies for what constitutes a legitimate or appropriate expenditure from a departmental budget. At the very least, expenses should be charged against the appropriate budget line or "object code." For example, if one were purchasing office supplies, the expense shouldn't be charged against travel and entertainment. With this in mind, one should understand the institution's policies for transferring funds from one line to another. Closely related to this is knowing whether or not funds budgeted for personnel can be transferred to non-personnel lines. In many institutions that is not permitted.

Another important departmental budget distinction, especially at state-supported institutions, is between what are commonly referred to as education and general (E&G) budgets and auxiliary budgets. E&G budgets are usually funded through state appropriations and from payments of tuition and fees. Auxiliary budgets are funds associated with "auxiliary" operations of the institution, such as housing and dining services and athletic programs. These are critical distinctions with which a student affairs administrator must be familiar.

Student Organization Budgets

These budgets are often handled in the same way that one's departmental budgets are, since, once funds are received, they are seen as institutional funds. Thus, some of the same considerations mentioned above apply to these budgets. However, the student affairs administrator who works with or advises student governments should determine whether these are managed differently. This would be especially appropriate if the institution's student government is a quasi-independent organization.

In the case of some student organizations, especially those that have a quasi-official relationship with one's institution, funds may be kept in a bank off campus. This arrangement adds an additional layer of complexity to the student affairs administrator's responsibility for overseeing the funds. In some cases, such funds may not be seen as institutional funds and, hence, not subject to the same policies and procedures as funds retained by the institution.

There may be some advantages to having funds deposited in an off-campus bank, such as accessibility at times when the institution is closed or in regard to the limit on the amount of funds that can be withdrawn at any given time. However, the lesser degree of oversight of such funds compared to those in an institutional account creates other types of risks and potential liability that may outweigh the advantages. Therefore, the student affairs administrator should determine whether such off-campus accounts are permitted at her institution. If they are, she should work closely with her institution's business office to assure that proper safeguards for oversight of the funds are in place. One such safeguard would be as easy as having the administrator's name on the account so she could have access to the account's records at any time.

Funds Received from Third Parties (Including Vendors) as a Result of Contractual Relationships

How these funds are managed by one's institution is generally determined by the terms of the contractual arrangement between the two parties. More often than not, the funds are designated for use within the area of the institution with which the contract is associated. For example, funds received from a company that provides dining services would normally be designated for use within the dining services program. In other situations, however, an institution may be given greater flexibility in how the funds can be used. Therefore, it is incumbent upon the student affairs administrator to know the terms of the contractual agreement for the use of such funds.

Funds Collected Through Ticket Sales for a Wide Variety of Events

How funds collected through ticket sales are managed is usually determined by the nature of the event. Here are some examples. A student government sells tickets to a homecoming concert in order to offset the cost of the performance. Proceeds from the ticket sales would normally go back into the student government's budget, at least until the budget reached a break-even point in relation to the cost of the concert. If additional proceeds were available, the student government's or the institution's policies would guide how they could be used.

Similarly, proceeds from the sale of tickets to a theatrical or musical performance given by those departments would likely be allocated to those departments to help support their activities. The same would typically apply to the proceeds from the sale of athletic tickets being allocated to the athletic department budget in order to offset some of its expenditures. However, various institutions address these issues differently, so the student affairs administrator should be sure to understand the policies pertaining to these types of fiduciary transactions.

Funds Received from Donations from Fundraising Events

The management of these types of funds is probably the clearest to understand. Virtually without exception, when an event occurs that is promoted as raising funds for a charitable organization, all of the funds raised are expected to be received by that charitable organization. Some charitable organizations make it clear that a portion of contributions received directly from the public are allocated to administrative expenses. However, in virtually every case where student organizations have an event to raise money for a charitable organization, it is understood that those involved are volunteering their time so that 100 percent of the money collected can go to the charity.

STEPS THAT SHOULD BE TAKEN TO REDUCE THE RISK AND LIABILITY OF HANDLING THE TYPES OF FUNDS DESCRIBED

Departmental Budgets

Quite simply, very soon after the student affairs administrator assumes a new position at an institution, she should meet in person with representatives of the business office and the purchasing office to review the budgets for which she has responsibility and to gain a clear understanding of the policies and procedures governing their administration and management. After this, the administrator should not hesitate to consult those individuals and/or the appropriate written policies about budget transactions. There will certainly be times when the student affairs administrator will be involved in authorizing expenditures, so he should be sure to adhere to his institution's guidelines.

For example, risk and personal liability are likely to come into play if such policies are violated. Here are some examples of how that could happen. A major purchase is initiated that is beyond the amount for which the administrator is authorized. A similar major purchase is initiated without the administrator realizing that her institution has a mandatory bidding process that first requires at least three competitive bids. The administrator submits a request for reimbursement of expenses related to travel to a professional association conference, but doesn't realize that prior supervisory approval was required before spending the funds. In connection with the same reimbursement request, the administrator submits expenses that are not authorized as reimbursable by her institution.

Student affairs administrators have been known to submit false information regarding institutional budget expenditures in an effort to receive funds to which they are not entitled. It should not need to be said that to do so is a violation of institutional policies and a crime—among the surest ways to be removed from a position and to have serious difficulty finding a new one.

Student Organization Budgets

Even though the responsibility for managing these budgets is usually delegated to students, the funds are usually regarded as institutional funds. Therefore, the administrator who is responsible for advising these organizations is ultimately responsible for the proper management of the funds. The student affairs administrator should make every effort to make sure that the students who have access to these funds also understand the institution's fiscal policies and procedures. Should they fail to manage them in accordance with those policies, the student affairs administrator charged with overseeing them would likely be held responsible.

Another way in which a student affairs administrator could be exposed to risk associated with an expenditure from a student organization's budget involves the administrator not agreeing with the expenditure. A good example would involve the administrator denying the expenditure for a speaker a student organization wished to bring to campus, because she disagreed with the speaker's topic or point of view. This would likely raise a variety of concerns around the issue of freedom of speech (Kaplin & Lee, 2007). The best course of action in situations like this is for the administrator to express her point of view to the students. However, if the students still wish to invite the speaker to campus and use their organization's funds to do so, the student affairs administrator would be well advised to approve the expenditure if it is in compliance with the institution's fiscal policies.

Funds Received from Third Parties (Including Vendors) as a Result of Contractual Relationships

In regard to these types of funds, it is imperative to manage them strictly in keeping with the terms of the contractual relationship. That seems simple and straightforward enough, but there are times when, in an effort to retain the business, the third party may suggest that the administrator could use the funds in some other way. Worse, the third party may offer a cash payment. Needless to say, such offers should be emphatically rejected, and the administrator should have a clear paper trail showing that both the amount and allocation of the funds received were in keeping with the terms of the contractual agreement.

Funds Collected Through Ticket Sales for a Wide Variety of Events

There is a significant opportunity for these types of funds to be in the form of cash. Risk and liability are greatest in the handling of cash, because of the potential lack of a paper trail. To reduce risk and potential liability when managing cash, the student affairs administrator should take extra precautions. There should always be at least two reputable employees involved at all times when cash is being handled, from the start of an event to confirm the starting amount in a cash box or cash register to the ending amount, when it might be secured in an institutionally approved safe (if kept overnight) or deposited with the institution's business office.

Funds Received from Donations from Fundraising Events

When student organizations engage in fundraising events for various charitable organizations, those who make contributions often do so with cash. As with cash transactions involving ticket sales, similar steps should be employed to reduce the risk and personal liability.

CONCLUSION

Student affairs administrators are very likely to have fiduciary responsibility for a wide variety of an institution's fiscal resources. Because of this, they need to interact with other employees within their institutions, students who work with student organization budgets, and third parties outside of their institutions. Each type of interaction presents its own unique exposure to risk if the management of the funds is not done so in accordance with the institution's fiscal policies, procedures, and guidelines.

To say that one was not aware of those policies, procedures, and guidelines is no defense if one's fiduciary management of resources is found to be in violation of them. Therefore, every student affairs administrator should take all appropriate steps to assure that she is fully informed of her institution's fiscal policies and the limit and scope of her authority to administer them. Beyond that, she should make every effort to follow them to the point that anyone who raised a question would immediately understand that what she did was strictly in keeping with her authority and her institution's fiscal policies, procedures, and guidelines.

REFERENCES

Kaplin, W.A., & Lee, B.A. (2007). "Students' Freedom of Expression." In W.A. Kaplin & B.A. Lee, *The Law of Higher Education*(4th ed.) (pp. 478–510). San Francisco, CA: Jossey-Bass.

ADDITIONAL RESOURCES

○ The institution's fiscal policies and procedures are usually available through the institution's business office.

○ The institution's purchasing polices are usually available through the institution's business and/or purchasing offices.

○ Professional organizations that provide information on money management include:

- The National Association of College and University Business Officers (NACUBO), whose web address is www.nacubo.org/,especially its section on risk management

- The National Association of College Auxiliary Services ((NACAS), whose web address iswww.nacas.org/

- The National Association for Campus Activities (NACA), whose web address is www.naca.org

CHAPTER 22

PHYSICAL ENVIRONMENT

DISASTERS AND CRISES

INTRODUCTION

Chapter Twenty addressed the range of risks and steps to be taken to reduce those risks associated with an institution's facilities. Reference was made to the fact that one might expect to have seen a discussion about the role that physical plant personnel, student affairs administrators, and others play in anticipating and planning for threats to the overall physical environment of the campus, whether they are natural disasters or threats from individuals. This topic is sufficiently complex that this chapter will be devoted to it.

Whereas Chapter Twenty addressed the risks associated with the day-to-day, ongoing operation of an institution's facilities, this chapter focuses on the overall physical environment of one's institution and the risks associated with (usually) a one-time event—either natural or caused by an individual or individuals—that would be of such seriousness that it could have significant negative repercussions for the institution, its students, faculty and staff, and even the surrounding community.

In the interest of clarity, these events will be considered *crises,* with the definition of a crisis as defined by Harper, Patterson, and Zdziarski as ". . . an event, often sudden or unexpected, that disrupts the normal operations of the institution or its educational mission and threatens the well-being of personnel, property, financial resources, and/or reputation of the institution" (Harper, Patterson, & Zdziarski, 2006, p. 5).

While the types of events encompass a broad range of threats (risks), this chapter is divided into two sections that provide a framework for addressing the threats (risks) with an eye toward minimizing the negative impact on all involved, including student affairs administrators. The first section addresses the prior planning associated with responding to a catastrophic event, emergency, or disaster and the deployment of resources once an emergency, crisis, or event presents itself. The second section focuses on the steps an institution should take following the event (the recovery phase), along with the post-event review aimed at returning the campus to its prior "normal" state and informing the campus community of what changes might be made if another similar event were to occur.

The greater the extent to which the appropriate individuals at an institution pay attention to these key elements regarding threats (risks) to an institution's physical environment, the greater the likelihood that liability associated with an event will be reduced. It goes without saying that student affairs administrators at all levels should be intimately involved in all stages, not only to reduce risk to their students and colleagues, but also to reduce the likelihood that they would be found liable for injuries associated with a disaster.

PLANNING PRIOR TO A CRISIS AND RESPONDING ONCE IT OCCURS

*Types of Events, Emergencies, and/or Disasters
an Institution Should Be Prepared to Address*

It would be virtually impossible to list every single type of event, emergency, or disaster with which an institution could be confronted. Geography plays a role in the likelihood that some natural events will occur. For example, campuses are more likely to be struck by a tornado in the central portion of the United States (often referred to as "tornado alley" when speaking of such phenomena) than are campuses in other parts of the country. Likewise, while flooding can occur in many parts of the country, campuses in coastal areas (especially along the Gulf and Atlantic coasts) are more likely to be affected by flooding caused by the storm surge from a hurricane than campuses in other parts of the country.

Without trying to compile an exhaustive list, here are just a few of the types of disasters, events, and emergencies for which campuses should engage in prior planning: natural disasters such as those mentioned above; a chemical spill; a uranium leak from a lab; a toxic gas cloud from a business near the campus; a meth lab explosion in a residence hall; a terroristic threat, such as a bomb in a stadium or arena; an active shooter (as, sadly, too many campuses have experienced); a major fire; and the list could go on and on. As a student affairs administrator, it could be productive to think about the particular types of events or disasters that could occur in your area and then read what follows with an eye to applying the points made.

An Institution's Crisis Management Plan: What to Do Before and During an Event

Although all of the types of events mentioned above are different, one common way of reducing the risks and liability associated with any of them, should they occur, is for one's campus to have a *comprehensive* crisis management plan (CMP) in place that "provides a clear basis from which everyone in the institution can operate in the event of a crisis" (Harper, Patterson, & Zdziarski, 2006, p. 18). Such plans can contain hundreds of pages because they generally include such components as: a flow chart to guide the response to a precipitating event; means of communication with people on and off campus; memoranda of understanding (MOUs) with off-campus organizations that might assist during an event; evacuation and shelter-in-place plans for literally every campus building; floor plans of buildings noting locations where hazardous materials are stored; locations of emergency supplies; evacuation routes and off-campus shelters; and tornado shelter areas, among others.

Pre-Event Resources

Arguably, one of the best resources for helping any campus address these issues is United Educators Insurance (UE), which refers to itself as a reciprocal risk retention group. According to its website:

> UE. . . was created by educational institutions for educational institutions with the sole purpose of providing a high-quality, specialized alternative to commercial insurance. UE understands the unique risk profile of schools, colleges, universities, and other educationally oriented organizations and our worldwide liability policies are specially designed and carefully written to cover the unique exposures of education. ("United Educators: Meet," n.d.)

However, UE doesn't just provide insurance. It goes much further and, to the point of this chapter, its website notes that "we help our members prevent losses from occurring. A core philosophy at UE is that sound risk management practices can reduce the frequency and severity of claims" ("United Educators: Meet," n.d.).

Key Components of a Crisis Management Plan

Just as no two campuses are alike, no two crisis management plans will be alike. However, many of the key elements will be common to all campuses. With that in mind, let us look at the first element of a crisis management plan (CMP), the people who make up the membership of what generically can be called an institution's Crisis Management Team (CMT).

While entry-level and mid-level student affairs administrators may not serve on the CMT, they play a critical role by making sure that the specific information about the facilities and other aspects of their areas of responsibility are known to student affairs administrators who are on the team. In some cases, student affairs divisions may have their own crisis management plans and teams, which become components of, and work in conjunction with, their campus-wide counterparts. In some cases, based on the nature of the crisis, the student affairs CMP and CMT will be all that's needed to address a crisis specific to the student affairs program (Harper, Patterson, & Zdziarski, 2006, p. 26).

Therefore, what follows also applies to all student affairs administrators involved in crisis management plans and teams specific to their student affairs programs.

1. In almost every case, such a group will have broad representation across an institution, which will likely include student affairs administrators from any number of areas, such as housing, student life, counseling, and so forth (Harper, Patterson, & Zdziarski, 2006, p. 12).

Among the many things a student affairs administrator should do fairly soon after accepting a new position is to become familiar with her institution's CMP, especially what her role is in relation to it. Some student affairs administrators will be members of the CMT charged with developing and updating the CMP, while others will be called upon to carry out certain responsibilities when the CMP is put into action. Failure to know what one's duties and responsibilities are could not only make the situation worse, but could present serious liability issues for the student affairs administrator.

2. Another element common to CMPs is the means of communication to be employed during an event. For example, will text messaging be used and, if so, how would those individuals who haven't signed up for that service be notified? Will electronic message boards be used? What will

be the backup plan if there is no electrical power? Will land line or cell phones be used? In either case, has a structure (often referred to as a "calling tree") been established so the student affairs administrator knows who to call next if he is called? If the student affairs administrator isn't familiar with the communication elements of his campus' CMP, precious time could elapse, greatly increasing risk to everyone affected by the event. Some student affairs administrators will be responsible for assuring that their buildings are evacuated, if an evacuation is the appropriate response to the event. Failure to communicate that in a timely manner could risk the lives of those in the building, resulting in potential liability for the student affairs administrator.

3. Closely related to the element of communication is the CMP's reporting structure or chain of command. The most basic aspect of that structure is who on campus determines that a precipitating event is of such a nature that the CMT should be called into action (Harper, Patterson, & Zdziarski, 2006, p. 19). What if the person charged with doing that is out of town? In a perfect world, every member of the CMT would be readily available if an event occurred. However, in reality, that is not likely to be the case. Therefore, to improve response time and reduce risk and subsequent liability, if a student affairs administrator is on the CMT, she should have two backups who would be called in case she was not available. Similarly, if a student affairs administrator would be expected to play a role during a precipitating event, he also should have two backups who would know how to fulfill his duties.

While certain events will certainly require that the full CMT convene, often it is the case that an event occurs resulting in a predetermined subset of the CMT convening to determine whether or not the full CMT needs to be called together. Depending on the nature of the event, various student affairs administrators could be called upon to help address and resolve the situation. Their actions might prevent an event from developing into a much more serious one. Again, especially in such situations, it is critical that the student affairs administrator know her role in order to reduce risk.

4. Another key element associated with reporting structures in any campus CMP is understanding the role that off-campus authorities play when called to aid in response to an event, emergency, or disaster (Harper, Patterson, & Zdziarski, 2006, p. 9). While each community may approach this differently, in the vast majority of cases, once civil authorities (police, firefighters, FBI, Homeland Security, bomb squad, or others) are called to campus and briefed on the situation, they take the lead in

determining the course of action. It would likely increase risk to others and therefore would be ill-advised for a student affairs administrator not to follow the directives of those authorities on the presumption that he knows the campus or his students better than the authorities from off-campus do.

5. Another important element of a campus CMP is knowing what resources are available and needed from both on and off campus, based on the nature of the event (Harper, Patterson, & Zdziarski, 2006, p. 12). One of the most important is having a place established where the CMT members go if called to convene. The location should, ideally, be reserved just for this purpose so that it can be equipped with all of the necessary documents, procedures, protocols, and means of communication needed. But even that's not enough, because the location could be impacted by the precipitating event, so at least one alternate location some distance away should be chosen.

6. Other resources, if properly deployed in an appropriate and timely manner, can significantly reduce risk by bringing the precipitating event to a beneficial conclusion. Depending on the student affairs administrator's duties, these could involve such things as knowing whom to call at her institution's police or security or physical plant department, knowing appropriate evacuation routes from her building or the places designated in the building, if the appropriate response is to shelter in place. Also, the student affairs administrator should have ready access to off-campus resources in the event that notifying one of them is the appropriate response. Such ready access would generally be found in the institution's CMP or a companion document readily available.

7. Another important element of a campus' CMP with which the student affairs administrator should be familiar involves the procedures to be followed before, during, and after a crisis. Without being overly simplistic, prior to an event or crisis, the student affairs administrator should be familiar with what her role would be and what procedures would be implemented *if* a precipitating event were to create a crisis. Once a crisis occurs, she should be equally familiar with what steps she would take (Harper, Patterson, & Zdziarski, 2006, p. 7).

8. One of the most difficult procedures during a crisis is handling communications with various constituencies who are affected by the crisis. One can imagine the calls (cell phone and otherwise) and the text messages from those both on and off campus, especially parents and the media, depending on the nature of the crisis. In addition to such inquiries, others familiar with the event may post information on their Facebook

pages, over which the student affairs administrator and his institution have absolutely no control. Worse, what is communicated may not be an accurate portrayal of the event.

As the saying goes, a lack of information creates a void to be filled. Because of that, the student affairs administrator should know who the CMP says the official spokesperson is. Sometimes, when the civil authorities take command of the event, that responsibility rests with them. In order to avoid making a bad situation worse by communicating incorrect or outdated information, the student affairs administrator should understand his role regarding communication associated with the crisis and act accordingly (Harper, Patterson, & Zdziarski, 2006, pp. 32–34).

9. Depending on the nature of the crisis, the student affairs administrator will also have a critical role to play after the event is over. Those affected by the event, especially students with whom the administrator has a close relationship, may be traumatized and need help processing what happened. This could affect the students' ability to continue their academic work or their ability to sleep. Here, the student affairs administrator should assist those affected only to the level to which he has been properly trained to do so, so as to avoid exacerbating the situation and creating the potential for risk and liability to himself and his institution.

10. The final element of a CMP is making sure that the campus—especially the CMT—routinely engages in what's called tabletop exercises. These are generally led by professionals trained to present them. A hypothetical, but potentially very real, event is presented that requires the CMT to convene and work through it, taking into account all that has been discussed up to this point. In order for such an event to be beneficial to the institution, those leading the exercise typically provide an after-action report critiquing the institution's response and providing suggestions for how their response could be improved. One can see how participating in such an activity on a regular basis could help reduce risk by improving the likelihood that a student affairs administrator and her institution's responses during a crisis were appropriate.

RECOVERY AND POST-EVENT REVIEW

Recovery

A post-event review may occur simultaneously with a campus's recovery from a crisis. Depending on the nature of the event, helping those affected recover from it (especially if they are students) may arguably be the most important factor to address first. To help illustrate that point, the nature of the crisis may have been such that student housing facilities were destroyed, some students may have been killed or seriously injured; alternative housing would need to be arranged; parents and other family members may have arrived on campus trying to find out what happened. As a result, a family resource center would likely need to be established on or off campus, and, in the midst of all of that, the news media would likely be there trying to get the story out as fast as they could. In such a situation, student affairs administrators would likely be intimately involved.

However, in order to reduce the level of risk to himself or others, the student affairs administrator should conduct himself according to his role as defined in (a) his job description and (b) his role as defined in his CMP. The student affairs administrator would likely be working closely with many others from across the campus and with those from off campus who were involved in the response.

While the student affairs administrator is involved in helping others recover from the event, she needs to be conscious of the fact that she also has been affected by it. Often, she's not aware of that, being so focused on the importance of taking care of others. So as soon as possible, she should seek whatever kind of help or support she needs. Not doing so only increases the likelihood that she will incur greater risk to herself and others as the recovery stage progresses. As a result, she might not be able to respond appropriately to related events as they occur, putting herself and/or others at greater risk.

Post-Event Review

Among the factors to be addressed in a post-event review are whether the responses that occurred were appropriate and, to the degree that they were not, what changes must be made to the institution's CMP. This is critical to being able to demonstrate that the student affairs administrator and the institution have taken steps to minimize risk and reduce liability in the future.

Second, the post-event review process should attempt to assess the potential short- and long-range impact that the crisis had on the students, faculty and staff, the institution itself, and the community in which it is located. Tragic events like the shootings at Kent State in 1970 and, more recently, at Virginia Tech remind us of the kind of impact such events can have—immediately and for years afterward.

CONCLUSION

A wide variety of events, both natural and those caused by people, can result in a crisis that can have a profound impact on an institution, its students, employees, and the community in which the institution is located. Regardless of the nature of the crisis, it is a certainty that student affairs administrators will have a role to play prior to it, planning how to address it should it occur, responding during it, and participating in the recovery and post-event review. Knowing what to do based on the institution's crisis management plan and understanding his role in relation to the institution's crisis management team will increase the likelihood that the student affairs administrator will be able to reduce risk to students and others at his institution and to himself.

REFERENCES

Harper, K.S., Paterson, B.G., & Zdziarski, E.L., II. (Eds.). (2006). *Crisis Management: Responding from the Heart*. Washington, DC: NASPA: Student Affairs Administrators in Higher Education.

United Educators: Meet UE. (n.d.). Retrieved from https://www.ue.org/meetue/offers.aspx

ADDITIONAL RESOURCES

Lake, P.F. (2011). "Managing the Institution of Higher Education Environment. Part I: Safety, Risk Management, Wellness and Security." In P.F. Lake, *Foundations of Higher Education Law & Policy* (pp. 91–178). Washington, DC: NASPA: Student Affairs Administrators in Higher Education.

Siegel, D. (1994). *Campuses Respond to Violent Tragedy*. Phoenix, AZ: Oryx Press.

United Educators: https://www.ue.org/home.aspx

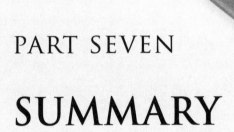

PART SEVEN

SUMMARY

The chapter in this part of the book summarizes the major points of the book. It presents a collection of sound practices that student affairs staff can employ to help manage the risk that is associated with their work, offers a conclusion to the book, and describes the principles of sound student affairs work and how they relate to risk management.

CHAPTER 23

PROMISING PRACTICES AND CONCLUSION

KEY PRINCIPLES OF RISK MANAGEMENT

Managing the risk of liability in development of programs and supervision of facilities is an increasingly complex task for student affairs administrators. The fact that there is risk is a given. Student affairs administrators assume considerable responsibility for the welfare of large numbers of students, virtually around the clock and for most of the year. Similarly, student affairs staff members have close relationships with students and are often in a position to be concerned for their physical well-being.

The relationship between institutions of higher education and students is complex. Several areas of law define this relationship. For example, because an institution of higher education is entrusted with the welfare of college students, the common law imposes a duty of care and a fiduciary duty upon the institution that defines its responsibilities. Liability for the negligent acts of the college or an employee is the most prevalent legal finding resulting from a breach of responsibility.

Since the civil rights movement and the student unrest of the 1960s, constitutional law has become more important in the college-student relationship. The constitutional rights of students have been explored and defined by a series of court cases. Those rights primarily relate to due process in disciplinary hearings, nondiscriminatory practices, search and seizure, and freedom of the student press. Contract law has also become significant for defining the college-student relationship. Implied contracts in the form of college catalogs and student handbooks, as well as actual contracts, such as residence hall contracts, are equally affected by this area of law. Finally, colleges have increasingly become responsible for compliance with various government regulatory programs.

Awareness of some areas of law impacting this relationship may help student affairs administrators understand their liability. This chapter presents a brief overview of several areas of concern for student affairs administrators regarding civil liability. It should be remembered that, although some examples are provided, proper legal determination of liability depends greatly on the jurisdiction and facts particular to each case.

Risk Transfer and Risk Sharing

As we described in Chapter Two, by purchasing commercial liability insurance, a student affairs administrator or, in a broader sense, an institution of higher education, may transfer its liability to another party. In this fashion, potential losses may be shifted to the insurance carrier in exchange for the payment of premiums. In many states, public institutions can claim governmental immunity from liability claims. However, it should be noted that the purchase of insurance by those institutions has been interpreted by some courts to constitute a waiver of that immunity to the financial limit of the insurance coverage. The current direction of the courts seems to be away from accepting governmental immunity as a defense. Student affairs administrators at a public institution should never act as if their actions were immune from liability.

It should be noted that, by entering into contracts with third parties, student affairs administrators may retain partial liability for the actions of those parties. Care should be exercised in entering into contracts with vendors of service or merchandise, and the actions of those vendors should be carefully monitored.

Search and Seizure

As we addressed in Chapter Four, another area of risk involves procedures relative to search and seizure in students' residential rooms. Cases over the past two decades have established that the Fourth Amendment protections must be carefully followed before criminal charges against any student can be successfully initiated. Further, evidence that may be used in disciplinary hearings should be obtained only after reasonable consideration is given to the privacy rights of students.

Freedom of Expression

Also, in Chapter Three, we explained that freedom of expression is an additional area of concern. Student life newsletters and other publications and the oral expression by students of their views are matters that have considerable protection from the courts. Student affairs administrators must remember that the constitutional right of persons to express themselves freely is not easily limited. It certainly should not be limited to views that are acceptable only to the majority. Although content-based restrictions of expression are risk-laden, student affairs administrators remain free to place reasonable restrictions on the time, place, and manner of any speech or program.

Regular Procedure Review and Promulgation

In Chapters Six, Nine, Fifteen, and Twenty-Two, we explained that sound student affairs work should include a routine review of procedures and practices related to risk management. Circumstances change, and the characteristics of the students we serve do also. Legislation and case law are continually altering the landscape of our work. Higher education is a dynamic industry, so the practices associated with the mitigation of risk need regular review to ensure that they are consistent with the current circumstances.

A review of risk management practices should be part of the orientation of new employees, as well as part of ongoing staff development. We cannot make the assumption that all staff members are consistently informed about risk management issues, so we must routinely provide updates about best practice and ensure that staff are prepared to address risk in responsible, consistent ways. Tabletop exercises that allow staff to walk through scenarios are good practice to improve staff readiness for real-life critical incidents.

Good Record-Keeping

In Chapters Seven and Seventeen, we described how many student affairs administrators may be inclined to informal and casual interactions with others. They may not keep records of discussions or of decisions, but good maintenance of records is an important part of risk management. Being able to show the content of an important conversation with a student or staff member may make the difference between enduring a challenging litigation and resolving a conflict without any adversarial proceeding.

Of course, not every aspect of the experiences of a student affairs staff member can or should be recorded, but knowing when a decision or an agreement should be noted for the record is an important aspect of risk management. The best guidance might be, when unsure about whether or not to note something for the record, do so.

Compliance with Government Regulations

In Chapter Six we explained how federal and state regulations are complex and can be regarded as burdensome, but they are not voluntary or optional. Responsible student affairs administrators should be aware of their duties regarding compliance with government regulations and should know when reports have to be prepared and to whom they have to be delivered.

Appropriate Supervision of Programs and Services

In Chapters Nine, Ten, and Fourteen, where we covered forms of tort issues, we explained how institutions of higher education have a duty to provide reasonable protection for their students. The courts have consistently held that an institution is obligated to take reasonable steps to minimize risk for the safety of its students. When a student has been the victim of attack, schools have been found liable for failing to protect the student from a reasonably foreseeable assault or failing to warn the student of a known danger. For example, a college can be held liable for failing to trim the foliage around the parking lot and stairwell or having insufficient lighting where an assault occurred.

The institution's duty to students not only relates to protection from harm by other persons, but under certain circumstances, may extend to protecting students from becoming risks to their own or others' safety (Kaplin & Lee, 2009, pp. 112–127). The conduct of students who become injured or cause injury after leaving college-sponsored events where alcohol is served may result in the institution's involvement in protracted litigation and a finding of liability. The extent of this liability varies from state to state and depends on the nature of the relationship between the host and guest. A college cannot ignore reasonable care in monitoring the consumption of alcohol at institution-sponsored events. Clearly, student affairs staff members who know, or should know, that students are consuming alcohol bear some responsibility for the actions of those students.

Policies, procedures, and facilities should be monitored with student safety and security in mind. The cost of litigation and the potential for liability also highlight the need for supervision of student affairs programs. Student affairs administrators must take care to monitor student activities and programs so that students and guests do not encounter hazardous or dangerous situations.

Full Disclosure and Accurate Representation of Fact

In Chapter Twelve, we discussed that an academic institution has a duty to release and fully disclose information in its possession, even if confidential, if it directly relates to an individual's safety. Because the duties of the student affairs staff involve counseling students, they need to be careful in fulfilling their legal obligation to notify an individual who might be the target of physical violence contemplated by a counselee (Kaplin & Lee, 2009, pp. 151, 454, 455). Obviously, such notification defies the canons of confidentiality. Depending on the situation, however, the court may find that the counselor had an obligation to notify the intended victim of potential danger. For example, if a student were to confide his intention to kill someone to a college counselor and then subsequently carried through on his threat, the college and the counselor would be held liable for failing to warn the victim.

Liability may also be imposed based on the misrepresentation of fact. The following hypothetical legal case illustrates this point. A university had represented its campus as a safe and secure place, but, in fact, a chronic pattern of assaults in the university community had occurred over a period of time. In a subsequent lawsuit brought by the victim of a crime, the court stated that there was a legitimate monetary claim against the institution due to its assertion that its environment was safe.

Occasionally, there may be aspects of or influences on student life that administrators may not wish to release due to public relations reasons, issues of confidentiality, or other factors. However, college students should be fully informed of hazardous or dangerous situations so that they, together with administrative personnel, can take all reasonable precautions to avoid risks. Events such as bomb scares, threats of death, and even newly waxed or wet floors, incorporate hazardous elements against which the campus community should be warned. Releasing information of a sensitive nature may be emotionally challenging for student affairs administrators, but weighed against the potential for injury or tragedy for students or their guests, such feelings should be set aside in favor of full disclosure of information.

Adequate Consideration of the Limitations of Program Participants

In Chapter Nine, we detailed how student affairs staff employed in campus activities exert great energy and considerable creativity in designing programming for students. These staff members, as advisors and sponsors, have an obligation, however, to ensure that program activities do not cause hazardous or dangerous conditions by demanding too much participant skill or knowledge. Amateur boxing tournaments, skateboard races, and tugs-of-war are examples of activities that might invite unqualified participants into potentially harmful situations. Student affairs personnel must take precautionary steps as programs are being developed and planned.

The mere use of waivers intended to absolve program sponsors of liability does not necessarily preclude claims to recover damages, although waivers may be sound educational tools to alert students to risks and hazards associated with an activity. As with any contract, whether or not a waiver of liability will be enforceable varies from state to state and depends on the terms of the waiver, the intention of the signor, and the circumstances under which it was signed. As a general principle, courts view waivers that purport to disclaim liability for one's negligence with disfavor and subject them to strict scrutiny.

Rights of and Responsibility for Visitors

In Chapters Twenty and Twenty-Two, we discussed that college campuses attract visitors with diverse purposes and perspectives. Students invite their personal guests, and both commercial and noncommercial solicitors see students as convenient and viable targets for their efforts. Thus, student affairs administrators must very carefully attend to their responsibilities regarding visitors.

Institutions of higher education, public as well as private, may adopt reasonable regulations restricting commercial, political, and religious solicitations on campus. Such regulations promulgated by public institutions are often attacked as being in violation of the constitutional privileges of freedom of speech and association. However, schools may adopt reasonable restrictions with respect to the time, place, and manner of such "speech." While such policies may be helpful in regulating and, to a certain extent, in controlling solicitation on campus, a few factors must be considered. First, any such policy must be "content neutral." This means that it must not allow solicitation by some groups and prohibit solicitation by others. Second, such policies, once promulgated, must be uniformly implemented. Arbitrary application may result in a violation in the right to due process. Third, various courts disagree as to whether such policies may be enforced in the nonresidential areas of student life (that is, the lobby, student lounge, and recreational spaces). Last, and perhaps most importantly, often the key factor in a court's decision is whether or not the institution has made provisions for alternate channels of communication.

Many campuses entertain visitors who are minors, sometimes as part of admissions recruitment and at other times through summer programs or sports camps. Minors form a protected class, and student affairs administrators have to be very sensitive to the risks associated with exposing them to material that may not be harmful to college students but might create challenges or be inappropriate for children. How unscheduled free time is managed; how transportation is handled; and whether there is Internet access: these all form aspects of risk and need to be considered when children are on campus, in residence halls, or in recreational facilities.

Finally, it should be noted that visitors who are allowed access to campus are entitled to many of the same considerations as students. For instance, the institution's duty to maintain its premises in a reasonably safe condition applies equally to the benefit of visitors, invitees, and students.

Housing Contracts

In Chapter Fifteen, where we addressed contracts, we specifically discussed the housing contract, or housing agreement form, an extremely important document in identifying and limiting the risk of liability of student affairs administrators and their employers. The contract should clearly articulate the rights and responsibilities of the institution and of the resident student. It should identify the parties to the agreement, establish the rate and method of payment by the resident, specify the dates of occupancy, and detail the services and offerings of the institution. Actions taken by student affairs administrators should be consistent with the written terms of the housing contract.

Appropriate Hiring, Training, and Supervision of Staff

In Chapters Sixteen and Seventeen, we discussed how the supervisory responsibilities of student affairs administrators require them to select and properly train staff. As an employer, the student affairs administrator and the academic institution may be held liable if they fail to use proper care in hiring, training, and supervising personnel. The doctrine of *"respondeat superior,"* which holds an employer responsible for the negligent acts of an employee, even if the employer took reasonable care in training and supervising the employee, makes adequate training and supervision even more important.

Student affairs administrators, of course, cannot be omnipresent in their hiring, training, and supervision of staff; however, they should evaluate candidates and employees carefully to ensure that staff actions closely follow expectations. In addition, those expectations should be delineated meticulously. Staff evaluations should be conducted on a regular basis, so that those individuals in need of attention or performance improvement can be provided with necessary assistance.

Disciplinary Proceedings

In Chapter Eighteen, we discussed how disciplinary proceedings comprise an area for which there may be considerable legal liability. Students are protected by procedural and substantive due process. Student affairs administrators who pursue disciplinary action against individual students must be aware of the codified procedures of their institutions regarding the rights and freedoms of students in the disciplinary setting. They should also ensure that those written procedures are consistent with the procedural standards established by recent litigation.

Ways to safeguard a student's due process rights in a disciplinary hearing are not precise. At least two elements are essential: (a) that the student is given an opportunity to respond and (b) that the decision-maker is impartial. Although there is some disagreement among the various jurisdictions, generally, a student need not be given an opportunity to cross-examine witnesses at a disciplinary hearing, as long as basic fairness is preserved.

Adequate Inspection and Maintenance of Facilities

In Chapter Twenty-Two, we described how student affairs administrators have an obligation to take reasonable steps to inspect and maintain buildings, facilities, and grounds so that those using them are protected from physical hazards. A wide range of cases reaffirm this obligation. Liability can be imposed when a student slipped and fell on ice, water, or cracked concrete. As noted above, a college can be held liable for damages to the victim of an attack by an individual who hides in foliage that obscures visibility from a stairwell adjacent to a school's parking lot.

Of course, in any such case, what constitutes reasonable conduct depends on the facts of that situation. It should also be noted that the standard of care under which liability will be imposed may differ from state to state.

Colleges need to ensure that the campus design does not facilitate criminal activity. Obviously, existing campus design places limits on what can be done; however, proper maintenance, lighting, and patrolling procedures may mitigate against liability. Certainly, when a particular design feature, such as the foliage in the above example, has become a hazard, design modification may be necessary.

In summary, student affairs administrators bear a considerable burden in maintaining the safety of facilities and grounds for which they are responsible. Such maintenance may not always be convenient, inexpensive, or even possible. Nevertheless, potentially hazardous conditions, such as waxed floors, icy sidewalks, and malfunctioning elevators, incorporate elements of undue risk for students, for which the student affairs administrator and the institution could be liable.

CONCLUSION

It will remain the burden of college attorneys to defend student affairs administrators and their employing institutions in the event of litigation. While those attorneys are best equipped to represent an institution in a lawsuit, student affairs administrators are best equipped to manage the risk of liability for their own actions.

Student affairs personnel should be cognizant of managing the risk of liability in several administrative practice areas. A concern for potential litigation, however, should not dominate an innovative, educationally sound student affairs administrative division. One might conclude that, as long as student affairs administrators conduct their duties in prudent and reasonable fashion and in good faith with an understanding of the principles of law as they relate to higher education, liability risks can be minimized.

Student affairs is a challenging field. It is populated by persons who genuinely care about students in the institutions they serve. Valuing learning above all other purposes of higher education, the profession celebrates diversity, inclusion, and a culture of excellence. Student affairs staff members see their campuses as very special places where people come to develop their talent and realize their potential for the future. Student affairs administrators do not shrink from challenges or fear difficult circumstances. They are planners; they are problem solvers; and they are decision-makers. They do what they must in order to manage the risks with which they are presented.

In this book we have reviewed the principles associated with risk and risk management in student affairs from a broad and general perspective. Clearly, the law is dynamic, and future court decisions, legislative initiatives, and practices in higher education will alter details associated with best practices for risk management in student affairs administration. The nature of the future is hard to predict, and student affairs professionals must assume responsibility for staying current on the law and risk management. Because the text of our book is intended to provide a general context for understanding risk management, it should remain relevant, even in a changing landscape.

In the context of these unsettled circumstances, student affairs administrators have to be tolerant of the ambiguity associated with risk management practices. Best practice depends on what is learned from case law, the nature of government regulation and policy, and the specific facts associated with the risk being measured.

It is almost certain that risk management challenges for student affairs administrators will occur with increased frequency in the future. We live in litigious times, and lawsuits will occur with increasing frequency. Risk associated with resources will increase, too, as property becomes more complex, technology becomes more dominant on college campuses, and financial management becomes more precious. Good planning, intentional and farsighted staff training, policies that are well grounded and clear, and, when appropriate, advice from legal counsel will help student affairs administrators craft intelligent strategies for risk management.

One aspect of risk management merits attention as it relates to the establishment of good relationships with students and student organizations. A student affairs administrator whose connections to students are characterized as trusting and fostering mutual respect is more likely to be informed on a timely basis about campus conditions or activities from which risk may evolve. When students trust administrators, they are more apt to alert them in advance to situations from which risk will evolve. Having the opportunity to engage a situation proactively, rather than reacting to an unfortunate event, is always a better strategy for risk management.

Risk cannot be avoided. Working with college students, whose values, beliefs, and place in society are taking shape, is a noble undertaking. However, it has inherent risks on an everyday basis. The very notion of eliminating risks associated with working with this high-energy, risk-taking population is simply not feasible.

Not all crises can be anticipated, but a risk management plan associated with one type of event can be used to deal with a different type of event. For example, student affairs practitioners can use their resourcefulness to apply the principles of a hurricane evacuation plan to respond to a student health epidemic on campus.

Risk comes in many forms, and a careful review of this text will help the student affairs professional see that risk is not just in the form of liability or lawsuits. Being sued is an unpleasant experience. It is adversarial and contentious, and it can take a great amount of time and emotional energy. Even the threat of a lawsuit is unpleasant, but, sadly, it is not uncommon. Conducting business in a prudent and careful way and staying alert to the specter of risk is sound practice, but focusing on students and their welfare and their success is the primary purpose of work in student affairs. The driving force in our lives is not avoiding lawsuits.

An additional form of risk is a risk to student safety or welfare. Activity that puts students in harm's way or threatens their good health must be avoided. Irrespective of litigation, activity that threatens the welfare of students must be avoided. This can be challenging, because many students, who are in their late adolescence, are risk takers. We know that, however, and that knowledge arms us with the realization that we need to look out for the students for whom we are responsible.

Another form of risk is associated with bad public relations outcomes. Damaging publicity, whether accompanied by other forms of risk or not, can be hard to recover from or almost impossible to refute. When our mistakes or criticisms of us become public, it can put us in an untenable position. A secondary effect of negative public relations can be an adverse effect on enrollment and student recruitment. Many times, bad publicity cannot even be rebutted. If the issue is associated with an unhappy former employee, student affairs staff might be unable to respond to questions or challenges if it is a confidential employment matter. Confidential student issues fall in the same category.

In addition, there is also the risk of property loss or damage. Fires, floods, or hurricanes can cause loss from which it can take years to recover. Natural disasters can be hard to predict and impossible to prevent, but good planning and intelligent management can help to manage the loss. In any event, understanding the wide spectrum of risk and its sources is sound practice in student affairs.

We hope readers find this book useful. We wrote it for practitioners in the field to try to help them understand risk in the big picture, rather than all of the subtle nuances and details that can come with a street-level view of risk so often tied to specific places and institutional contexts. We also wrote it for students who are entering the field and would benefit from a broad understanding of the principles of risk and strategies for avoiding or managing it. We hope that the book has served those purposes.

REFERENCE

Kaplin, W.A., & Lee, B.A. (2009). *A Legal Guide for Student Affairs Professionals* (4th ed.) (pp. 112–127, 151, 454, 455). San Francisco, CA: Jossey-Bass.

ADDITIONAL RESOURCES

Kaplin, W.A., & Lee, B.A. (2007). "Alternate Dispute Resolution." In W.A. Kaplin & B.A. Lee, *The Law of Higher Education* (4th ed.) (pp. 79–84). San Francisco, CA: Jossey-Bass.
Kaplin, W.A., & Lee, B.A. (2007). "Institutional Management of Liability Risk." In W.A. Kaplin & B.A. Lee, *The Law of Higher Education* (4th ed.) (pp. 85–93). San Francisco, CA: Jossey-Bass.
Lake, P.F. (2011). "Managing the Institution of Higher Education Environment. Part I: Safety, Risk Management, Wellness and Security." In P.F. Lake, *Foundations of Higher Education Law & Policy* (pp. 91–178). Washington, DC: NASPA: Student Affairs Administrators in Higher Education.

ANNOTATED RESOURCES

Council on Law in Higher Education. Accessible online at www.clhe.org/clhe/
home. This resource is a subscription-based publication that is published
regularly and routinely and provides a discussion of case law or legislative
initiatives, including legislation at the state level.

Harper, Kristin S., Paterson, Brent G., & Zdziarski, Eugene L., II (Eds.). (2006).
Crisis Management: Responding from the Heart. Washington, DC:
NASPA. This is an excellent summary of steps to take in face of a crisis,
from the perspective of senior student affairs administrators who have had
first-hand experience.

Kaplin, William A., & Lee, Barbara A. (2007). *The Law of Higher Education*
(4th ed.). San Francisco, CA: Jossey-Bass. This book addresses legal issues
in higher education from a broader perspective than their other book. In
addition to addressing how the law interacts with the student/institutional
relationship, it provides a more thorough coverage of academic issues,
faculty matters, employment law, and policy concerns.

Kaplin, William A., & Lee, Barbara A. (2009). *A Legal Guide for Student
Affairs Professionals* (4th ed.). San Francisco, CA: Jossey-Bass. This text is
one of the most important resources for practicing professionals and students learning about legal issues in student affairs. It is technically sound
and quite thorough and very well organized. Also see the authors' other
book on this list.

Lake, P.F. (2011). *Foundations of Higher Education Law & Policy.* Washington,
DC: NASPA: Student Affairs Administrators in Higher Education. This book

provides a fine discussion of how the law informs practice in student affairs. It is written in a relaxed, conversational tone and is a comfortable read.

Pavela, G. *The Pavela Report.* Saint Johns, FL: College Administration Publications. Accessible online at http://collegepubs.com/the_pavela_report. This excellent subscription-based weekly publication provides current and timely discussion of case law, regulatory developments, and best practice associated with law and policy.

Sun, Jeffrey C., Scott, Lynn Rossi, Sponsler, Brian A., & Hutchens, Neal H. (2014). Understanding Campus Obligations for Student-to-Student Sexual Harassment: Guidance for Student Affairs Professionals. *Legal Links: Connecting Student Affairs and the Law*, 1 (1). This is a very good discussion of approaches in the face of sexual harassment between students.

The Catholic University of America, Office of General Counsel. Accessible online at http://counsel.cua.edu. There is no better or more current discussion of federal regulatory issues that affect student affairs than this one. The site includes a calendar for compliance and a set of excellent discussions and interviewed experts on associated issues.

About the Authors

Thomas E. Miller is the vice president for student affairs at the Tampa Campus of the University of South Florida. He is also an associate professor in the College of Education at the Tampa campus of the University of South Florida. He previously held student affairs positions at Eckerd College, Canisius College, Indiana University, and Shippensburg University. His scholarly work has been focused on the themes of student expectations and persistence in higher education.

Miller holds a bachelor's degree from Muhlenberg College and master's and doctoral degrees from Indiana University. He received the Scott Goodnight Award for Outstanding Performance as a Dean from NASPA in 2001 and was chosen as a Pillar of the Profession in 2004. He has been on more than a dozen institutional accreditation teams and NCAA Certification review teams.

He received the Elizabeth Greenleaf Distinguished Alumnus Award from Indiana University's Higher Education and Student Affairs Program in 1989. Miller has served as a member of the boards of directors of NASPA, BACCHUS/GAMMA Peer Education Network, and of the National Consortium for Academics and Sports.

He and his wife, Carol, have two sons, Drew and Justin, and three grandchildren, Logan, Julie, and Wesley.

Roger W. Sorochty has spent more than four decades as a student affairs administrator while serving as a vice president during more than half of that time. His career began with the State University of New York and continued at Kent State University, Newman University, Eckerd College, St. Bonaventure University, and, from 2001 until 2013, as vice president for enrollment and student services at The University of Tulsa, from which he retired.

He holds a doctorate in educational administration from the University of Ottawa, Canada, a master's degree in student personnel administration from Syracuse University, and a bachelor's degree from Hobart College, Geneva, New York.

He currently serves as the Senior Associate for Higher Education in the Center for Conflict Dynamics at Eckerd College, on the editorial board of NASPA's *Journal of Student Affairs Research and Practice*, as a Peer Reviewer for the Higher Learning Commission of the North Central Association of Colleges and Schools, and has presented regularly at regional and national student affairs professional meetings.

In June of 2014 he and his wife, Barbara, celebrated forty-four years of marriage. They have two children, Matthew and Michelle, and five grandchildren: Ryan, Anna, Riley, Will, and Morgan.

INDEX

If you enjoyed this book, you may also like these:

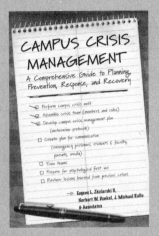

Campus Crisis Management
A Comprehensive Guide to
Planning Prevention, Response,
and Recovery
by Eugene L. Zdziarski II,
Norbert W. Dunkel, J. Michael
Rollo & Associates
ISBN: 9780787978747

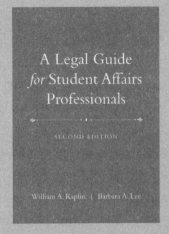

A Legal Guide for Student Affairs
Professionals
by William A. Kaplin
Barbara A. Lee
ISBN: 9780470433935

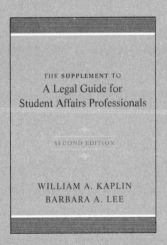

The Supplement to A Legal Guide
for Student Affairs Professionals
by William A. Kaplin
Barbara A. Lee
ISBN: 9781118031872

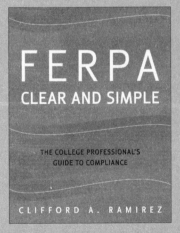

Ferpa Clear and Simple The
College Professional's Guide to
Compliance
by Clifford A. Ramirez
ISBN: 9780470498774

Want to connect?

Like us on Facebook
www.facebook.com/JBHigherEd

Subscribe to our newsletter
www.josseybass.com/go/higheredemail

Follow us on Twitter
http://twitter.com/JBHigherEd

Go to our Website
www.josseybass.com/highereducation